43 Essential Policies

for Human Services Professionals

Gerald V. O'Brien

NASW PRESS

National Association of Social Workers
Washington, DC

Cheryl Y. Bradley, *Publisher*
Rachel Meyers, *Acquisitions Editor*
Julie Gutin, *Project Manager*
Laurel Vincenty, *Copyeditor*
Juanita Ruffin Doswell, *Proofreader*
Matthew White, *Indexer*

Cover by Ashley Slade
Interior design, composition, and eBook conversion by Rick Soldin
Printed and bound by Books International

First impression: November 2021

Library of Congress Cataloging-in-Publication Data

Names: O'Brien, Gerald V., author.
Title: 43 essential policies for human services professionals / Gerald V. O'Brien.
Description: Washington : NASW Press, 2021. | Includes bibliographical references and index. | Summary: "For potential use at both the BSW and MSW level, the book provides thumbnail descriptions of key social welfare problems and policies in the United States, starting with the Elizabethan Poor Laws of the 1600s to Japanese internment, through the Patient Protection and Affordable Care Act of 2010, to COVID-19 relief and the Black Lives Matter movement. One feature of the book, Analysis Elements, address issues such as unintended consequences, goal development, and target efficiency"—Provided by publisher.
Identifiers: LCCN 2021029430 (print) | LCCN 2021029431 (ebook) | ISBN 9780871015747 (paperback) | ISBN 9780871015754 (ebook)
Subjects: LCSH: Social legislation—United States—History. | United States—Social policy.
Classification: LCC KF3300 . O27 2021 (print) | LCC KF3300 (ebook) | DDC 344.7303—dc23
LC record available at https://lccn.loc.gov/2021029430
LC ebook record available at https://lccn.loc.gov/2021029431

Printed in the United States of America

This book is dedicated to all the MSW and BSW students
I have had in policy classes over the past 25 years, and
especially the 500 or so who have accompanied me to
Lobby Day activities in Springfield, Illinois.

Contents

Note to Instructors

A 45-page Instructor Appendix is available as a separate PDF. This teaching resource includes two components for each chapter: (1) questions for further discussion and (2) research and questions related to analysis elements. The Instructor Appendix can be used for assigning student research, paper topics, and class discussions, and includes cross-policy and cross-concept analysis, occasionally referencing concepts and policies not covered in this text. To request a copy, send an e-mail to press@socialworkers.org.

Acknowledgments

I am grateful to my faculty colleagues in the Social Work Department and throughout Southern Illinois University Edwardsville for their support of my research over the years, and also to the college and university administrators. Special thanks to Jill Schreiber, chair of the Social Work Department; dean emeritus Gregory Budzban and current dean, Kevin Leonard; Provost Denise Cobb; and Chancellor Randy Pembrook. Much of this book was completed during a fall 2020 sabbatical, and I am appreciative of all those who supported my sabbatical proposal. Thanks also to Kathleen Tunney, Duff Wrobbel, and Andy Theising. I am also appreciative of Rachel Meyers at NASW Press, who worked with me over this sabbatical to see this book through the publication process. This is my second book that Rachel has shepherded through, and I am grateful for her time and effort. Thanks also to others at NASW Press who have had a hand in supporting my work.

Over my 25-year academic career, I have primarily taught policy courses at both the undergraduate and graduate levels, and I am dedicating this book to my students. Although I hope they have learned some things about the importance of policy analysis, I know I have learned much from their own engagement both in class and in related lobbying activities. Social policy is broad and deep, and is constantly changing. Even after many years, there is still much in the way of new information that I learn from my students. For approximately 16 years, I have prepared students for their legislative Lobby Day in Springfield, Illinois, and this is often a highlight of my academic year because I am able to watch students try to navigate the policy terrain as they analyze the bills they have chosen. For many, this is their first engagement with social policy and is an anxious time, especially for those who have never even been to the Capitol or met with a legislator. I am always proud of them, and they never fail to represent both the university and the profession extremely well. It makes me happy to know that some, including Ashley Stewart and Janet Wiley, have decided to serve their local communities in elected positions. Thanks also to all the current and past Illinois politicians who have been so responsive to my students, especially Representatives Jay Hoffman, Katie Stuart, La Shawn Ford, and Mary Flowers, and Senators Bill Haine, Rachelle Crowe, and the late Evelyn Bowles.

An interest in politics came naturally to me, and I thank my mother, Kay O'Brien, and my late father, Dan O'Brien, for stoking my curiosity about the political world and especially for instilling in me the importance of politics in the course of social and economic justice. As a child, I handed out campaign literature at our precinct before I could vote. My dad was especially fascinated by the Watergate proceedings, so I remember following that quite closely along with him. He was a councilman in our city of Hazelwood, Missouri, and ran for a seat as our state representative. My uncle, Father Tom Michel, an expert on Christian–Muslim relations, also has had a great influence on me, especially in my passion for social justice.

I owe a huge debt of gratitude to my wife, Jean, who has always supported my research even when it consumes too much of my time and attention. Jean has herself been involved in the advance of racial justice within our own community, and I am proud of her work to that end. Thanks also to the rest of my family—Shannon, Mark, Kevin, Jade, Quinn, and Willow—as well as to my siblings and extended family.

My primary social policy interests center around disability policy, eugenics, historical issues in social welfare policy, and metaphor analysis. I am grateful to those scholars whom I have known personally or whose writings have influenced the direction of my policy research. These include James Trent, George Lakoff, Mark Landau, David Mitchell, Sharon Snyder, Rosemarie Garland-Thomson, Brenda Breuggemann, Nick Haslam, Otto Santa Ana, Yoosun Park, Andreas Musolff, Sam Keen, and Sander Gilman.

Introduction

I HAVE A FEW CLARIFICATIONS BEFORE I BEGIN. FIRST, ALTHOUGH THIS BOOK lists "43 policies" in its title, this is actually false advertising. One chapter (on eugenic sterilization) focuses on state policies rather than one federal policy, the Pierce veto chapter discusses a proposal that was vetoed, and the chapter on Elizabethan Poor Laws describes the importance of this set of British regulations for the United States. In addition, the book ends with COVID-19 and Black Lives Matter (BLM). These topics were highly important and will continue to affect policies at various levels. They are not policies, but their recent importance necessitates their inclusion in this book. For the most part, though, I have tried to choose those specific policies that I believe are most important for social workers and other human services professionals to be aware of. Many of these policies are important in terms of eligibility for services, or the advancement of social and economic justice and others for their historical effect, or because of the discussions or controversies they give rise to.

Now, if one were to ask a group of rock music aficionados to name the 20 best rock albums or avid baseball fans to give you their list of the 10 best players, you would have spirited disagreement and contentious debate. There would perhaps be more disagreement than agreement. The same is true here. Although most policy instructors would support the inclusion of many of these policies in such a list, there would also be strong arguments for adding others or deleting some of these. I have tried to include the most important policies from the broad range of social work areas (child welfare, housing, aging, disabilities, mental health, and so on), but a number that I would like to have included missed the cut. I have included information on some of these within the related chapters or as follow-up questions in the Instructor Appendix (available by request; see Note to Instructors on page vii).

Approximately half of the book chapters include at the end an example of a policy analysis component in relation to the social problem or policy. In the Instructor Appendix, the second section for each chapter provides questions that require students to generalize particular analysis elements to that particular problem or policy. For some, such as policy goals, this is fairly straightforward. For other examples, however, such as horizontal versus vertical service delivery or social engineering, students might want to review the example provided before attempting to apply the analysis component to a different social problem or policy issue.

Most chapters in this book provide a brief historical overview of the issue or problem along with basic elements or goals of the social policy and some information on effectiveness. It is impossible to go into too much depth in a brief chapter, so I have tried to be as economical as possible. My goal is that the book provides a general introduction to important social welfare policies for students.

It is easy for students and practicing social workers to become callous about politics and policy in an era of increasing divisiveness that too often spills over into anger and contempt. Policies continue to guide both practice and funding; however, and for this reason alone, social workers need to remain policy advocates. Policy is incremental, and victories take time, but they do come with perseverance. As I write these words, the U.S. House of Representatives has just passed The Equality Act (H.R. 5—117th Congress: Equality Act, 2021), a bill that would ban discrimination against people on account of their gender identity or sexual orientation. It is a goal of President Biden to see this bill passed and signed into law during his first term. After more than a decade of stagnant wages and decreased purchasing power, it seems certain that the minimum wage will also finally be increased, although it is still unclear by how much. These gains in social or economic justice may seem painfully slow in coming, but the time and effort it takes to reach them can make them all the more sweet when they do come.

CHAPTER 1

Elizabethan Poor Laws

◖1601◗

Historical Overview and Nature of the Social Problem

The Elizabethan Poor Laws were established in Great Britain centuries ago, yet they had a great deal of influence on the response to people in need both before and after the Revolutionary War in the United States. Thus, their inclusion here is important in providing the groundwork for social welfare policy in the United States. First formalized as The Poor Relief Act of 1601, the "Elizabethan Poor Laws" (or "Poor Laws"), as this act was called, constituted an attempt to define what groups should be provided with governmental assistance, the form of assistance to be given, the responsibilities of those who were given assistance, and methods of dealing with potentially dependent "visitors" and beggars who were deemed undesirable of assistance.

Although people in both Great Britain and the American colonies recognized the responsibility to take care of the poor, this was seen fundamentally as the responsibility of the family (Day, 2006). Some early community policies attempted to force or shame family members into caring for their indigent members. For those without families or whose families were also poverty stricken, the Poor Laws provided some guidance as to how the community or town was to deal with them. Before the establishment of the Poor Laws, communities dealt with vagrancy in their own, often harsh, ways. According to Kelso (1969), during the 1500s, unlicensed vagabonds in England were often disgraced by tattooing a large *V* on their chest. Nash (2004) added that this practice carried over to the New World, where, in the early 1700s, the poor in New York were forced to wear the letters *N:Y* on their clothes, delineating that they were dependent on the city. Green (2003) noted that, in some cases, such markings were a way to delineate the "worthy" from "unworthy" poor.

The Poor Laws were developed in part to discourage indiscriminate charity by organizations or individuals because it was assumed that this would only foster dependency (Mencher, 1967), and thus a set of standards was required to properly funnel support to the poor. Over time, the problem of poverty largely came to be viewed as an urban problem in both Great Britain and the United States partly because people without work often traveled or were forcibly brought to, and thus increasingly congregated in, larger cities. This also fostered the need to develop aid policies, because it became more difficult to track and "warn out" beggars in the midst of a large population. As Piven and Cloward (1971) noted, even in these early years, poor support was often used as a way of pacifying the poor and preventing large-scale rebellion, especially in harsh economic times.

Policy Overview

Two primary elements of the Poor Laws were (1) the categorization of those in poverty based on the presumptive cause of their dependency and their ability to work; and (2) the establishment of residency requirements as a way of ensuring that the town, village, or city had the ability to control the settlement of people who might require support. As is famously known, categorization related primarily to separation of the "worthy poor" from the "unworthy poor" (Day, 2006; Mencher, 1967). The worthy poor group usually included children, the elderly, and people with obvious disease or disability conditions that affected their ability to work. It was often the members of this group who could receive a license to beg (Kelso, 1969). The unworthy poor group primarily included anyone who could presumably work but did not. In the case of this group (as well as many in the worthy poor category, too), work, either in a poorhouse, almshouse, or other supervised setting, was often the primary requirement for assistance (Katz, 1996). In both the United States and Great Britain, such custodial facilities were developed largely to control the work and behaviors of aid recipients (Trattner, 1999).

Settlement laws, a central element of the various early poor laws, were the primary way of ensuring that only residents of a town or village received aid. Those who did not live in the community for the requisite amount of time were banished, often following a public display of humiliation (for example, being placed in stocks, whipped). At times, vagrants who were recent immigrants were even deported back to their home country (Green, 2003). Newly arrived individuals were frequently required to register with a town official to ensure that they would not become beggars (Kelso, 1969). They frequently had to post a bond or demonstrate that they had a close relationship with a resident who could vouch for them and ensure their financial independence. As Abramovitz (1988) wrote, slaveholders, too, had to post a bond when they freed slaves as protection against their becoming a public charge. The children of poor families, and especially of unmarried women, were often removed from their families and required to become apprentices (Abramovitz, 1988; Green, 2003). In addition to other logistical problems, however, settlement laws were increasingly difficult to enforce because they restricted individual freedom, and movement into a community was often important for employment purposes (Kelso, 1969).

Effectiveness

Even though the Poor Laws are generally viewed today as highly draconian, this was not necessarily the case during the time they were in force because they largely just formalized standard practice in relation to those in need of assistance. Some critics felt that if private or public providers were overly generous in their assistance, this would lead to dependency of the poor on the community or the state. One of the principal critics of the Poor Laws in Great Britain was Thomas Malthus, who was the leading population theorist of the time and who wrote the seminal *An Essay on the Principle of Population* near the beginning of the 19th century (Malthus, 1798/1967). Malthus believed that public assistance of any type (or even widespread private charity) would not only increase dependency but, moreover, would support increased procreation and thus population growth among the lower classes. If their children were to be supported by the public treasury, he felt, the poor would have little natural disincentive to childbearing. In addition, those in the middle and upper classes would presumably spend an increasing amount of their own money on taxes to support this growing population. As a result, persons in both these classes might then have fewer children because their resources would then be depleted; thus, a vicious cycle would develop, whereby an ever-increasing number of poor individuals would be supported by a progressively decreasing number of productive taxpayers (Malthus, 1798/1967).

Not only were Malthus's arguments taken up at the end of the 1800s by social Darwinists (Spencer, 1904), eugenicists (Kevles, 1985), and others, but they also have continued to be a staple in political discussions related to welfare reform of all types. Many of those calling for limited federal involvement in support of the poor have held, as did Malthus, that, in a democracy, the growing sector of "dependents" will eventually constitute a voting majority and potentially take over society by voting in a wide array of assistance packages. This issue is revisited in chapter 36.

Analysis Element: Individual Deservedness

A central element of the Elizabethan Poor Laws was the delineation of the deserving versus the undeserving poor. Questions about who should and who should not receive governmental assistance continue to be an inextricable part of public policy as distinguished by the frequent debates related to eligibility for Aid to Families with Dependent Children (AFDC) (established by the Social Security Act of 1935, P.L. 74-271; see chapter 7) and Temporary Assistance for Needy Families (TANF) (created through the Personal Responsibility and Work Opportunity Reconciliation Act of 1996, P.L. 104-193; see chapter 36) benefits or other forms of public assistance (Goldberg & Collins, 2001).

One of the major difficulties related to our judgments of deservedness, however—aside from how presumptuous it is to stand in judgment of someone else in the first place—pertains to the fact that we generally consider this issue on an individual basis, whereas large bureaucratic entities naturally categorize potential recipients with a broad brush. Consider, for example, a young unemployed new mother who did not finish high school. Our tendency may be to say that she should have made better decisions about her life and not brought children into the world if she could not support them. Of course, the more questions we ask about someone in this situation and get to know about their life, the more difficult these judgments become. What if the pregnancy was the result of rape or incest? What if, knowing that an abortion would also be a viable option, she decided to carry the child to term? What if her failure to finish high school was necessitated by a difficult pregnancy that required months of bedrest?

The point is that making judgments based on the stereotypes we develop is not only easy but also provides us with a continuous stock of convenient scapegoats (Macek, 2006). Once we begin looking a little more closely at individual circumstances, things tend to get foggier. Deservedness relates closely to individual and societal values as well as our cultural views of certain needs as necessities or luxuries. For example, those nations that perceive basic medical care to be among the fundamental necessities of life will view their citizens as deserving of such care, regardless of individual circumstances.

CHAPTER 2

Dorothea Dix and the Pierce Veto

1854

Historical Overview and Nature of the Social Problem

Dorothea Dix was a tireless advocate for people with mental illness, and during her struggle to increase interest in and implement policies related to such people, strong advocacy was indeed needed. These were days long before the availability of any effective pharmaceutical, medical, or psychological treatment (or even accurate diagnostics), and much of what passed for treatment would more aptly be defined as torture today. During the 1830s and 1840s, when Dix was most heavily involved in attempting to solicit state and federal support for people with mental illness, they were most frequently either warehoused in settings such as almshouses or poorhouses, or simply left on their own (Katz, 1996). As noted in chapter 1, many communities engaged in "passing on," whereby their mentally ill and other "dependents" were brought, often under cover of night, to a neighboring town and abandoned there. Other communities, especially those that were too small to build a poorhouse or almshouse, "auctioned" people with mental illness to a family from the community that would be responsible for their care; in return, the family would be given a modest monetary contribution from the town (Dix, 1843/1976). Because the lowest bidders "won," the point was to see how cheaply such people could be maintained.

Dix was a firm believer in "moral treatment" in relation to people with "insanity." This concept was an outgrowth of the Enlightenment in Europe (Lightner, 1999) and was initiated in the late 18th and early 19th centuries by professionals such as William Tuke in Great Britain and Phillipe Pinel in France. *Moral treatment* held that great gains could be realized by people with even chronic mental illness if they were treated with kindness but firm authority and control in small institutional settings (Whitaker, 2002). Dix felt that such treatment could improve and even cure most of those with long-term mental illness (Dix, 1863) but that, outside of institutions, such people were a potential danger to themselves and others. She also advocated for early treatment before a person's mental illness got to the point at which institutionalization would be required (Dix, 1863).

Dix began her social welfare work in the early 1840s, reporting on the treatment of prisoners and advocating for better care for them (Trattner, 1999). For the remainder of the 1840s and into the next decade, she visited a number of states to assess the various ways in which people with mental illness were treated. She reported her findings, including graphic details of maltreatment, to state legislatures and other interested parties (Dix, 1843/1976, 1863; Lightner, 1999). As she noted repeatedly, these individuals were frequently dealt with in an animalistic manner (O'Brien, 2019). Poorhouses or almshouses often provided care to a wide range of poor, disabled, and elderly people; however, they were not specifically designed to respond to the particular problems of people with mental illness. Therefore, Dix argued, specific institutions for people with mental illness needed to be developed—with moral treatment as the basis of care.

The first hospital in the United States developed specifically for people with mental illness opened shortly before the Revolutionary War in Williamsburg, Virginia. Its primary purpose, Rothman (1971) wrote, was to "preserve the peace of the community, to keep the insane from roaming about" (p. 43). During the decades between the opening of facility and Dix's advocacy efforts, a number of other state facilities were developed, but little real progress had been made in treatment. Dix sought support from the states to expand institutional development and also professionalize care based on the tenets of moral treatment. She was successful in obtaining assistance for her cause in many states, and early institution-building was supported in large part because of her advocacy efforts. She began her efforts in the eastern United States and was instrumental in the development of facilities in Massachusetts and other states. She moved to the Midwest for a time, working with legislators in Illinois to develop asylums in that state. Dix felt, however, that the best way of working toward her goal was to take a more sweeping federal approach.

Policy Overview

The policy Dix brought before the federal government, then, was her most important initiative, and she spent years fighting for its passage. The bill, called The Land-Grant Bill for Indigent Insane Persons (1854), would provide more than 12 million acres of federal land to be set aside in various states for the development of mental institutions, or to be sold by the state, with the earnings used to support institutional development and treatment costs (T. J. Brown, 1996; Gollaher, 1995). Dix reasoned that because the government was beginning to cede land to railroads, corporations, homesteaders, and other private interests, it made sense for them to support her noble cause.

However, after passage by both the House and Senate, President Franklin Pierce, who Dix felt had assured her he would sign the bill (Tiffany, 1891), vetoed it. A major reason for the veto is that Pierce believed that the policy would set a dangerous precedent: If the federal government began providing assistance for those in need, the states and private charities would wash their hands of the poor and look to the federal government to provide such support. Tiffany (1891) described Pierce's philosophy of government: "Begin with doing anything for the indigent insane, and soon will the federal government have on its hands the support of every sick man, every vagabond, every drunkard, in the land!" (pp. 199–200).

Unlike the other examples in this book, then, here, we are not talking about a policy but rather a proposed policy that was vetoed. However, this was arguably the most important veto in the history of social welfare policy, because it set the stage for decades of nonintervention in social welfare issues by the federal government. Throughout the remainder of the 19th century as well as the first decades of the 20th century, the government was unwilling to involve itself in public welfare provisions—with only a few minor exceptions. As further discussed shortly, the prevailing belief was that issues such as poverty, housing, food, and other basic human needs should be provided for by family, charitable organizations, churches, and possibly the local community or state government, but not by the federal government.

Having worked so hard and come so close to her goal, the veto was a devastating blow to Dix. She made overtures to legislators in an effort to gauge the possibility of overriding the veto, but this did not appear to be likely

(Schlaifer & Freeman, 1991), especially because, as T. J. Brown (1998) noted, only one presidential veto had been overridden up to this point.

Analysis Element: Role of Government

Although the Pierce veto occurred more than 150 years ago, the principal policy issue that relates to the veto remains with us today in only slightly different garb. There are continuing questions about the proper role of the federal government, specifically surrounding its role in education, welfare, health care, and other such areas. Contemporary debates surrounding the proper purview of the government are strikingly similar to the ones that took place during Dix's time. Indeed, many of the policies that we discuss throughout this book focus on the question of how involved the federal government should be in relation to the funding, implementation, and evaluation of services and benefits, and whether such provisions are even harmful in their effects by causing dependency on the government.

Recent efforts at *devolution*, or the movement of funding and authority from the federal to state governments, are typical of efforts to diminish the scope of the federal government. One example is the TANF program, passed in 1996, which allowed states to determine specific components of what previously had been the AFDC program. Those arguing for such policies contend that state lawmakers and bureaucrats know the people of the state better and thus can more appropriately provide services. Another important rationale is that cutting out a level of bureaucracy will both save money and ensure a greater degree of efficiency. On the other hand, states frequently institute draconian spending cuts for basic need programs, especially during tough economic times, and often do not include the necessary oversight or may provide benefits in an overtly biased and discriminatory fashion. The reason that many programs have come under federal control in the first place is because of such problems. Most state-operated or state-funded institutions for people with mental illness or mental retardation, for example, were historically deplorable facilities and required federal oversight to force the provision of a humane level of care.

To complicate matters, some combination of federal, state, and county, local, or city authorities can all have a degree of control over policy making, funding, implementation, and evaluation as is the case with elementary and secondary school education policy. In addition, questions arise about whether implementation of policies (for example, service or benefit provision) should be provided by the government or by nonprofit or for-profit private agencies or corporations. Fully developing these issues would easily take its own book.

CHAPTER 3

State Eugenic Sterilization Legislation

◖1907◗

In 1907, Indiana passed the first eugenic sterilization policy in the nation (Reilly, 1991). Many other states followed, and by the time the eugenics movement had run its course, the majority of states had policies in place that allowed for involuntary sterilization for eugenic purposes, especially targeting people diagnosed as "feeble-minded" or "insane," along with other groups that were deemed to be a burden on the community (Reilly, 1991). These policies were not federal measures, yet I have included them in this book because they form one of the most egregious examples of public policy as a means of social control over a vulnerable community group. Involuntary sterilization as a method of "protecting" the nation from the rapidly expanding population of "deviant" or "defective" people also provides an important example of the various ways that vulnerable populations can be framed as an important threat to society and demonstrates how the basic rights of such individuals can be limited because of this threat.

Historical Overview and Nature of the Social Problem

Involuntary sterilization policies were passed within the context of the American eugenics movement, which lasted from 1900 to approximately 1930. Based on the writings of England's Sir Francis Galton (1870), eugenics held that for society to thrive, a program of differential reproduction must be supported. Eugenicists argued that policies needed to be in place that reinforced greater breeding among the more "fit" members of the population (termed "positive eugenics") and diminished breeding among those who were deemed "unfit" (termed "negative eugenics"). Eugenic thinking took hold in the United States in 1900 following the rediscovery of Gregor Mendel's writings on genetics, and a movement to support eugenic policies grew rapidly over the next few decades (Kevles, 1985).

By 1910, eugenicists had zeroed in on presumably feeble-minded people, and particularly "morons," the highest functioning subgroup included in the feeble-minded designation (the others were "idiots," the lowest functioning, and "imbeciles"), as the most appropriate targets of eugenic control (O'Brien, 2013). Eugenicists argued that such individuals, many of whom were presumably immigrants, procreated in large numbers and that they and their progeny were responsible for a host of social problems, including poverty, alcoholism, crime, venereal disease, and prostitution. Such individuals were measured by means of early (and faulty) intelligence tests, and advocates of control frequently spoke of the damage that procreation among such groups might bring to the nation (Trent, 1994).

The first major form of eugenic control was widespread institutionalization; many states attempted, some successfully, to pass policies that would require the involuntary institutionalization of people who were diagnosed as feeble-minded ("Feeble Minded Boys," 1915). Indeed, one of the reasons that the feeble-minded population was targeted by eugenicists more so than those diagnosed as insane was because policies were already in place to allow the institutional control of people in the insane group.

Policy Overview

Following the introduction of the vasectomy in the late 1800s and the salpingectomy (tubal ligation) soon after, sterilization became a palatable eugenic option for many medical professionals, agency superintendents, politicians, and others. As the procedure became more acceptable, states began introducing legislation allowing for the voluntary and even mandatory sterilization of feeble-minded people. By 1931, 30 states had passed eugenic sterilization laws (Popenoe, 1934). Not everyone, however, waited for such laws to be passed before engaging in sterilization and even castration. F. Hoyt Pilcher, the superintendent of a Kansas asylum, for example, wrote in his annual report in 1894 that he had castrated a number of charges, mainly "confirmed masturbators" (p. 7).

Although some eugenicists preferred institutionalization over sterilization, most came to view the sterilization as either preferable to commitment or as a useful complement to it. According to Theodore Robie (1934), a supporter of eugenic sterilization laws, a 1930 survey of the members of the American Association for the Study of the Feeble-Minded found that 227 out of 243 respondents supported the practice (p. 203). This preference for sterilization was primarily a result of its cost benefits relative to institutionalization. Many hoped that it would become a method of reaching that segment of the feeble-minded population that had not come under institutional control, especially in rural communities. The leading advocate of the state laws was Harry Laughlin of the Eugenics Record Office in Cold Spring Harbor, New York. Laughlin developed a model sterilization policy and traveled to a number of states in a largely successful effort to develop and lobby for passage of such laws (Laughlin, 1925).

In many states, institutionalized feeble-minded people who could live in the community were routinely "paroled" once they "voluntarily" agreed to submit to sterilization. In some institutions, residents could not even go on short vacations or family visits unless they first received the operation (Popenoe & Johnson, 1933). Realizing that the substantial cost of building an institution often stood in the way of large-scale segregation, many eugenicists believed the facilities would be more economical if they had a "revolving door" policy, serving larger numbers of people for brief periods and sterilizing anyone who was transferred into the community.

One of the primary reasons sterilization won support from many eugenicists was that it was widely viewed to be a humane measure. The procedure would allow the individual to live outside of the institution and possibly even to marry, and, therefore, it could be justified as being in the best interests of "paroled" individuals. Sterilization, one eugenicist contended, "would interfere with the real liberty of the individual less than custodial care" ("The Jukes in 1915," 1916, p. 474). Difficulties arose, however, when authorities questioned the constitutionality of some of the state laws, usually because they were alleged to be cruel and unusual punishment or violated the due process or equal protection clauses of Amendment XIV to the U.S. Constitution (U.S. Const. amend. XIV). The U.S. Supreme Court sought to settle the question in its infamous 1927 *Buck v. Bell* decision.

Carrie Buck was a resident of a state institution in Lynchburg, Virginia. J. D. Smith and Nelson (1989) contended that, like many poor young women of her day, Carrie's "immorality," as evidenced by her bearing an illegitimate daughter, was the real reason—rather than her intellectual capacity—she was targeted for sterilization. They also questioned whether Carrie or her daughter—who was given an IQ test when only eight months old—merited the feeble-minded diagnosis they were given (Smith & Nelson, 1989). The Supreme Court found in the state's favor and, in an eight-to-one decision, held Virginia's law to be constitutional, even when it was not voluntarily applied. The majority opinion, which included the infamous phrase "three generations of imbeciles is enough," was written by the famous jurist Oliver Wendell Holmes, Jr. (Dudziak, 1986). Once *Buck v. Bell* (1927) was decided in favor of Virginia, other states that had previously been unwilling to enforce their existing sterilization laws began to expand their employment of the procedure, some dramatically, because it had been given the blessing of the Court.

Effectiveness

By January 1935, more than 20,000 people were sterilized in the United States, and the majority of these operations took place in California (Reilly, 1991). Procedures continued into the 1970s, and about 60,000 people eventually were subjected to involuntary eugenic sterilization within the nation. The major goal of these policies was to diminish the spread of feeble-mindedness and other "degenerate" conditions. In this regard, these policies were an abject failure. Eugenic solutions to social problems were seriously flawed because they viewed heredity as almost fully explaining human behavior, and they were based on a simplistic reading of Mendel's laws and how these laws could be used to transform the course of human evolution (Kevles, 1985). In addition, the policies used extremely rudimentary, highly biased, and unscientific intelligence tests as the primary measure of intelligence (Trent, 1994).

Many eugenic supporters came to believe that large-scale sterilization would not solve major social problems, yet they did feel it would be beneficial in individual situations to save potential children from parents who had severe mental illness, mental retardation, or otherwise were deemed inadequate parents. As Kline (2001) noted, this is why involuntary sterilizations continued decades after eugenic thinking fell into disrepute in some professional and scientific quarters. In a number of states, eugenic sterilization gradually evolved into the forced sterilization of poor and minority women, especially targeting those on AFDC or other forms of "welfare" (Roberts, 1997).

The eugenic movement in the United States did have an effect on the development of Nazi eugenics under Adolf Hitler. Hitler (1925/1971) had expressed support for eugenic thinking in his early manifesto *Mein Kampf*. Although the Nazi programs certainly would have been implemented regardless of the American movement, the design and course of these programs, especially their 1933 sterilization law (Peter, 1934; Proctor, 1988), was based largely on the U.S. example. This law was passed shortly after Hitler took office, and under the policy, hundreds of thousands of Germans, largely people diagnosed as feeble-minded or insane, were involuntarily sterilized. In 1939, the Nazis developed their most destructive eugenic program when they had gas chambers installed in six mental institutions. For the next several years, they transported patients from asylums and hospitals throughout Germany to meet their end in these facilities (Proctor, 1988). These gas chambers were used by the Nazis to test out the most efficient means of mass murder and to set the stage for carrying out the Holocaust.

Following the Nazi experience, eugenics became a taboo topic of discussion for several decades. More recently, however, a highly contentious conversation about the role of eugenic thinking has reemerged. To a large degree, this is because of the development of eugenic or "quasi-eugenic" policies in the United States and other countries. Many have argued that current bioethical procedures, such as prenatal testing coupled with abortion, do not constitute "eugenic" practices because they are the result of parental decisions and are not imposed by the state. However, others have contended that such practices, whether they are the result of individual parental decisions or are incentivized or mandated by the state, are driven by cultural values that derogate disability and thus bear a close resemblance to historical eugenics (O'Brien, 2011).

Analysis Element: Social Engineering

Nations may, at times, attempt to engage in *social engineering*, described here as efforts to either encourage or discourage—through policy development—social roles, such as parenthood; the occupational or educational paths individuals may take; where they choose to live; and other individual choices. One can argue that the nation has a vested interest in such decisions and therefore should have the right to affect them. The country might, for example, pass a policy to pay off student loans for medical professionals who agree to work in underserved areas for a certain length of time. Sterilization policies can be viewed as an example of social engineering.

The primary rationale behind involuntary sterilization policies was a eugenic attempt to enhance the quality of the U.S. population through an early (and flawed) form of controlled human breeding. Criticisms over human rights violations were dismissed by the belief that the good of the nation was being served and that the "burden" of an expanding population of "unfit" people was economically and socially harmful to others. "Morons" were thought to be procreating in much greater numbers than the rest of the population, a supposition that has frequently been made about minority and immigrant groups, and therefore had to be controlled.

Forms of social engineering are more prevalent in communitarian nations, where individual desires and goals are generally taken to be less important than the societal good. In the United States, where individualism and personal freedom are held in high regard, and where many are suspicious of the expansion of the government to manipulate the public, social engineering is less obvious but still may be enforced in less noticeable ways, such as manipulation of the tax code in a way that benefits certain groups and harms others. Childbearing in particular may be incentivized or disincentivized, depending on the group, through various policies.

CHAPTER 4

Workers' Compensation

◖1911◗

Historical Overview and Nature of the Social Problem

A central concern of many progressivists during the early decades of the 20th century was work-related injustices. Child labor, extremely long work days, union busting, and the "assisted immigration" of low-wage workers were examples of occupational problems of the time. One of the most important issues was the lack of support for injured workers. Because this period was before safety regulations or inspections and many poor and immigrant workers were employed in risky jobs, injuries and even deaths were common in a number of work environments (Fowler, 2013; Sanchez, 2006). Many businesses had access to a steady stream of low-wage workers who could take the place of hurt or sick employees, and most of those who were unable to continue working had neither medical support nor any form of assistance from either the employer or the government. Given that males were most often the primary or sole "breadwinner" of the family, these accidents often swept already poor families into dire poverty. Injured males had little support, but the situation was even worse for working women, who were less likely to be protected by a union and were often employed in jobs that were just as risky (Abramovitz, 1988).

Accounts, such as Upton Sinclair's (1906/1981) book *The Jungle* and New York's Triangle Shirtwaist Factory fire, described in more detail later in this chapter, led activists to work to support the unionization of workers and the development of occupational safety legislation. Activists, such as Mother Jones, also played an important role in pressing workplace safety as an important sphere of government interest. Mother Jones was a longtime supporter of workers in particularly dangerous jobs, including the coal mining industry and factories (Gorn, 2001). As with other areas of social welfare during the Progressive Era, occupational safety regulations were opposed by corporate interests and many politicians, who referred to such policies as a form of socialism.

Policy Overview

The important concept behind workers' compensation is corporate responsibility: If a workplace is responsible for causing an accident, it also holds some degree of responsibility to provide for the individual during a rehabilitation period or on a long-term basis, depending on the nature of the injury. As with many social insurance policies, the United States was influenced by policies that had been previously developed in Europe. Prussian Chancellor Otto von Bismarck developed a system of compensation for injured workers in the late 1800s, and this was followed by initiatives in Great Britain and other nations (Fowler, 2013). In the United States, Wisconsin was the first state to develop such a policy, in 1911, and others soon followed. By 1948, every state had some form of workers' compensation (Fowler, 2013). Although many of the policies delineated in this book are partnerships between the state and federal governments, this policy largely is the responsibility of the various states.

Workers' compensation was designed to benefit both employees and employers. For employees, it provides them with some measure of financial support when injured on the job. For employers, it protects them from protracted litigation and potentially expensive legal costs related to injured employees. The exclusionary principle of workers' compensation basically formalized this agreement: If the worker is fairly compensated, they will not be able to sue (Janoski, 2013; Larson, 1989; Reno, Williams, & Sengupta, 2003/2004). Of course, many compensated workers would contend that their compensation was not "fair," but the exclusionary principle stands as a primary component behind the policy.

Because workers' compensation is state based, the various states provide differing levels of coverage for even the same injury. Approximately two-thirds of an injured worker's usual pay is provided (Hunt, 2003/2004) as well as medical or rehabilitation benefits related to the injury and death benefits to dependents in the case where the injury led to the worker's death (Fowler, 2013; Janoski, 2013). The state oversees funding, which is provided by the business with rates set based on the type of industry and likelihood of various forms of work-related injury (Reno et al., 2003/2004). Workers may be required to engage in rehabilitation in those cases in which rehabilitation is needed for the worker to regain the ability to work.

Workers' compensation injuries are often delineated by the cause of the injury and its effects. For example, the most common type is a physical–physical claim in which a physical event (for example, falling down the stairs) has a physical effect (for example, a back injury). As one might assume, the more problematic cases involve either a mental etiology or a mental effect (for example, inability, because of a panic reaction, to use a machine that previously cut off a coworker's hand). Different states have varying ways of attempting to deal with such claims (Janoski, 2013; Tucker, 2010). Many, for example, require that the initiating event must be highly unusual and shocking for that particular work environment (Tucker, 2010). For example, viewing a shooting death may be grounds for a claim for a social worker but less so for a police officer, which may be viewed as a more likely expectation of a police officer's job (Janoski, 2013).

Another issue of controversy relates to potential employer deceit in informing workers of likely risks. Deception may occur especially when the risks might be the result of long-term exposure or the specific nature (for example, potential violence) of work activities (Larson, 1989), the possible effect of work-related exposure to chemicals or toxic substances to fetuses, and subsequent company liability for birth defects as well as the companies' ability to fire pregnant workers because of such a risk. More recently, the possible use of genetic testing to see whether particular workers may have a predisposition to various risk factors has become a subject of much discussion (Sedo, 2007).

Effectiveness

A key difficulty with any scheme of workers' compensation is deciding whether an injury actually occurred in the workplace. Although an injury is often apparent, many injuries, such as carpal tunnel disease or other repetitive motion injuries, take place over an extended period and are contributed to by both work and other activities—which is also true with mental conditions. Workers may experience undue stress or various forms of mental trauma in their employment setting that may be layered on top of other stressful situations. These issues are particularly important for social workers, who often work in situations in which they may experience the abuse of themselves or others, be subject to particularly heavy workloads or expectations, or be exposed to other stressful factors. Janoski (2013) noted that, in some states, the work environment must contribute at least 50 percent to the injury. However, accurately quantifying injury etiology, and especially mental or emotional injuries, is an impossible task.

Another concern surrounds possible exploitation of the policy by workers who either are feigning or overstating their injuries, or are attempting to pass off as a work-related injury an injury that occurred outside the workplace. Although a physician examination is required for workers' compensation, some injuries are simply difficult to adequately diagnose. An important example is a back impairment, which falls especially high on the list of workers' compensation claims. It is largely because of such hard-to-diagnose conditions that fraud is a particular problem in regard to workers' compensation.

Often, too, employees contend that the physicians to whom they are referred are friendly to the business so are not apt to support the claim, whereas employers, for their part, may contend that many other physicians are too lax in upholding an injury claim. Employers frequently hire investigators to look into claims, particularly when they believe the person may be overstating the degree of the injury to collect benefits. Therefore, privacy considerations often arise in assessing how the policy is carried out.

Analysis Element: Trigger Events

Trigger events are important situations that garner public attention to a particular social policy. Government funding relates as much to the public attention drawn to an issue as it does to rational thinking and objective research about the effects of particular problems relative to other social problems. At any given time, there is a wide range of policy issues that we could focus attention on, so we need to prioritize. In a real sense, social policies and those who have a stake in them compete with one another for public attention because recognition of the importance of a problem paves the way for policy development and funding. Even within a large social problem area, the stakeholders in "subareas" compete with one another. For example, within the disability community, advocates for diabetes research and services compete against those advocating for many other disability-specific concerns. A large public relations infrastructure is often developed in an effort to bring a particular problem to the fore by attempting to focus public awareness on specific relevant trigger events.

Often trigger events are not anticipated but simply occur (for example, Hurricane Katrina, 9/11 attacks, COVID-19), and the large-scale effect of an event draws attention to the way that politicians do (or should) respond a particular problem. Trigger events can include not only specific tragedies such as the aforementioned ones but anything that draws massive public attention to an issue, including books, movies, songs, and personal stories. Two important trigger events related to workers' compensation policy were the book *The Jungle* and the Triangle Shirtwaist Factory fire. Both of these events drew sustained public attention to the problem of workplace safety and fostered relevant policy efforts.

Upton Sinclair's (1906/1981) book *The Jungle*, published in 1906, famously described the state of one unsafe work environment: the Chicago stockyards. Jurgis Rudkus, the main character in the book, was a Lithuanian immigrant who worked in the stockyards. Sinclair described in horrid detail the unsanitary and dangerous conditions of the work as well as the degree to which Rudkus was viewed as simply one in a long line of "disposable" immigrant workers. The book had an important effect not only on unionization efforts but also on the implementation of the Pure Food and Drug Act, passed later as the Federal Food and Drugs Act of 1906 (34 Stat. 768). Of course, reformers were not the only ones concerned about the employee safety issues Sinclair discussed. The unsanitary conditions in meat production gave a wide range of consumers a vested interest in policy change.

Another pertinent example of a trigger event was the 1911 fire at New York's Triangle Shirtwaist Factory, where almost 150 women and girls were killed when fire quickly consumed the facility, and workers were trapped in the building. They could not escape because the doors had been locked to lessen employee theft and to keep union organizers from entering the building. The fire sparked outrage, and in addition to supporting unionization efforts, it fostered policies related to sweatshop safety initiatives (Sanchez,

2006). A newspaper headline on the fire did not refer to those "killed" in the fire but, rather, used the term "murdered" (Burt, 2004). The inadequate safety regulations and employer callousness were together responsible for the deaths.

Although other examples from the period supported worker safety legislation, these two were important ones. Sinclair's (1906/1981) book used an attractive form of media, fiction writing, to push home a serious point. The Triangle Shirtwaist Factory fire gained the attention of the public not only because of the large number of deaths in the heart of a public place but also because accounts of the disaster included descriptive information about those killed, thus personalizing the trauma.

CHAPTER 5

Immigration Restriction Legislation

1921 and 1924

Historical Overview and Nature of the Social Problem

Whether it be the expulsion of the sacrificial scapegoat, supported or assisted immigration of criminals, the "passing on" of vagrants, or the development by a nation or community of selective immigration or deportation laws, the restricted entrance into or forced removal from a community has often been a primary means of dealing with undesired elements of the population or of otherwise controlling the demographics of a country. Organized opposition to immigration in the United States began in earnest before the Civil War and waxed and waned for the next few decades. However, toward the end of the 19th century and during the first several decades of the 20th century, demands for immigration restriction grew markedly. Calls for restriction were bolstered primarily by the rapid increase in immigration, which approached or surpassed a million a year following the turn of the century (Abbott, 1924).

In addition to the increasing number of immigrants, the immigrants were denigrated because of their presumed inferior quality. Even though the majority of the American population comprised people from northern and western European nations, such as Great Britain, Germany, and France, the proportion of those coming from southern and eastern European nations increased dramatically between 1880 and 1910. On the West Coast of the United States, immigration of Chinese and then Japanese people also greatly expanded during this period. Advocates of restriction policies argued that people from these various countries did not share the values and moral fiber of those who "built the country" and that they were primarily poor and uneducated. In addition, many workers were afraid that low-paid foreigners were taking the jobs of Americans, a concern that was especially strong at a time when unions were struggling to gain a foothold and some large industries were supporting immigration to break the unions. Coming on the heels of the Bolshevik revolution in Russia and growing support for socialism and anarchism in Europe, restriction advocates expressed concern regarding the potential immigration of large numbers of "radicals" intent on inciting insurrection. Related to this, following World War I, concerns about the likely increase in refugees from war-torn southern and eastern Europe increased, and public support for more restrictive measures grew ("The Threatened Inundation from Europe," 1920).

These new immigrants, it was argued, were largely to blame for many social problems, such as crime, immorality, and urban poverty. Eugenicists and White nationalists also contended that the percentage of people with feeble-mindedness and insanity was much larger in the immigrant class than for those born in the United States (O'Brien, 2003). Because these newer immigrant groups congregated in urban areas, such as New York, Philadelphia, and Boston, rather than spread themselves throughout the nation, many feared that these groups could not effectively assimilate into the "social body" or might come to politically, culturally, and economically take over the large cities. Supporters of restriction assured Americans that the country could not continue to absorb such a large number of newcomers without harming itself and that a policy to limit immigration was the only way to preserve the existing culture (Ross, 1913).

Policy Overview

With the exception of anti-Chinese legislation that was developed in the 1880s because of mobilization of restrictionists in California, the immigration restriction policies in the United States before the 1920s focused not on race or nationality but on those immigrants who possessed "undesirable" characteristics, such as contagious diseases, "insanity," or "feeble-mindedness," or who were believed to be unable to support themselves. Before the race-based restrictions of 1921, probably the most controversial measure to restrict immigration was the literacy test, which passed in 1917 and required that immigrants be literate either in English or in their native language (Curran, 1975). The immigration laws, developed before 1921, served to keep out immigrants with apparent diseases, disabilities, and certain other undesirable characteristics; however, to most supporters of restriction, these laws failed to deal with the most pertinent problems of immigration: high numbers and the presumed inferior quality of immigrants.

The primary component of the 1921 immigration restriction law, called the Emergency Immigration Act of 1921 (P.L. 67-5), was the development of a national origin quota. By means of this quota, annual immigration from specific countries would be limited to 3 percent of the total number of foreign-born people from that country living in the United States according to the 1910 Census (O'Brien, 2003). Because quotas were determined on a month-by-month basis, ships carrying immigrants from those countries whose numbers were most restricted would race to New York Harbor in the first hour of a new month. According to Viola Paradise (1922), "a single minute would make a tremendous difference in the lives of hundreds of immigrants" (p. 505).

The 1921 policy was intended to be a temporary law, and it was superseded by the more permanent measure, the Immigration Act of 1924 (P.L. 68-139). The 1924 law was even more restrictive than its predecessor because it used the 1890 Census figures (number of immigrants by country of origin) as the baseline from which percentages would be established and reduced the percentage of allowed immigrants to 2 percent per nationality (M. Grant, 1933). Because relatively few immigrants from the "nonpreferred" nations were in the country before to the turn of the century, their numbers would be severely limited by the 1924 policy.

Effectiveness

Given the nature of the national quota law, especially when the 1890 census figures were used as a baseline from which to determine the number of accepted immigrants from each country, immigration from "undesirable" nations was dramatically curtailed. Madison Grant (1933) favorably noted that this law not only sharply reduced immigration but also "favored the European Nordic, whose people made the United States what it is," as opposed those belonging to the "Alpine" and "Mediterranean" races, who "were late comers and intrusive elements" (p. 271). Countries, such as Great Britain and France, seldom came close to reaching their quotas, whereas the vast majority of those from Russia, Poland, and other nations in Eastern and Southern Europe were frequently not allowed to emigrate because of the quotas. For all practical purposes, the policy also halted the immigration of most Asians to the West Coast (Takaki, 1989). Immigration was further reduced by the onset of the Great Depression in 1929, when employment opportunities within the nation fell dramatically (M. Grant, 1933).

A good argument can certainly be made that immigration into the United States needed to be restricted or controlled at this point in the nation's history. The vast numbers were difficult for authorities to process, and, considering that immigrants were not disbursed throughout the country but rather settled largely in urban enclaves, unrestricted immigration added to the infrastructure problems (for example, sanitation and disease control, tenement development) that beset New York and other large cities (Frazer, 1923). The number of unskilled workers arriving in the country surely harmed union development, and many large industries financially supported immigration for this reason.

Analysis Element: Unintended Consequences

Unintended consequences may be described as any effect from a policy other than what was primarily intended. These usually are described as negative effects, but they can be positive. They frequently but not always are unanticipated at the time the policy was signed into law and implemented but often are expected. In this case, a primary unintended consequence of the 1921 and 1924 immigration policies was completely unanticipated at the time they were passed but involved the eventual destruction of potentially tens or perhaps hundreds of thousands of innocent lives.

It was not coincidental that those Eastern European nations from which immigration was largely closed off by the 1921 and 1924 acts were countries, such as Poland, Romania, Hungary, and Russia, that were populated by large numbers of Jews. A strong undercurrent of anti-Semitism was contained within the immigration restrictionist movement, and it nicely dovetailed with the American anti-Semitic campaign championed by Henry Ford, which reached its peak of influence in the early 1920s ("The International Jew," 1920).

When Adolf Hitler became chancellor of Germany in 1933, much of the Jewish population within the country became highly anxious because Hitler's vocal anti-Semitic views had already been made plain in his 1925 book *Mein Kampf* (Hitler 1925/1971). Interestingly, in that book, Hitler praised the American immigration policy, saying that "by refusing immigration on principle to elements in poor health, by simply excluding certain races from naturalization, it [the United States] professes in slow beginnings a view which is peculiar to the folkish state concept" (Hitler, 1925/1971, p. 440), that is, an effort to maintain racial and ethnic homogeneity. As the power of the Nazis grew within Germany, they were able to develop increasingly restrictive laws against the Jews—policies that they would "export" to neighboring areas of Europe that they would take over, beginning with Austria in 1938. Many of those Jews who had left Germany soon after Hitler gained control of the nation found themselves again within Nazi territory as the Nazis expanded their domain throughout much of Europe.

Between the mid-1930s and the early 1940s, hundreds of thousands of Jews likely would have left Germany and Eastern Europe, and Hitler would have likely allowed this departure (for a hefty price, of course), had the Jews been able to relocate a nation that would accept them (Bauer, 1994). Most European and other nations, however, followed the lead of the United States and fought hard to keep large numbers of Jews from entering their borders. The United States made a concerted effort to maintain immigration restrictions, even against children and even after it became obvious that the Jews of Europe were in grave peril (Morse, 1967).

When the war began in 1939, emigration from within Germany and the conquered territories became restricted. Hitler had purportedly been considering forcing the Jews out of German territory, and the Nazis had actually toyed with the idea of sending all Jews within their control to Madagascar (Bauer, 1994). With the onset of the war, however, resources were directed elsewhere, and Hitler knew that he needed to look to other avenues for solving the "Jewish question." He also realized that the war provided the cover he needed to carry out these more extreme measures.

Although the United States, operating under the 1924 act, was only one player in this international drama that ended in mass horror, it was an important one. Amid the fighting and upheaval of war, European nations were themselves in a worse position to take on large numbers of Jewish immigrants, and many of those who fled Germany for other parts of Europe found themselves in harm's way eventually anyway. In failing to assist vulnerable refugees as well as interning many of its own citizens for dubious reasons, the United States demonstrated that social justice may fall by the wayside during times of war.

CHAPTER 6

Unemployment Insurance

◖1935◗

Historical Overview and Nature of the Social Problem

Although unemployment is a fact of life that a portion of the population faces, it becomes a more obvious problem during times of large-scale financial stress. The Great Depression, which began with the 1929 stock market collapse, forced policymakers to focus intently on ways to increase employment because, toward the height of the Depression, almost one in four workers was without a job. Most of these workers had little in the way of savings and did not have much, if any, financial support from government programs. In addition to its effect on individuals and families, the Depression fed on itself because having so many people with little money (or who feared losing their job) had a detrimental effect on national spending, which exacerbated decreased production and led to additional job losses.

Another potential problem with periods of high unemployment is worker dislocation or movement (Blaustein, O'Leary, & Wander, 1997). If workers move frequently because of occupational availability (or lack thereof), this could have a problematic effect on housing and even community stability as well as on families (for example, if children are forced to move from their schools or couples are forced to live apart) (Estey, 1937).

Other major effects of the Depression and large-scale unemployment included desertion by fathers so the family could receive minimal governmental support and an increase in homelessness. These issues were magnified by the Dust Bowl, which left much of the farmland in the Great Plains unable to produce food.

Herbert Hoover, U.S. president at the time the Great Depression hit, had strong ideological concerns about governmental efforts to either create jobs or provide financial support for unemployed people. Hoover felt that the economy would eventually bounce back if left alone and that support needed to be provided on a local or state rather than federal level or through charitable sources. Even though he initiated the Emergency Committee for Employment to study the problem, few resources were provided in the form of government support to help unemployed people (Katz, 1996). Trattner (1999) noted that, in 1930, Hoover "approved a congressional appropriation of $45 million to feed stricken livestock of Arkansas farmers [but he] opposed an additional $25 million to feed the starving farmers and their families" (p. 277). Homeless and unemployed individuals had frequently set up "Hooverville" tent cities as an ignominious slap at the president's inaction in the face of growing unemployment.

Policy Overview

Some states and industries had small unemployment insurance (UI) programs, but those programs failed to have much effect on most workers, especially those who might have been out of work for an extended period. UI was passed as part of the Social Security Act of 1935 (P.L. 74-271) (see chapter 7) and as a central component of Franklin D. Roosevelt's New Deal. As noted in chapter 5, mobilization on the part of unemployed people was instrumental in forcing the government's hand. When unemployment occurred before the Depression, policymakers could chalk it up to individual problems, such as laziness, poor attitude, and alcoholism, or region-specific problems, such as droughts. With the extent of unemployment that took place during the 1930s, however, it became more obvious that large-scale economic and even international forces affected workers' ability to attain and maintain employment. This was particularly true because so many previously prosperous white-collar employees were now also out of work.

Roosevelt had developed an interest in UI options from his tenure as governor of New York, which occurred at the beginning of the Depression (Blaustein, Cohen, & Haber, 1993). In 1934, after becoming president, Roosevelt created the Committee on Economic Security not only to provide recommendations for UI but also to design a policy recommendation for the provision of Social Security to retired workers. As noted in chapter 7, one way of expanding employment opportunities for younger workers was to provide financial support to older workers so they could retire. The younger workers could then step into some of these positions.

The major question the committee had to come to terms with was whether an unemployment program should be wholly operated by either the various states or the federal government, or whether a joint federal–state program was best. An important argument for at least partial federal involvement was that some economic downturns hit certain regions of the country more so than others, and the federal government could spread resources around better than the individual states. States might also be wary of taxing their employers more heavily than neighboring states, which could result in a loss of businesses (Blaustein et al., 1993). As with many other social policies, the federal government develops broad standards for UI and allows the states a degree of flexibility in specific aspects of policy implementation (O'Leary & Rubin, 1997). States, for example, set out requirements recipients must follow in a job search, and states may extend benefits for a time beyond what is required during periods of high extended unemployment.

Most aspects of UI have remained largely intact since its passage, although some changes have taken place. To qualify, workers must have been laid off or fired from a job. If fired, the firing cannot be because of misconduct or illegal activities (P. M. Anderson, 1997). This requirement provides some control over people purposefully getting themselves fired to collect benefits. The other major requirement is that individuals who are receiving benefits must be actively searching for another job and be registered at an employment office (P. M. Anderson, 1997).

Eligibility for UI requires that workers have a substantive recent work history, which, in most cases, includes a "base period" from which the amount of UI is determined. This generally requires a full year or more of recent employment. UI covers approximately one-third to one-half of a recipient's regular salary, and benefit levels are tied to previous earnings (K. Kahan & Wentworth, 2012; O'Leary & Rubin, 1997). As O'Leary and Rubin (1997) noted, benefits need to be high enough to support out-of-work families but not so high that unemployed people refuse to look for a job.

In addition to the provision of a means of support during difficult economic times, the UI program serves to stimulate the economy and help keep economic crises from deepening (Blaustein et al., 1997). In periods of high unemployment, such as the 2007 recession or 2020 COVID-19 pandemic (see chapter 42), either the federal government or the states can decide to extend the length of time UI can be received. As a result of the extended recession that began in 2007, benefits were extended in many states for up to 99 weeks (Mazumder, 2011).

Effectiveness

Certainly, most recipients, especially those receiving UI on a long-term basis, would argue that UI is an essential government program. One benefit of the program is that it guards against underemployment—that is, someone with a graduate degree, for example, should be working in the area of their specialization rather than as a barista, unless this is by choice. Not only is the person directly harmed by such underemployment, but the community loses when expertise gained by years of education is wasted. UI allows people to engage in an extended job search to find a position that is more fulfilling and in keeping with the person's individual talents and skill.

As one might expect, it is especially entry-level and low-wage workers who have problems during times of unemployment, even if they qualify for benefits. Such workers receive lower benefits (because they had lower base earnings), and they are less likely to have savings to fall back on. Many families in this situation, therefore, are likely to look toward means-tested programs, such as TANF, to survive economically (Sales, 1995; Shaefer & Wu, 2011). There are also important gender differences in the system because women are less likely to be employed in positions for which UI benefits are offered or are more likely to be part-time employees. When they are eligible for benefits, they generally receive lower payments based on lower average wages (Mitchell, 2010; Shaefer & Wu, 2011).

Critics often argue that a large number of recipients take advantage of the program and refuse to actively engage in a job search until their money runs out. These concerns are not new and go back at least to the 1950s (Yoder, 1956). Because many recipients may be living in a household with at least one other worker, the desire to find a job quickly may be less than it was when UI was developed. During the recent recession, Republican legislators were generally wary of extending the length of unemployment benefits, arguing that many recipients were simply not looking for work. Most Democrats, however, contended that the job market was so difficult that finding any reasonable job was unlikely. Furthermore, states have varied in their policies related to refusal to look for or accept work as well as what might be considered a "suitable job" (P. M. Anderson, 1997).

CHAPTER 7

The Social Security Act

◖1935◗

Historical Overview and Nature of the Social Problem

Elderly people have always been particularly susceptible to living in poverty. As people age out of the workforce, they may not have the requisite savings to live on, especially when unexpected health care or other expenses arise. This is particularly true for people who lived in poverty or barely above the poverty line when they were employed. At the time the Social Security Act of 1935 (P.L. 74-271) was passed, for example, approximately three quarters of a million elderly people were on public relief (Douglas, 1936), and millions of others were living in dire poverty. In addition, there is one important unknown factor that relates to one's economic standing following retirement: how long a person (as well as their spouse) may live. This makes planning for retirement somewhat of a gamble.

The Great Depression, which began with the 1929 Stock Market crash, provided evidence in support of the adage that desperate times call for desperate measures. The Social Security Act and other social reform measures signed into law as part of President Franklin D. Roosevelt's New Deal would not likely have been passed except for dire economic circumstances. As Piven and Cloward (1971) noted, it is in times of mass struggle that the government must respond to basic human needs—for the self-preservation of politicians, if no other reason. Massive need means public disenchantment and the possibility of organizing and perhaps even rebellion on the part of the poor—and thus pressure for social reform. The era therefore provided a political atmosphere that was conducive to old age assistance and other forms of government assistance that had traditionally been perceived as radical.

Policy Overview

In a broad sense, the Social Security Act as it was developed in the United States was based on similar programs that had previously been in place in Germany and other European nations (Estes, Rogne, Grossman, Solway, & Hollister, 2009). Before the Depression, such schemes were largely viewed in the United States as socialist measures. The plan was also informed in certain ways by private pension programs that were in operation at the time (Domhoff, 2009). With the bank closures that occurred in the wake of "Black Tuesday," when the Stock Market crashed, problems related to private savings came to a head because many lost their life savings on their bank's collapse.

A primary motivating factor for the policy was the pressure brought to bear by those advocating on behalf of the unemployed. This was typified by the Townsend Plan, named after a California physician. This plan called for a monthly stipend to be given to elderly people under the requirement that it be spent within a short period. This, Francis Townsend said, would both stimulate the economy and allow many elderly people to retire, helping with the employment problem among younger workers (Béland, 2003). With unemployment at record levels during the Great Depression, both arguments were frequently made to support some form of old age assistance. The Townsend Plan gained a great deal of support throughout the nation and pressured the federal government to fast-track Social Security. Similarly, the "Share the Wealth" movement of U.S. Senator Huey Long of Louisiana was a large-scale plan to redistribute money to diminish the gap between rich and poor in the country (Altmeyer, 1966).

Although a number of states and private industries had developed their own versions of retirement or pension systems, these were a patchwork of programs, and it became obvious that a federal program was necessary, especially because workers often changed jobs or moved; thus, such programs would be logistically problematic. Work on an old age policy began when Roosevelt gave an executive order creating a Committee on Economic Security in June 1934 (Altmeyer, 1966). The committee studied various forms of social insurance in the public and private sectors and eventually came up with a rudimentary version of the current system. The Social Security Act was primarily opposed by certain business interests, but these stakeholders had less sway during the Depression.

The Roosevelt administration considered a larger package that would include universal health insurance, but it was dropped out of fear that it would bring down the entire policy (Altmeyer, 1966). Despite concerns about its massive scope and the logistics of implementing the policy, it passed in August 1935.

The Social Security Act has undergone extensive changes over the years, yet the basic elements remain as they always have been, and the program is now the cornerstone of economic security for elderly Americans. I certainly do not have the space here to detail all aspects of the program. The vast majority of workers in the United States pay into the system, along with their employers, and they are able to draw out money when they reach the requisite age so long as they have paid into the system for the full-time equivalent of at least 10 years. The Social Security system is largely progressive, "which means that a lower-income individual receives a higher rate of return on his investment in the system than does a higher-income individual" (Blahous, 2000, p. 112). Dependents or survivors (widows or widowers) may receive benefits, although not as extensive as recipients themselves.

As most readers are aware, the major issue with Social Security over the past few decades relates to viability of the trust fund. Many younger earners are particularly concerned about whether they will be able to recoup the money they have already or will put into the system. To a large degree, this concern arises because of the large number of baby boomers who are retiring and the ratio of future retirees to current workers, often referred to as the "dependency ratio" (Gorin & Armstrong, 2012).

The following major recommendations have been put forth for maintaining the viability of the system into the future:

- Require all workers (and their employers) to pay a higher percentage of their earnings into the system.
- Freeze the amount that current retirees can take out (stop cost-of-living increases), especially for more financially well-off retirees.
- Gradually increase the age at which retirees can draw money out of the system (for example, to 69 or 70).
- Increase the number of years workers need to pay into the system to be eligible for Social Security (for example, from the current 10 years to 12 years).

- Diminish the ability of the federal government to dip into the Social Security Trust Fund to pay its bills.
- Allow future retirees to invest at least a portion of their money into private investment accounts.

This final recommendation is particularly controversial and is explored in some depth in a later section.

Social Security reform will undoubtedly include a variety of the types of changes delineated in the preceding list, along with others. Although reforms will have an adverse effect (that is, require higher contributions, lower payouts, or both) on both current workers and future retirees, one might assume that current workers will bear the brunt of the burden for ensuring continued viability of the system. Not only do elderly Americans vote in larger numbers (relative to their population size) than younger voters, but, more importantly, they tend to be single-issue voters. They primarily focus on two related policy areas: Social Security and Medicare. Spreading their votes among both parties in relation to a much larger range of issues (for example, gun control, the economy, war/military, abortion, children's issues, welfare), younger voters have less of a political voice when it comes to Social Security and how it should be reformed.

Effectiveness

Social Security has certainly been an effective government program, especially in its primary goal of removing senior citizens from the poverty rolls. Over the past half century, the poverty rate of elderly people has dramatically declined. Social Security is not wholly responsible for that decline, but it has had an important positive effect on the economic status of retirees. Some might argue that it has been too successful. Many people look to Social Security as their primary source of income in retirement, and therefore the program's continuation is crucial. This leads to large-scale public fear any time reforms are discussed. Larry Polivka (2012) noted that although the poverty rate among elderly people has diminished in the long term, more recently, retirement income has fallen, especially with the 2007–2010 economic downturn and loss of much investment income. Social Security is often called the "third rail" of politics; the metaphor pertains to the electrified rail on a subway or "L" track that could electrocute anyone who touches it. The message to lawmakers is if they fool with Social Security, they face the consequences at the polls (Blahous, 2000). Even minor recommendations may be exploited by political opponents through fearmongering.

Increasing life expectancy over the years has also harmed the viability of the system because the amount of money placed into the system has not kept pace with this increase. Importantly, however, the number of years' extension of life expectancy differs based on one's income, according to Gorin (2012). As he noted, growing up in poverty can lead to any number of long-term health problems, such as diabetes or other risk factors, and such individuals are less likely to have had access to preventative health care.

Analysis Element: Corporate Involvement and Privatization

In chapter 2, I discussed the continuing questions surrounding the proper role of the federal government. An important aspect that pertains to this discussion is the extent to which private entities—either for-profit or not-for-profit—should be involved in carrying out various governmental programs. It has been traditional for all levels of government to contract out specific implementation or service components to private agencies or corporations. Questions relate to the process of how these service providers are to be chosen, what accountability mechanisms are in place to ensure efficient implementation, and how to keep conflicts of interests from occurring. Because of its recent political importance in the United States, this issue of contracting out to private agencies is of great importance, and I discuss it relative to Social Security privatization.

The privatization of Social Security would take one of two approaches. The first would allow those who oversee trust fund money in the Social Security Administration to have a wider range of investment options and place much of the trust fund money into stocks and bonds (A. Monroe, 1996). The major type of privatization that I focus on here would allow workers themselves to be able to invest a portion of their Social Security in private investment accounts, such as money market accounts, under the assumption that such a measure would enhance individual autonomy, support the economy, and hopefully provide a better return on investment than the Social Security trust fund provides.

Although privatization was discussed extensively during the President George W. Bush administration, and the president supported calls for at least partial privatization, these discussions died out as the economy faltered during his second term. Many politicians opposed to privatization argued that an economic downturn could severely undercut any privatization scheme. Investors may indeed make more money than the trust fund would allow, but they could also lose much. The government would have to strictly control what type of investments might be allowable to keep people from taking large gambles with their money. This is also a primary rationale for only allowing a portion of Social Security to be privatized. As Svihula and Estes (2009) noted, privatization would shift much of the risk related to Social Security from the government to citizens.

Another concern related to privatization measures arises from the close relationship between large corporations and politicians. As corporate support for political campaigns and parties continues to grow at a rapid pace, there are good reasons to be concerned that the actions of lawmakers, especially their support or opposition to various proposals, will be connected to their need to keep large contributors placated (Drew, 1999). This brings up a potential conflict of interest related to privatization. Because some arm of the federal government would have to control the type of investments recipients would be able to make, is it feasible to believe that politics will not contribute heavily to how these decisions are made?

Yet another implementation concern related to privatization plans would be that future retirees pay into the system to support current retirees. Any money that was transferred into private accounts would not be available in the trust fund. For this reason, most recommendations related to privatization would go into effect gradually to ensure they did not destabilize the existing trust fund (Dreyfuss, 1996; Marsh, 2005). Some critics are also concerned that because the more well-off recipients would have more knowledge of the economic system and basic elements of investment, they would have a "knowledge benefit" on other investors, and thus Social Security could be yet another means of enhancing the gap between the rich and poor in the country.

CHAPTER 8

Works Progress Administration

◖1935◗

Historical Overview and Nature of the Social Problem

As noted in other chapters on Franklin D. Roosevelt's New Deal policies, when the Great Depression hit, few governmental safeguards were in place to support either the mass of unemployed workers or the large number of businesses that themselves were suddenly struggling to remain viable. As stocks plummeted, banks closed their doors, and consumer purchasing diminished, the entire business sector of the economy was in serious jeopardy.

A potential policy response in such a situation is to advance the governmental development of jobs; obviously, though, this is problematic for a number of reasons. First, government jobs programs are frequently opposed as a form of socialism, just as were many of the initiatives of the New Deal. This was especially of concern during the 1930s because it was a decade marked by a fear of Communism (Lyons, 1970). Second, it is difficult to find areas of government-supervised employment that are not in direct competition with businesses and unions. Such competition would do further economic damage to already struggling companies. Third, because government jobs generally would not operate based on the normal rules of supply and demand, they could be viewed as an especially unfair form of competition for private industry to contend with.

On the other hand, given that businesses were laying off millions of workers and were unlikely to begin hiring in the foreseeable future, the government was left with few options to support the large number of unemployed people. Many of the programs developed by Roosevelt early in his first term were more in the nature of public assistance programs as opposed to work programs. Those in dire poverty needed some immediate support for basic necessities, which would also provide at least a little fuel for the economy. In addition, work programs would require time to logistically plan and set up. He saw both the public assistance and the public employment programs as emergency measures only, and he felt that long-term dependency on the government would further demoralize those without jobs (Edsforth, 2000).

Policy Overview

Among the rather large number of "alphabet soup" programs developed during the New Deal, the Works Progress Administration (WPA) stands out as one of the most important and ambitious. The program, later called the Work Projects Administration (Howard, 1973), was created in 1935, the same year as the Social Security Act (P.L. 74-271) (see chapter 7) and unemployment compensation program (see chapter 6). The WPA was a massive federal jobs program designed to provide employment for many of the millions of unemployed during the Great Depression. The program was headed by Harry Hopkins, a social worker and a principal aide to President Franklin D. Roosevelt. The WPA was preceded by the Civil Works Administration, a more temporary works program. Another similar program was the Civilian Conservation Corps, which provided occupational opportunities for young males who lived in boot camp–style communities.

The WPA supported state-based works programs that employed more than three million unemployed people during the height of the Depression (Bartik, 2001). These projects primarily focused on infrastructure improvements, such as building roads and bridges, bringing electric to rural homes and communities, and undertaking construction projects (Hopkins, 1938). Efforts were made to ensure that these projects did not compete with private businesses (Teaf, 1938), but this is problematic, and over the course of the program, a number of companies and trade unions contended that the government was taking over their jobs (Millett, 1938). As Howard (1973) noted, the inability to engage in competition with private industry meant, among other things, that the particular skills of many workers could not be used to the best advantage of the program. Although the WPA was intended to fit workers into jobs matching their skills and knowledge (Hopkins, 1938), in the case of people who had been previously unionized or who had worked in positions dominated by the private sector, it was difficult to ply these skills (Teaf, 1938). In some cases, the program worked in parallel with industry and even served as a "reservoir of labor" and source for training when particular private jobs became available (Coyle, 1939).

More recent federally supported works programs, such as the Comprehensive Education and Training Act of 1974 (P.L. 93-203), have experienced similar problems in attempting to assuage unemployment by providing federally supported employment (Bartik, 2001). As with many policy areas, critics regard the federal government as a poor and inefficient provider of services and contend that the jobs that are created are often unimportant and provide little in the way of useful skill development.

Effectiveness

The WPA was quite controversial, yet it did fulfill its primary goal of pumping money into the economy and supporting a large number of public works. In a number of geographic areas, the program was unfortunately coopted by various bureaucrats and used for patronage purposes. Writing at the time, Aikman (1936) contended that WPA money was primarily funneled to those who operated Democrat-led political "machines" and that powerful political leaders would only give funding to those individuals and groups that shared their political persuasion. Although some critics at the time said that too much of what the WPA was engaged in was largely inconsequential make-work, many of their projects were not only beneficial to communities but have also stood the test of time (Noah, 1982).

There is little doubt, however, that much of the work of those hired under the program would not have been completed had the program not been available. Among the other projects that the WPA supported were art projects, including the completion of murals in public buildings, and support for individual artists, actors, and writers. Harry Hopkins had a particular interest in supporting poverty-stricken artists, and by "1943 tens of thousands of impoverished painters, sculptors, musicians, actors, and writers" had been provided with some support through the program (Edsforth, 2000, p. 224). This funding supported more than 1,000 books written as part of the Federal Writers' Project, including a large variety of reference and guidebooks (Bold, 1999; Leuchtenburg, 1963). One of the more historically important programs of the Writers' Project was collecting first-person narratives from surviving slaves. Because slavery ended in the United States approximately 70 years before the campaign, the vast majority of those who had been slaves had died, and this project was an effort to collect stories from survivors of their lives under slavery (Strickland, 2014).

Government support for the arts is a particularly controversial issue that continues today with debates about funding for the National Endowment for the Arts, public radio and television (TV) broadcasting, and other such endeavors. Many disparage government funding for particularly controversial projects, especially those considered to be immoral or sacrilegious. Although freedom of expression is a fundamental constitutional right, they contend that this does not mean that the government should be a party to supporting all forms of expression. Edsforth (2000) noted that many conservatives hated the WPA-supported Federal Theatre Project "because it finances radical new plays" (p. 225).

On the other hand, advocates might say that the federal government supports all types of businesses, including lucrative ones, through various forms of "corporate welfare." In addition, expression through the arts is likely to be controversial. One might even argue that all great art is by its very nature liable to be unusual or cutting edge. Music, art, and writing often focus on divisive or uncomfortable subjects, and much of what we today accept as classical works of art or music were controversial in their own time. The WPA also supported many African American artists and musicians who, although talented, experienced barriers in getting their products out to the general public (Edsforth, 2000).

Questions surrounding governmental support for the arts may seem to be unrelated to social work interests, yet they lead to a broader issue that does more closely connect with the profession. There are certain areas of social work and other helping professions that can be viewed as more art than science. One might contend that all areas of any profession first make their appearance as something experimental, creative, and perhaps controversial because of their novelty; in other words, they appear as a form of art. Science comes in as these creative forms of engagement are subject to research and become accepted elements of the profession. These issues frequently arise when we consider which particular types of services or programs will be acceptable to government or private funders.

CHAPTER 9

Fair Labor Standards Act

◖1938◗

Historical Overview and Nature of the Social Problem

The employment system established in the United States has traditionally been characterized by at will employment, which has provided employers with a great deal of latitude to set the policies related to employment, particularly in relation to hiring, promotion, and discharge decisions. Employers have also had a great deal of latitude to set the other terms of employment, including issues such as salary and benefits, schedules, and various other policies. The assumption behind this is that employees are "free agents" who can investigate these conditions of employment and make a personal choice about what jobs to apply for. Those holding this view also contend that if certain employees are being exploited or are underappreciated, they have the right to search for an employment option where they are treated better.

Over the years, however, certain elements related to employer discretion in operating their businesses have been called into question, and various governmental policies have restricted their decisions in certain regards. For example, in 1935, before the Fair Labor Standards Act of 1938 (FLSA) (P.L. 75-718), the federal government passed the National Labor Relations Act (NLRA) (P.L. 74-198), which allowed employees to unionize (A. Cohen, 2009). Passed during the Great Depression, both the FLSA and NLRA were efforts to empower manual laborers and other low-wage employees who historically could be fired if they called for better pay or working standards.

This was especially likely to be true for unskilled and semiskilled workers when a large number of potential replacement employees could be used in their place. Especially during the latter half of the 19th and beginning of the 20th centuries, many large companies attempted to attract laborers, first from Europe or China (especially for railroad construction), and supported their immigration to the United States to fill low-wage jobs. When much of the

European workforce was cut off by World War I in 1914, many of these businesses went to southern states, paying railroad passage for African Americans to come to large northern cities to serve as replacement workers. What came to be called the Great Negro Migration was in large part supported by corporate efforts to fight unionization (Shaffer, 1923). A number of the race riots that took place in northern cities during this period were largely the result of labor struggles that arose from this supported migration (Grossman, 1989).

Before the 1930s, then, the government generally had a hands-off approach to business operations. Pay and benefits were within an employers' purview, and the assumption was that the best workers could leave for better opportunities if offered a more attractive option. Potential collusion among employers in certain industries to maintain low pay, however, was seen as a problem that the federal government might intercede in. Many argued that government intrusion into business decisions was inappropriate and would harm the ability of companies to operate in a free market economy. Others, though, recognized that low-wage employees were often mistreated and exploited. In addition, some employers took extensive efforts to ensure that their workers would not unionize, including bringing in paid strikebreakers (R. M. Smith, 2003). Especially during the Depression, then, calls were made to support the humane treatment of workers and to provide a restructuring of the balance in the employer–employee relationship.

Policy Overview

The FLSA was supported by the President Franklin D. Roosevelt administration and in particular by Frances Perkins, his labor secretary, as well as by groups, such as the National Consumers League, which advocated for low-wage workers, especially women (Storrs, 2000). Perkins, the first female to be named to a cabinet post, was a social worker who had long advocated for the rights of the working class (Downey, 2009). The policy passed in 1938 by a large margin in both chambers, although only after certain elements of the policy were watered down (Andrias, 2019; Storrs, 2000). Among other policy elements, the FLSA set the minimum wage and included provisions against child labor. Historically, one approach to depressing the wage scale was to have children fill certain unskilled jobs often in high-risk industries, such as mining, farming, and factory work. Families, and especially immigrant families, frequently supported this approach because adults received such poor compensation and, therefore, other family members needed to earn money (Stadum, 1995). In addition, immigrant families often came from nations where compulsory education was not standard practice, so not being enrolled in school was not unusual.

The 1938 act included a minimum wage of 25 cents an hour, which was gradually increased to 40 cents an hour by 1945 ("Minimum Wage Overview," 2013). Downey (2009) noted that 25 cents an hour was lower than the vast majority of businesses were paying anyway and did not provide for a living wage. The policy also created the Wage and Hour Division within the U.S. Department of Labor as a bureau to investigate businesses that failed to abide by the standards of the policy; the policy also required overtime pay for most jobs that was higher than the standard pay rate ("Minimum Wage Overview," 2013).

The policy allowed certain waivers related to both its child labor and minimum wage provisions. Some of these waivers remain in place, although they have been revised in various ways over time. Adolescents may work in family businesses, such as farms and restaurants, for example, but the number of hours is restricted, and such work is not supposed to negatively affect the child's education. Subminimum wage can be paid for certain work, especially when the person makes tips to supplement their regular salary.

One waiver area that has become fairly controversial over the past few decades is the ability to pay subminimum wages to people with disabilities. The argument in support of this practice is that people with especially severe intellectual or emotional disabilities will not be hired for jobs unless such a rate is allowed. Traditionally, sheltered workshops or rehabilitation centers and other places of employment are supposed to test the productive capacity of these individuals relative to nondisabled people and pay a percentage of the standard wage for that work that coincides with their productivity ("Minimum Wage Overview," 2013). Some contend that these workers are being exploited, whereas others counter that there are no viable regular job options for them and that any work is preferable to no work.

Over the past few decades, there have been increased calls for the provision of a living wage that is markedly higher than the current minimum wage. The primary arguments against minimum wage increases are that it will decrease the number of low-wage jobs as employers find ways to minimize the number of workers and that it will increase prices as wage increases are passed along to customers (which includes many of those minimum-wage workers). Hill and Romich (2018) noted that another opposition argument is that if employers are forced to pay workers more, they may respond by decreasing the benefits they provide. As Romich (2017) noted, wages are only one aspect of an employee–employer relationship, and the entire package of benefits needs to be considered in its entirety rather than simply focusing on hourly pay. Yet another problem that this author pointed to is that some low-wage workers receiving certain governmental assistance programs, such as the Supplemental Nutrition Assistance Program (or SNAP) (see chapter 15) and Earned Income Tax Credit (EITC) (see chapter 26), may not be helped by a minimum wage increase because their benefits may be diminished as a result of the extra income they receive.

Effectiveness

The FLSA was an important policy for protecting employees from exploitation and helped to raise some families out of poverty. One problematic area of the policy is that, unlike the cost-of-living allowances that are attached to Social Security, minimum wage does not carry with it standard inflationary adjustments. As of 2021, for example, the federal rate has not increased since 2009. The $7.25 hourly rate is worth much less than a decade ago because of inflation. States have the capability to legislate their own increase over and above the federal level, and many have. Moreover, certain cities can themselves have a higher rate than the state (if the state allows) under the assumption that the cost of living is higher than in other areas of the state (Soergel, 2020). According to Hill and Romich (2018), since "2014, 18 states updated their minimum wages, and more than two dozen localities—including Chicago and Los Angeles—created minimum wages above federal and state levels" (p. 109). Many groups had taken up the fight for a higher minimum wage, usually with a goal to eventually increase wages to $12 or $15 an hour after annual incremental increases over a number of years (Soergel, 2020).

Another problem area that the Department of Labor is struggling with in relation to FLSA is illegal work, especially by minors. One estimate is that several hundred thousand minors are illegally employed in the United States during most years (Hindman, 2006). Some of these youth workers may be undocumented immigrants, but many are not. Hiring individuals illegally saves costs for employers because benefits do not have to be paid. Clearly, the child labor and minimum wage elements of the FLSA are important policies now as they were when they were passed, although both are only piecemeal efforts at enhancing worker rights.

CHAPTER 10

Japanese Internment

◖1942◗

Historical Overview and Nature of the Social Problem

To fully understand the internment of Japanese people in America during World War II, it is helpful to consider the history of Japanese immigrants in California and other areas on the West Coast during the four decades that preceded internment. There actually were two stages of agitation against Asian immigrants: The first took place against Chinese people during the last few decades of the 19th century (Pfaelzer, 2007), and the second primarily targeted Japanese people at the beginning of the 20th century. Although aspects of the first stage of anti-Asian discrimination carried over to and influenced the second, in some ways, these were two disparate movements.

Overt hostility against Japanese people in America began shortly after the turn of the century and was primarily situated in California, although restrictionist campaigns were also waged during the first few decades of the century in Washington and Oregon as well as on the west coast of Canada. The first major conflict in relations between the Japanese and American people within the United States centered around efforts to segregate Japanese students in the public school system, particularly in San Francisco during the first decade of the century, when the city was devastated by an earthquake and widespread fire. President Theodore Roosevelt became involved in the affair and sought to avoid "causes of irritation" with the increasingly powerful nation. California lawmakers, on the other hand, contended that they had legal grounds to decide state matters (Steiner, 1917). As a result of this contentious situation, the "Gentleman's Agreement" was established in 1908 between the Emperor of Japan and President Roosevelt. The agreement included a promise by Japan that it would not permit the emigration of its laborers to the United States (Rowell, 1913).

Many of those who wrote in opposition to having Japanese people in America, however, were not appeased by the agreement. They believed that those who were already residing in the country posed a menace, and they called for further restrictions. Supporters of restriction argued that, like their Chinese predecessors, the Japanese people were an immigrant group that could not assimilate into the United States. They were said to both threaten race purity through intermarriage and to have larger families than native Californians, thus they were becoming an increasingly imposing and dangerous minority population (Stoddard, 1922).

Many also feared the increasing influence of Japanese immigrants within the agrarian sector over the first two decades of the century. This was a widespread concern because, as they expanded their ownership of arable land, especially in California, they were viewed as "taking over" a larger share of the coastal region. In response, the state passed laws in 1913 and 1920 that restricted them from owning land (Buell, 1923). In 1922, their ability to become citizens was revoked when the nation's Supreme Court, in the case of *Ozawa v. United States*, found that "the naturalization statutes which limited applicants for naturalization to 'free white persons' and 'persons of African descent'" precluded Asians from gaining citizenship (Daniels & Kitano, 1970, p. 53). The Immigration Act of 1924 (P.L. 68-139) (see chapter 5), in addition to limiting immigration from southern and eastern European nations to the East Coast of the United States, also excluded Japanese people from immigrating to the United States.

Interestingly, fear of a Japanese invasion of California predated Pearl Harbor by several decades. A 1920 article from *The Literary Digest*, for example, noted that many in the state believed that such an invasion was a real threat and that if the federal government did not take action to control the Japanese people, Californians would have to take matters into their own hands ("California's Anti-Japanese Campaign," 1920). Six years before Pearl Harbor, Carey McWilliams (1935) wrote that local legend held that

> the Japanese have an enormous fleet of fishing boats operating out of California harbors; these boats, being constructed in Japan, may be instantly converted into minelayers and torpedo boats; the entire fleet is manned by Japanese naval officers disguised as fishermen. (p. 735)

Even earlier, another author described a movie called *Shadows of the West* (Hurst, 1921). This early film "depicted a ridiculously mysterious room fitted up with a wireless apparatus by which a head-Japanese ticked out prices which controlled a state-wide vegetable market" and "invented a Japanese spy system" and the American-based "headquarters of a secret government" (Buell, 1923, p. 71).

Policy Overview

Immediately following the December 7, 1941, attack on Pearl Harbor, calls were made to control the Japanese people and their descendants who were residing within the United States. A particular concern was the *kibei*, the children of Japanese immigrants; these children had been born in America, but many had returned to Japan for their education. Internment supporters said it was this group that had been inculcated with a love for the emperor of Japan and hatred of the United States. They were described as spies who were waiting for the proper moment to play their part to assist the Japanese invasion of the coast (Baldwin, 1944; Bendetsen, 1942).

Although the *Congressional Record*, numerous media reports, and other sources described accounts of presumed or expected sabotage and treasonous activities by Japanese people in Hawaii and California, either in conjunction with or following Pearl Harbor, few of these reports were substantiated (Baldwin, 1944; 88 Cong. Rec., Pt. 2, February 24, 1942, p. 1565). Calls to force all Japanese and their American-born descendants away from the coast quickly hit a fever pitch, and some legislators even recommended the deportation of all Japanese people who were residing in the country (88 Cong. Rec., Pt. 1, February 18, 1942). President Franklin Roosevelt signed Executive Order 9066 in February of 1942, which included a voluntary removal and the restriction of "alien enemies" from certain sensitive zones (for example, near power plants, military bases, factories) and the complete removal of all Japanese people, regardless of length of residency in the country or citizenship status, beginning in April 1942. Two "reception centers" were built to send internees to temporarily, and 10 "relocation centers" were eventually established, some as far away from the coast as Arkansas. In all, 110,000 people were interred as part of the program, which included 40,000 nonnaturalized

Japanese immigrants and 70,000 of their descendants. Most of those people removed, therefore, had been born and raised in the United States (Daniels & Kitano, 1970; Park, 2008; Thomas & Nishimoto, 1946).

Interestingly, in Hawaii, the territory where Pearl Harbor was located and where a much higher percentage of people of Japanese descent lived than on the West Coast, the Japanese people were, except for those deemed to be potentially dangerous, "allowed to remain at liberty and to go about their business" (Daniels & Kitano, 1970, p. 62). Roger Baldwin wrote (1944) that there was no concerted effort to evacuate, deport, or segregate them, even though Hawaii was much more vulnerable to attack than California and was a vital military base for the Pacific Theater.

Effectiveness

Internees owning businesses or homes were forced to quickly sell all their possessions, and the combination of a huge sell-off and a quick removal deadline meant that speculators could purchase these properties at dirt-cheap prices, resulting "in something close to disaster for virtually every Japanese American businessman" and farmer (Thomas & Nishimoto, 1946, pp. 16–17). Within the camps, internees were paid a nominal wage if they could perform necessary labor, and many were given furloughs to work in the surrounding area, although these people, too, were paid the menial government wage. From the money they earned, internees were required to "pay the Government for expenses incurred in [*sic*] behalf of their dependents who may remain at Relocation Centers" (Bendetsen, 1942, p. 544). A particular irony is that a number of internees of military age were allowed to enter the military.

Many who were forced into camps attempted to develop a sense of normalcy and make the best of their situation, yet they also realized that what was happening to them was highly un-American. Many had lost everything they had worked their entire lives for and were treated as foreign enemies not because of any actions they had taken but simply because of their race. Eventually, many citizens and politicians came to question the need for internment, but by this point, it was too late.

Analysis Element: Problem Framing

To believe that those of Japanese descent were interred only because of anger over Pearl Harbor and the presumptive threats these people posed to the West Coast is to misread history. For decades before the onset of the war, the Japanese people were reviled in California and elsewhere. Internment followed on the heels of a series of oppressive measures and fit neatly into an overall decades-long pattern of anti-Japanese hysteria that had been fueled by nativist groups, such as the American Legion and the Sons of the Golden West, and politicians who realized they could further their careers by supporting anti-Asian xenophobia (Baldwin, 1944; Buell, 1923; "California's Anti-Japanese Campaign," 1920). Internment was based as much on economic opportunity and long-standing racial animosity as it was on fear.

An important aspect of policy analysis that relates to vulnerable populations is group or problem framing that is based in part on media images and aversive writings about such people. Within the context of such images and writings, metaphors and other "picturesque" language as well as pictorial images are used to define the group as a subhuman or threatening social force, bent on harming the "general population" in some way (O'Brien, 2009, 2018). Japanese immigrants and their progeny were described as a racial population that could not assimilate into the United States. They were "an immoral people" who threatened "mongrelization" of California (Ogawa, 1971) and the eventual takeover of California (Phelan, 1919).

One particular example of a negative metaphorical image of the Japanese people pertained to their involvement within the food industry. Metaphors related to the inability of the nation to "digest" such immigrants (Deford, 1935) may have been particularly apt in describing Japanese people because of their involvement in food production. A 1924 cartoon in *The Literary Digest* shows Uncle Sam turning back a plate labeled "Japanese immigration," saying it gives him "digestive trouble" ("End of the 'Melting-Pot" Theory, 1924). These images had already been familiar when internment was on the horizon. It is not at all surprising that among the other fears of Japanese people and Japanese Americans remaining "at large" in California was the belief that they were able, when the time was right, to poison a substantial amount of the food on the coast, rendering the population helpless to ward off an attack. Earnest

Hauser (1941) wrote that in the paranoid minds of those supporting internment, "Japanese farmers, having a virtual monopoly of vegetable production in California, will send their peas and potatoes and squash full of arsenic to the markets, throwing the population into a panic" (p. 689).

Aversive metaphors frequently work on a subconscious level, and this is a good example. We have a strong fear of potentially harmful "foreign" elements entering our bodies and vigilantly guard what we eat to ensure that we do not ingest impurities. There is a strong connection between protecting our body from poisonous or harmful elements and protecting the "social body" from immigrant populations that we believe may be damaging (O'Brien, 2018). In addition, in the case in which a population can be viewed as potentially harmful, the "burden of proof" is on that group to prove that this is not the case, which is impossible. Individual human rights are often abrogated when a great threat is assumed to be present.

CHAPTER 11

Servicemen's Readjustment Act (G.I. Bill)

1944

Historical Overview and Nature of the Social Problem

It stands to reason that the United States, or any nation for that matter, owes a debt to those who put their lives on the line for the nation by serving in the military. This debt is particularly obvious when it comes to those who are required to join as a result of a draft during time of war. One can argue that certain rights should accompany the grave personal sacrifice from the individual on behalf of the entire community

The sacrifice of military service came to be seen in a much different light in the United States as a result of World War I. It was always apparent that physical disabilities and death were obvious effects of war, but "shell shock" also came to be seen as a consequence of battle at this time. Because Great Britain was involved in the war before the United States was, shell shock was seen there first. In 1917, British writers Smith and Pear discussed this consequence of war and noted,

> We have chosen to use [the term] rather than the more satisfactory, but less widely employed term "War Strain." . . . Whenever the term shell-shock appears in these pages, it is to be understood as a popular but inadequate title for all those mental effects of war experience which are sufficient to incapacitate a man from the performance of his military duties. . . . Never in the history of mankind have the stresses and strains laid upon body and mind been so great or so numerous as in the present war. (pp. 1–2)

Shell shock would continue to evolve as a concept, going through various terms and definitions and most recently being described as a form of PTSD (E. Jones & Wessely, 2005).

Those in the military face not only physical and mental/emotional stressors but other sacrifices, too. They may have to forgo education, starting a family, purchasing a house, and so forth, and the training they receive in the military may not transfer well to a viable job opportunity in the private sector. In addition, those who died in combat or have been left unable to work may have families who require continued assistance.

Although some measure of support had been provided to veterans before World War II, this support was generally minimal and took the form of "widows pensions" or the provision of property in undeveloped areas of the frontier (Frydl, 2009). Many who had served in World War I were disappointed with the lack of support the government provided following the war; this disenchantment grew with the onset of the Great Depression, which found many veterans destitute. The "Bonus Army" was a group of such veterans who created a tent community on the National Mall as a show of protest. They were forcibly removed on the order of President Herbert Hoover (Frydl, 2009). However, with a more deadly war on the horizon, the United States realized that it needed to provide greater support to those who were willing to risk their lives in combat.

Policy Overview

A confluence of issues, then, came together to support momentum to provide more than token support to those fighting in World War II. There was greater "widespread recognition of the damaging effects of service" (Frydl, 2009, p. 110). Advocacy groups, such as the American Legion, had developed to fight for policies, and the Great Depression and subsequent New Deal had led to greater recognition of the federal government's role in providing support to its citizens. In addition, with more than 10 million members of the military reentering the civilian population within a fairly short time, the government needed to be involved in organizing this massive transition (Levine & Levine, 2011).

The question, then, was not whether to provide meaningful support to veterans of the war but, rather, how much and in what particular areas. The

Government Issue Bill ("G.I. Bill") passed as the Servicemen's Readjustment Act of 1944 (P.L. 346-268) shortly before the end of the war. The policy primarily provided financial support for higher education and low-interest loans to support home ownership. Neither of these provisions, though, could be viewed as simply altruistic. With the nation entering a new technological age and being in competition with the Soviet Union and other nations, a more technically advanced workforce was viewed as essential. In addition, many civilian workers would lose their jobs with the slowdown in defense production (Levine & Levine, 2011), so the nation was facing a large-scale transition in its workforce. Assisting veterans in purchasing homes for their families was not only beneficial for community and neighborhood stability. With the baby boom beginning, suburban communities outside the large cities needed to be developed.

Nam (1964) wrote that shortly after the end of the war, approximately 70 percent of the males enrolled in colleges and universities were veterans on the G.I. Bill, and many others used their benefits to learn a trade. Levine and Levine (2011) added that, under the policy, more than two million home loans were made following the war. Updated versions of the G.I. Bill have been passed periodically since the initial law, particularly following the conflicts in Korea and Vietnam. Questions continue in regard to the nation's obligation to combat as opposed to noncombat veterans and the form of benefits that should be provided (J. Cohen, Segal, & Temme, 1992). For example, according to Mark Boulton (2014), the American Legion fought a Vietnam-era proposal because it would have provided similar benefits to all veterans, including those who had not engaged in battle. Boulton quoted President and former General Dwight D. Eisenhower as saying that "those who serve in peacetime undergo fewer rigors and hazards" than those engaged in battle, and therefore, they deserved fewer benefits (p. 61). A further question is how much support the government should provide to injured veterans, including those suffering from PTSD (Carlson, Stromwall, & Lietz, 2013).

Effectiveness

Many analysts have contended that the G.I. Bill, in conjunction with other factors, such as unionization and the expansion of higher education, helped to create the American middle class and led to a vast improvement in the economic standing of a large number of Americans (Smith-Osborne, 2009). These gains, though, did not cut across racial lines. Although the policy itself did not discriminate racially, and, in theory, it provided benefits to all veterans regardless of race, those benefits could not be used by many African Americans. It did little good to provide housing assistance if communities were racially segregated, and university vouchers were not helpful if the university did not accept you in the first place. "As southern Black veterans attempted to gain from these new benefits, they encountered many well-established and some new restrictions" (Katznelson, 2005, p. 121). Southern legislators only supported the policy when it was clear that racial segregation would not be threatened (Altschuler & Blumin, 2009; Frydl, 2009). Even though enrollments at historically Black colleges grew greatly, these veterans were still limited in terms of which programs were open to them, and these degrees unfortunately did not carry much weight with many employers.

Moreover, highway development and suburban sprawl supported segregation throughout the nation. All-inclusive communities, such as the massive Levittown development in New York, were White only, and as these large suburban communities developed and families moved outside the cities, businesses followed (Levine & Levine, 2011). The postwar period was extremely prosperous for the nation, and the G.I. Bill did much to close the economic gap between working-class and professional Whites while simultaneously extending the racial gap.

The greatest benefit of the G.I. Bill seemed to accrue to those who fought in World War II. According to Boulton (2014), Vietnam-era veterans, even those who served in battle, received lessor benefits than their predecessors. Moreover, the support the Vietnam-era veterans received for mental health conditions arising from the military were insufficient, and the government famously questioned taking responsibility for the physical effects of Agent Orange, a dangerous herbicide to which many soldiers were exposed.

More recently, controversy has arisen regarding the experiences of female soldiers, especially related to sexual abuse, including the lack of support by the military for either legal action against perpetrators and the provision of counseling and other services (Carlson et al., 2013). The most well-known of these incidents was the 1991 Tailhook scandal, which involved sexual assault of a large number of women in the U. S. Navy. Finally, the decades-long controversy over the military's Don't Ask, Don't Tell policy (Obama, 2011) has affected the ability of lesbian, gay, bisexual, transgender, and queer (LGBTQ) members to not only receive benefits but even serve their nation at all.

CHAPTER 12

Head Start

1965

Historical Overview and Nature of the Social Problem

It has long been accepted that the earliest years of a child's life are extremely important in regard to their physical, intellectual, and emotional development. It is just as true that numerous environmental, cultural, and family issues could either stunt or enhance this development. Poverty especially puts young children at risk of not reaching their full potential, as do related problems, such as the lack of adequate food and nutrition, access to medical care, and suitable housing. Families struggling to meet basic needs often are not in a position to place a high priority on education and are apt to live in communities where day-to-day survival is valued over more long-term investments, such as education.

Even though for decades, child welfare and education experts have expressed the need for early childhood education, policymakers began listening to them in the 1960s and 1970s for a variety of reasons. Reasons included the increase in both single-parent families and poor families in which one or both parents were employed in entry-level, low-wage jobs; increasing concerns about poverty and environmental neglect; and rising optimism regarding the potential benefit of early education (Zigler & Muenchow, 1992). Regarding the increase in optimism, Rose (2010) wrote that "Head Start was born in a time of enormous optimism, both about the impact early innovation could have on children's development and life trajectories and about the federal government's ability to solve deep-seated problems of poverty and inequality" (p. 13).

Policy Overview

Although a small public preschool program was initiated during the 1930s as part of Franklin D. Roosevelt's New Deal, this was a temporary program and was discontinued in 1943. Vinovskis (2005) wrote that the program was beneficial in supporting government work programs during the Great Depression but that it also was beneficial to society when World War II began and many women entered the workplace to assist with the war effort. For a number of reasons, early childhood education was an important goal of both the President John F. Kennedy and President Lyndon B. Johnson administrations. The Cold War with Russia and subsequent competition to innovate (for example, related to space exploration) to gain an advantage in science and technology led Kennedy and others to believe that the potential of all children should be a national priority (Vinovskis, 2005). He also became concerned about the effects of poverty and other forms of deprivation on young children. Writings, such as Michael Harrington's (1962) *The Other America*, brought Kennedy face-to-face with the degree of poverty in the United States (Trattner, 1999). The civil rights protests also brought home to the rest of the country the problems faced by poor children, particularly those in minority populations (Ceglowski, 1998).

As these administrations viewed it, an early education program would meet several important goals. First and foremost, it would provide a stimulating educational experience and give at-risk children a jump start that would assist them when entering elementary school. Second, it would provide unemployed single parents living in poverty with the ability to perhaps gain at least part-time employment because their children would be in a safe environment. Third, it would offer an opportunity for important services outside of education, such as health and dental checkups; vaccinations; parenting support and training; and the dissemination of information regarding beneficial social policies, such as the Special Supplemental Nutrition Program for Women, Infants, and Children (WIC), housing assistance, and EITC benefits.

When President John F. Kennedy was assassinated in Dallas in November 1963, the job of creating an early education program fell to Johnson, who viewed it as a central element of his larger "War on Poverty." Early education was also part of a broad approach to federal involvement in education at other levels. Education had previously been left almost completely in the hands of the state and local governments, but President Johnson felt that the federal government needed to have some involvement, especially when it came to schools in high-poverty regions and states. These schools had few resources to draw on, and the children who attended them were at a distinct disadvantage compared to other children. In the same year that Head Start was created, Johnson pushed for passage of the Elementary and Secondary Education Act of 1965 (ESEA) (P.L. 89-313), which was the first major federal policy designed to provide financial and other support to primary and secondary schools (Vinovskis, 2005).

Head Start was passed on the heels of Johnson's Economic Opportunity Act of 1964 (P.L. 88-452), and Johnson pegged Sargent Shriver to spearhead the development of Head Start. Shriver was John F. Kennedy's brother-in-law and was also instrumental in the implementation of Kennedy's Peace Corps program. As an aside, Shriver also was chosen to run as George McGovern's vice presidential candidate in 1972 when the original choice, U.S. Senator Thomas Eagleton of Missouri, was dropped from the ticket following reports of clinical depression and electroconvulsive therapy treatments. And, yes, Shriver was also Maria Shriver's father and thus the future father-in-law of the future governor of California, Arnold Schwarzenegger.

Shriver was extremely interested in developing as large a program as possible, so he delegated a planning committee with the responsibility to design Head Start. Although Shriver was passionate about the potential benefit of the program, he was probably overly optimistic about the potential benefits of Head Start and the government's ability to quickly implement such a large program without major problems arising (Rose, 2010; Zigler & Muenchow, 1992). As discussed further later in this chapter, many local Head Start programs were unclear about both operational logistics and the prioritization of program goals.

The initial program was only offered during the summer, but within a few years, many of the centers expanded to year-round operation (Ceglowski, 1998). The primary target population for Head Start is children who live in poverty, but about 10 percent to 15 percent of the children served have diagnosed disabilities (Zigler & Styfco, 2004). A major revision to the Head Start Program was the development of Early Head Start in 1995, which was designed to serve even younger children than the original program (L. Olsen & DeBoise, 2007). This program also was connected with the Individuals with Disabilities Education and Improvement Act of 2004 (P.L. 108-446) as a response to the disproportionate number of poor children who have recognized disabilities (Azzi-Lessing, 2010).

Effectiveness

To a large degree, effectiveness related to Head Start pertains to which of its goals is presumed to be most important. If the principal goal of the program is to enhance the intellectual capacity of children, it did not appear to be successful; if it was to close the knowledge gap between children living in poverty and other children, it appears to have had some short-term success that was not maintained over an extended period; if it was to provide supportive services (for example, dissemination of medical, nutritional, and other information) to poor families and children, it was largely a success. Because of confusion over goal development and prioritization, I explore this issue in greater depth shortly.

Because of its rapid development and implementation, Head Start came to mean different things to different local programs. As Zigler and Muenchow (1992) wrote, "The rapid expansion of Head Start also had a price, namely the sacrifice of consistent quality. It is a price we are still paying, in the uneven nature of Head Start programs today" (pp. 28–29). Even today, legislators themselves seem to view Head Start from widely varying perspectives. Some perceive it to be an important and beneficial educational and social services program, whereas others hold to the position that there are "wide disparities" in relation to the quality of differing programs (Zigler & Muenchow, 1992). According to Zigler and Styfco (2004), quality control standards were built into the program during the 1970s, but there was insufficient monitoring to ensure that all centers were abiding by these standards.

Analysis Element: Goal Development

It seems exceedingly obvious to say that goal development is an important element of policymaking. To understand whether a policy has been effective, we need to clearly delineate the important goal(s) of the policy. One of the major problems with Head Start is that goal development was unclear. The program spelled out a range of different goals but offered little clarity about prioritization regarding which of these goals was most important for the program to be viewed as a success (Rose, 2010). In addition, the program was initiated on a large-scale basis within a fairly short time, which did not allow for much experimentation to find the best type of program. The funding that was initially provided was also much lower than what was needed to reach important goals (Ceglowski, 1998). As with other War on Poverty programs, funding was diminished in part because of the need to fund the expanding war in Vietnam. In effect, the real war adversely affected effectiveness of the metaphorical one.

A core emphasis of Head Start was local involvement. Many of its founders saw the program as a community organization approach to ending poverty as much as an educational program (Bates, 1966; Payne, Payne, Mercer, & Davison, 1973). Because a wide range of community members were employed as teachers, these individuals did not necessarily have expertise in the education of children, and they were generally poorly paid (Ceglowski, 1998).

A grassroots approach to the program also meant that individual programs varied widely in their organization. Because of this variance and because different programs could be focusing on different goals, it was extremely hard to determine whether the overall program itself was successful, what factors might be significant in leading to successful outcomes for particular centers, or whether positive findings related to any particular center could be generalized to others. The various community action programs that arose during Johnson's administration, such as Head Start, included the concept of *maximum feasible participation*—that is, community members were to be actively engaged in having a voice in the direction and operation of the programs. Although maximum feasible participation enhances community self-determination and is important for a number of reasons, a primary negative side effect is that widely divergent programs may arise, thus making comparisons between centers extremely difficult.

Head Start was initiated during a period when there was a high degree of optimism about the effects of early education, especially related to children who lived in poverty. Many supporters even contended that Head Start could enhance children's IQ levels. According to Zigler and Muenchow (1992), Shriver himself testified before Congress in 1966 that the program could lead to IQ gains "as much as 8 to 10 points" after only six weeks of participation (p. 26), and even Lyndon Johnson and First Lady Claudia Alta "Lady Bird" Johnson embraced the potential for IQ development. When the program was implemented and such gains were not seen, Head Start was open to criticism.

As Rose (2010) noted, although the 1960s was, in general, marked by a degree of optimism regarding the effects of education and the environment on intelligence, the 1970s saw a reversion to a largely hereditarian and conservative perspective. The prospect of raising IQ as a goal of Head Start was based largely on misleading research and was a side effect of both wishful thinking and a need to "sell" the program. It is important that policy goals are not only clear but also reachable, especially because evaluation studies that fall short of expectations could place the program in jeopardy.

CHAPTER 13

Community Mental Health Centers Act

◖1963◗

Historical Overview and Nature of the Social Problem

Efforts to identify and provide custodial care or some type of effective treatment to people with mental illness date back centuries. In the United States, political concern over federal provisions for those with chronic mental illness can be traced back to the efforts of Dorothea Dix, described in chapter 2. Because Dix's efforts were vetoed by President Franklin Pierce, care of people with mental illness remained almost completely a state responsibility for the next century. Although most states had developed large institutions during the 1900s or early in the 20th century, the federal government first became highly involved in the problem during World War I, when the issue of shell shock, or "war neurosis," brought psychiatrists onto the government payroll to decide whether such conditions were truly a form of mental disease or simply malingering or "cowardice." These early researchers also attempted to discover an effective treatment and determine if there were certain characteristics of conscripts that predicted who was more likely to be stricken (Culpin, 1920; "Strange Vagaries of Shell-Shock," 1918).

The war arose around the same time that Freudian psychotherapy was first coming to be embraced by many American psychiatrists. A central element of mental illness for Freud and others was that at least some forms were not inherent or genetic but were caused by one's experiences, especially early in life, and thus could be amenable to treatment. A degree of optimism was also supported by the writings of Clifford Beers, an advocate for humane treatment of people with mental illness. In his book *A Mind That Found Itself*, Beers (1930) wrote of his own experiences in a mental institution and proposed changes that would lead to more benevolent treatment and the beginning of a self-advocacy movement.

Despite these signals of potential positive change, however, mental institutions became increasingly large throughout the first half of the century, and treatments were frequently ineffective and harmful. Perhaps the most well-known such procedure was the frontal lobotomy. Developed in Portugal in 1935 by Egas Moniz, who would win the Nobel Prize in Physiology or Medicine in 1949 for his development of the procedure, the lobotomy—originally called leucotomy—was popularized in the United States by Walter Freeman (El-Hai, 2005). Freeman performed a large percentage of the operations in this country and became its most important advocate (Freeman & Watts, 1950). He "sold" the operation in large part by vastly overstating its positive effects on his patients (El-Hai, 2005).

Policy Overview

The Community Mental Health Centers Act (CMHCA) (1963) (P.L. 88-164) was preceded by the National Mental Health Act (NMHA) (P.L. 79-487), passed in 1946. This first major federal mental health policy primarily supported research on the various forms of chronic mental illness and increased training of mental health professionals (Grob, 1991). The policy was spearheaded by Robert Felix, a physician who directed the National Institute of Mental Health (NIMH) from 1949 until 1964 (Grob, 1991). NIMH was created as a result of the 1946 act and would become the national center for research related to mental health–related issues. Over the course of his time with NIMH, Felix would support many of the provisions that would later be included in the CMHCA.

The CMHCA was passed in 1963 following the development, under President John F. Kennedy, of a presidential commission to study problems related to mental illness and the best approaches to solving those problems (Dixon & Goldman, 2004). President Kennedy pushed for policies related to mental illness and mental retardation in part because of his family's experience with his sister, Rosemary, who may have been diagnosed as either feeble-minded (intellectually disabled), mentally ill, or both. She received a lobotomy while in her twenties (by the aforementioned Freeman), which failed miserably and left her largely incapacitated. It should be noted, however, that diagnostics related to mental illness and intellectual disability were rudimentary at the time Rosemary was growing up, and the Kennedy family went to a great deal of trouble to obfuscate Rosemary's situation, so we really know very little about an actual diagnosis (O'Brien, 2004).

In addition to President Kennedy's interest in the subject, mental illness was becoming a hot policy topic for additional reasons. First, exposés of institutional abuses during the 1960s and earlier decades shed light on the poor treatment in many facilities and served to increase public awareness (Deutsch, 1948/1973; Grob, 1991). Second, parent support groups had begun to advocate for better services and increased funding to treat those with chronic mental illness. Third, the development of antipsychotic medications, beginning in the 1950s, led many professionals, patients, and family members to believe that people who had been confined to institutions could thrive in the community (Whitaker, 2002). Many state politicians felt that the closure of large state institutions would save them money, especially if the federal government assisted in paying for community-based care (Mechanic, 1999).

Advocacy for the bill, therefore, was fairly widespread and supported both for humanitarian and pragmatic political and economic reasons. The bill passed relatively easily (Grob, 1994), and primary goals of the policy included not only the provision of mental health services within outpatient community settings but also increased training of mental health professionals and expanded research into mental illness.

The push to fully implement the act and depopulate mental institutions was supported by a number of important lawsuits during the 1970s and 1980s brought on behalf of involuntarily institutionalized individuals (Shannon, 1997). These legal claims were given impetus by the previous exposés of institutions, the burgeoning civil rights movement, and the writings of Erving Goffman (1961), Thomas Szasz (1970), and other supporters of individual rights for people with mental illness. These suits, which included *O'Connor v. Donaldson* (1975) and *Youngberg v. Romeo* (1982) (Shannon, 1997), dealt with a number of civil liberties issues but primarily the right of individuals to not receive forced treatment unless they proved a threat to themselves or others and the requirement that institutions provide meaningful efforts to provide services that would allow those with chronic mental illness to gain the skills necessary to allow them to move into the community.

Effectiveness

Scholars seem to agree that the CMHCA was largely ineffective in reaching its primary goal of supporting the treatment of people with mental illness within community-based settings. Some have argued that the basic premise of the policy was fairly sound but that defunding of the policy, once it was implemented, led to its downfall. E. Fuller Torrey (1988), Specht and Courtney (1994), and others wrote that there were few incentives in mental health policy for clinics and providers to treat people with long-term chronic conditions, and many professionals primarily focused their attention on the "worried well," people with more treatable short-term mental conditions.

The policy was dramatically underfunded, especially during the President Richard M. Nixon administration, and the Vietnam War served to both take public attention away from many domestic problems and to direct federal funding into supporting the war effort. This was somewhat ironic, of course, because many soldiers would later return from the war and require community-based mental health treatment themselves. The economic downturn of the late 1970s further depleted funding as did the decision during the President Ronald Reagan administration to develop block grants as a means of returning mental health services to a state responsibility (Mechanic, 1999).

Evaluation Criteria: Self-Determination

As introduced above, the major controversy related to community-based versus institutional care surrounds those individuals with chronic mental illness who have problems living outside an institution, but who do not pose imminent harm to themselves or others, and thus cannot be confined against their will. This relates to individual self-determination, and the question of when the state can remove a person's right to make personal choices. This controversy can be framed by the writings of E. Fuller Torrey (1988) and Thomas Szasz (1970), two of the most well-known adherents of each position.

In his book *Nowhere to Go*, as well as other writings, Torrey (1988) argued that the pendulum has swung much too far in the direction of preserving the individual rights of those with serious mental illness. He contended that it is of no benefit to weaken commitment laws if those who would otherwise be forced into inpatient facilities instead wound up on the streets, living in dilapidated housing, and were incapable of engaging in basic self-care and were highly vulnerable to victimization. He frequently cited fellow psychiatrist, Darold Treffert (1973), who wrote that in "the zeal to impeccably protect the patient's civil liberties and rights, an increasing number of troubled and psychotic patients are what I choose to term dying with their rights on" (p. 1041).

On the other hand, Szasz (1970) and others (Whitaker, 2002) contended that forced commitment has often been used for political purposes or to enforce conformity and that there is always a good likelihood that this will happen again if laws are changed to make it easier to involuntarily commit people with mental illness. Szasz (1970) continued that most mental illnesses, with the exception of those that can be proven to have an organic or medical basis, are in large part socially and politically constructed to provide jobs to diagnosticians and service providers, promote the power and authority of the psychiatric profession, and pump money into the pharmaceutical industry.

An outgrowth of this view that mental illness diagnoses are socially and politically constructed is the development over the past few decades of the Mad Pride movement. Focusing on both the issue of self-determination and the power and control issues that Szasz (1970) and others have written and spoke of, Mad Pride groups, similar to other disability rights groups, contend that people who have experienced chronic mental illness and have been involved (sometimes begrudgingly) in the system are the best mentors and advisors for those currently exhibiting symptoms rather than psychiatrists and other mental health professionals. They advocate for alternatives to psychotropic medications and the training of law enforcement personnel on how better to engage with people with mental illness (Quinn & Otteson, 2019). Regardless of where social workers and other helping professionals fall related to these issues and to our proper role as mental health professionals, it is important that we are mindful of how such concerns may be viewed from the standpoint of clients.

CHAPTER 14

Civil Rights Act

1964

Historical Overview and Nature of the Social Problem

Within the confines of this text, I cannot recount the long history of overt and covert racism against African Americans in the United States. This includes, but is certainly not limited to, slavery, medical experimentation (Washington, 2006), lynchings, the Jim Crow laws (Kennedy, 1973; Woodward, 1957), "sundown" laws (Loewen, 2006), restrictive covenants ("Anti-Negro Covenants II," 1947), redlining, poll taxes, and educational segregation (Jacoway, 2007). Although there are certainly many parallels between discrimination and oppression in relation to African Americans in the United States and movements against other minority populations, here, I primarily discuss maltreatment against African Americans because this type of discrimination was the principal focus of the Civil Rights Act of 1964 (P.L. 88-352).

With the civil rights demonstrations of the 1950s and 1960s, which began in earnest following the 1954 *Brown v. Board of Education* case and the 1955–1956 Montgomery bus boycott, the realities of segregation and unfair treatment of African Americans was forced on the attention of the American public. As images were distributed through the media of police dogs and water cannons being set on peaceful protesters and Freedom Riders being badly beaten, public sympathy came to rest increasingly with the protesters (Arsenault, 2011). Even the outright murder of civil rights workers often went unsolved in the South, leading political leaders at the federal level to realize they had to get involved.

It is important to note that racial discrimination was not merely tolerated before the Civil Rights Act. In many areas (and not only in the Deep South), it was mandated, particularly relating to the Jim Crow laws. In many areas, restaurants and other businesses could not cater to an integrated customer population even if they wanted to; instead, they were required to segregate.

Restaurants, for example, often had strict and specific standards for partitioning the races, including the use and storage of separate dinnerware and glassware (*Civil Rights—Public Accommodations*, 1963). Similarly, even after cities could no longer segregate where African Americans could live though legal and policy restrictions (de jure discrimination), many communities took it on themselves to maintain segregation through more covert private measures (de facto discrimination).

Policy Overview

A civil rights bill was proposed and defeated during the last half of the 1950s, largely because of the efforts of U.S. senators such as Strom Thurmond of South Carolina. Although John F. Kennedy had some interest in the promotion of civil rights policy, being born and raised in New England and having spent several years living abroad or serving in the military, it is likely that he was somewhat naive about the extent of discrimination in the southern states, where the most egregious forms of abuse were taking place. In addition, on taking office, he was beset by other problems (for example, Cuba, the Cold War) that diverted attention from the struggle (Rosenberg & Karabell, 2003).

Many political leaders at the beginning of the 1960s held that discrimination because of race, ethnicity, gender, or religious affiliation was wrong, but a number of them questioned whether it was really the role of the federal government to develop policies in an effort to ameliorate such practices. The call for civil rights legislation was for a different form of social policy than the government had previously enacted in that such legislation was primarily dealing with the private actions of employers, landlords, school officials, and other people with "property rights" and was forcing the federal government to intervene in matters that traditionally were left to the states. Many White leaders called for patience, but Martin Luther King, Jr., and other leaders of the civil rights movement said that they had already waited too long to act, and King's advocacy for nonviolent passive resistance was taken up by protesters throughout the nation.

The Civil Rights Act was arguably the most contentious federal policy in the history of the nation. This is true not only because of the strong emotions on both sides of the issue but also because southern lawmakers decried what they felt was the federal government's intrusion into the states. Southern Democrats formed the basis of opposition to the law and maintained a lengthy filibuster in their efforts to defeat it (Loevy, 2004; Whalen & Whalen, 1985). Certainly, one of the major long-term political implications of the policy is that, following its passage, political control in the South transitioned rather dramatically from the Democratic to the Republican party. Although other issues were of some importance in this transition, the support of the Civil Rights Act by the Democratic party (and advocated and signed into law by President Lyndon B. Johnson, a Southern Democrat) played a large role. As Loevy (1997) noted, support for the policy also served to endear many African Americans to the Democratic party.

Among other arguments, those opposed to the bill contended that it violated states' rights; that discrimination was virtually impossible to prove and stop; that the owners of private businesses had the right to make decisions about their business, such as whom to hire and serve; that businesses forced to integrate in many areas would have difficulty remaining open; and that constitutional rights (for example, the right to a jury trial) were being eroded (Butler, 2004) through the bill. One of the more interesting arguments waged during the Senate filibuster was that Amendment XIII to the U.S. Constitution (U.S. Const. amend. XIII) outlawing slavery also meant that the federal government could not coerce someone to provide services to another person that they did not want to serve. This was said to be a form of "involuntary servitude" (Civil Rights Act of 1964).

The policy, which was passed in July 1964, outlawed discrimination in hiring and had provisions for community services and education. It also provided some support for voting rights, especially in areas of the South where poll taxes, literacy tests, and other mechanisms had been used to make it difficult for African Americans to vote, although voting access would be expanded the following year by the Voting Rights Act of 1965 (P.L. 89-110) (Loevy, 2004). The Civil Rights Act opposed discrimination based on race, color, ethnicity, gender, and religion. Although some supporters called for protection based on age discrimination, this protection was not included and would come about later with the Age Discrimination in Employment Act of 1967 (ADEA) (P.L. 90-202).

Effectiveness

A central problem with any antidiscrimination policy is that gauging effectiveness is extremely difficult. Within the context of any major social problem and policy response to it, a plethora of additional social, economic, political, and other issues can intertwine when attempting to judge the effect of the policy on the problem. Furthermore, these problems expand when dealing with discrimination, a concept that is notoriously hard to delineate and harder yet to accurately measure. Absent a "smoking gun" (for example, oral or written communication to the effect), proving that a particular "adverse action" was related to prejudice is extremely difficult. Even demonstrating how strong the connection is between prejudice, which is a feeling or attitude, and discrimination, which is an action or behavior, is itself problematic.

More recently, controversy in the area of antidiscrimination policy largely relates to affirmative action programs. Although there is not adequate space to detail here the various arguments in support of and opposition to affirmative action, it is important to note that this remains a highly contentious issue, and the backlash against affirmative action programs has grown substantially over the past several decades (J. [Juan] Williams, 2006). An important issue pertaining to this debate is that affirmative action does not generally necessitate quotas, although many people wrongly assume that they do. Another important question is whether affirmative action, if it is supported, should be based on racial or other (for example, family or community economic) factors.

During the height of the civil rights protests, the feminist movement was becoming another important force in American politics calling for equal treatment. Although feminist leaders, such as Betty Friedan and Gloria Steinem, had their primary effect during the decade following the Civil Rights Act, the 1964 policy did recognize the core argument of the feminist movement: that equal treatment based on gender was an important factor in establishing a moral foundation for the nation. Similar rights movements took place around the same time or later in the Native American, Hispanic, disability, gay/lesbian, and other minority communities. These movements all shared similar concerns about oppression but also differed in important ways and sometimes worked at cross-purposes or viewed one another as competing interests.

Analysis Element: Covert Rationales

Often, covert rationales for policy support are known but play a secondary role in the arguments for passage of the legislation. The primary rationale for passage of the Civil Rights Act was the blatant discrimination against African Americans as well as women and other minorities. However, an underlying issue that had a great deal of effect on passage was the Vietnam War and the relationship between the war and discrimination that was taking place in the United States at the time.

In one sense, this disconnect could be visualized in the example (used periodically by supporters of the bill) of the African American soldier from a southern state who had laid his life on the line for the country, came back on leave to his home airbase, went to the nearest restaurant, and was refused service. Stories like this one held sway with many (especially northern Republican) lawmakers, who were otherwise uncomfortable with the policy because of the intrusion on states' rights and because various types of discrimination were certainly prevalent outside the southern states.

Added to this was the realization that the nation went to war "on behalf of" the South Vietnamese because we found Communism to be an abhorrent form of government. The domino theory was an important metaphor used in support of the war: It held that the Communist takeover of Vietnam would lead to the entire region, one nation at a time, being overrun by Communists unless the United States or other Western nations intervened. The policy of the United States was that in democracy, it had a better mode of governance and that the people of Southeast Asia would be more capable of embracing their inherent rights under a democracy. This rationale for entering the war was countered when the people of Southeast Asia were shown photographs, videos, and other propaganda material of African American demonstrators being beaten for protesting, being refused the right to access the voting booth, being educated in poor and decrepit schools, and being maltreated in numerous other ways. Many politicians realized that so long as these conditions existed in the United States, they would be exploited by the enemies of the United States and form a viable argument in opposition to American-style democracy.

CHAPTER 15

Food Stamp Program/Supplemental Nutrition Assistance Program

1964

Historical Overview and Nature of the Social Problem

We might like to think it is a "given" that all citizens of one of the wealthiest nations in the world should have the basic right to at least a minimal amount of food. Even this right, however, is frequently subject to debate. Those in poverty often experience difficulty affording or accessing sufficient food. Even when such people have access to government programs, such as food stamps or WIC, or both, they often live in areas with few full-service groceries (these areas are known as "food deserts"), or their limited resources serve to support only a nonnutritive diet. Ironically, even those areas that produce the most food—small rural communities—may constitute food deserts (Harnack, Valluri, & French, 2019; Lloyd, 2019).

Hunger or food insecurity often leads to a number of poor health outcomes for adults and children, and may thwart the full physiological and educational development of children (Coleman-Jensen, 2010). Many would assume that the obesity problem in the United States provides demonstrable proof that hunger is not a problem. We misconstrue caloric intake, however, with nutrition: People can easily be overweight but still experience nutritional deficiencies. Living in a food desert may lend itself to obesity and related health problems because of limited nutritional food options.

Policy Overview

The Food Stamp program was preceded by a surplus food allotment program that provided some measure of assistance to the large mass of unemployed and poverty-stricken Americans during the Great Depression. The more formal program, however, was developed as a pilot program during the John F. Kennedy presidency and was made permanent in 1964 as the Food Stamp Act of 1964 (P.L. 88-525) as part of President Lyndon B. Johnson's War on Poverty ("Food Stamp Timeline," 2010). In testimony related to the 1964 act, it was made clear that a primary goal of the program was not only to provide food support to poor families but also to "strengthen the agricultural economy" by expanding the market for food production ("Food Stamp Act of 1964: Hearing," 1964).

During the first few decades of its existence, the Food Stamp program grew substantially both in the number of recipients and the overall budget. This growth led to a backlash against the expanding program and questions about eligibility, especially for Food Stamp program recipients, such as college students, the nonworking poor, and long-term recipients ("Should Congress Limit the Present Scope," 1975). Restrictions now especially target able-bodied adults without dependents and may include time limitations on the program or require them to either be working or in job training programs (D'Angelo, Libal, Seymour, & Hamel, 2017). As d'Amora (2016) noted, states have a good amount of discretion over various operational aspects of the SNAP program. Many of these limitations were included within the Personal Responsibility and Work Opportunity Reconciliation Act of 1996 (P.L. 104-193), which gave rise to the TANF program (Biggerstaff, Morris, & Nichols-Casebolt, 2002).

A 2008 reauthorization of the policy (Food and Nutrition Act, P.L. 110-246) included a change in the title of the Food Stamp program to SNAP ("Supplemental Nutrition Assistance Program," 2010). Currently, the program generally enrolls between 6 percent and 9 percent of the population, and, as one might expect, sees increasing numbers during difficult economic periods—for example, during the 2007 recession (Hoefer & Curry, 2012; Libal, Tomczak, Spath, & Harding, 2014). Time limitations or work requirements may also be relaxed during difficult economic times.

Because food stamps are a public assistance program, recipients are required to complete a means test to qualify for the benefits. In many states, those who qualify for supplemental security income (SSI) automatically qualify for food stamps (Trenkamp & Wiseman, 2007). As with other public assistance programs, female-headed and, in particular, single-parent households are at increased risk of experiencing food insecurity (Coleman-Jensen, 2010; Hoefer & Curry, 2012).

Effectiveness

Among other issues, effectiveness of the Food Stamp program/SNAP relates to target efficiency—whether there is a good match between actual recipients and those who are most vulnerable to hunger—and nutritional adequacy. The first effectiveness issue relates to fraud within the program and ensuring that those who are designated to use the program are indeed using it. For much of its existence, the Food Stamp program has come under fire because of the widespread belief that many recipients sell off all or a portion of their stamps, which are then used by ineligible individuals. Primarily as a result of this practice, states during the 1980s and 1990s began issuing electronic benefit transfer cards to replace the coupons.

The second effectiveness issue, nutritional adequacy, primarily pertains to whether the Food Stamp program enhances the nutritional intake and thus the health of its recipients. The assumption that recipients are going to increase their nutritional outcomes is only valid if the program provides additional nutrition over and above what it otherwise would have had. In other words, Food stamps can be either a supplement to or a substitute for the usual food purchases of recipients. Poor families receiving food support might decrease their own food purchases to the extent that they add SNAP purchases and use money that otherwise would go for food or other basic needs.

According to Mabli and Worthington (2014), SNAP has reduced food insecurity for children, which is one of its primary goals. The program has also lifted several million people slightly above the poverty line (Nestle, 2019), although many of these recipients are vulnerable to moving back into poverty, given a reduction in benefits or family emergencies. Rank and Hirschl (2005) wrote that approximately half of those who are eligible for the program do not apply. The reasons may be stigma, the perhaps realistic belief that their situation is temporary, difficulty in applying, alternative sources of food support, and so forth. Rank and Hirschl (2005) also contended that almost half of all adults will, at some point in their lives, receive SNAP benefits. As one might assume, for many, such receipt would be only temporary.

Analysis Element: Control of Benefits

A significant quandary in social policy relates to how much control the government is to have over the benefits provided by a program. This quandary can be viewed as striking a proper balance between recipient self-determination and program accountability. Regarding self-determination, one might argue that the recipients of assistance should be able to make decisions about how to best use the services or benefits derived from the policy. Furthermore, it could be viewed as paternalistic to be overly prescriptive of how benefits are used. As I note later in chapter 36, if we do want to support recipient dependence, we should foster individual decision making. On the other hand, many would argue that because the government provides the benefits in the first place, it has not only the right but the obligation to prescribe how the benefits are to be used. This may be viewed as a basic element of policy accountability. Beyond this argument is another: Because taxpayers are paying for the services, conservative stakeholders, in particular, have argued that the general public through elected and agency representatives has the right to set such limits.

Within the context of the Food Stamp program/SNAP, this argument pertains primarily to fraud prevention (that is, those who are supposed to use the benefits do indeed do so) and secondarily to the specific types of purchases that are made. This is an area of increased focus within our culture because of the increasing obesity problem along with such related health problems as diabetes and heart disease. Questions frequently arise about whether strict options need to be set under SNAP to fight the obesity problem and to further support the goal of providing the proper nutritional diet.

Related to these health and nutrition issues lay concerns about recipients purchasing junk food. As D'Angelo et al. (2017) pointed out, though, it is extremely difficult to adequately specify exactly what products constitute "junk food." Moreover, as mentioned earlier, many food deserts lack fruits, vegetables, and other, more nutritious options. It is difficult for the government to micromanage the program by specifying what products are acceptable without ensuring reasonable access to those products. It is also difficult, if not impossible, to ensure that politics will not play a role in dictating which products are deemed acceptable.

CHAPTER 16

Medicare

◖1965◗

Historical Overview and Nature of the Social Problem

Obviously, health concerns rank high on the list of problems that often occur with advancing age. Although we can do much to help stave off health problems that may arise as we grow older and we should refrain from stereotyping elderly people as fragile, the simple fact is that there is a positive correlation between health problems and their associated costs and age, especially at the upper end of the age scale. Add to this that most people, as they get older, retire. Because our health care system traditionally tied insurance to employment, that posed a problem for retired people before the advent of Medicare (Friedland, 2005). When individuals on a fixed income lost their insurance coverage on moving into retirement, they frequently could not get affordable private insurance because of their age and often because of preexisting medical conditions (Moon, 1993). Medicare is tied to Social Security, although many workers who are outside the Social Security system are also required to pay into and so receive Medicare benefits on retirement. As with Social Security, Medicare is paid for by a percentage payroll tax on employees, which is matched by an employer contribution.

At the time of Medicare's passage in 1965 (P.L. 89-97) as an amendment to the Social Security Act of 1935 (P.L. 74-271), health costs were keeping many elderly people in poverty (Moon, 1993). For retired people who were living barely (or even reasonably) above the poverty level, any large medical or pharmaceutical expense could place them into poverty. This was a constant fear that a large number of older Americans lived with at the time. Until the 1960s, poverty was more frequent among older Americans than people in any other age group (DiNitto, 2005). Medicare was preceded by the 1960 Kerr-Mills Social Security Act (P.L. 86-778), which provided a smaller degree of support—and only to elderly people who were poor (Cassel, 2005; Greenfield, 1968; Oberlander, 2008).

Policy Overview

In 1965, when President Lyndon B. Johnson realized he did not have the political support to get a larger universal health package passed, he decided to propose these two separate programs: Medicare and Medicaid (Ball, 1998; Lawlor, 2003; Maioni, 1998; Moon, 1993). As with other large-scale health care changes over time, primary opposition came from the American Medical Association along with other stakeholders in the health arena (Greenfield, 1968; Oberlander, 2008). Interestingly, even though many coalitions of elderly Americans formed the basis of support, the AARP—a nonprofit that, today, focuses on issues affecting Americans 50 and older—was not strongly in favor of the bill, according to Marilyn Moon (1993, p. 29). Christine Cassel (2005) noted that, at this point, that group was not heavily focused on political activism.

Medicare originally included two major provisions. Part A is required and provides support for basic hospital costs and some rehabilitation or home health care. Part B is optional insurance that pays for many of the treatments that Part A does not cover, particularly outpatient services. Initiated in 1997, Part C of Medicare is a voluntary program that provides a managed care option (now called Medicare Advantage) covering certain services for recipients (Friedland, 2005). Part D of Medicare, the prescription drug benefit, was signed into law by President George W. Bush in 2003 under the Medicare Prescription Drug, Improvement, and Modernization Act (P.L. 108-173) (Bakk, 2015; Friedland, 2005). This provision was quite controversial both because of its high cost as well as the heavy-handed nature of legislative supporters in getting the law passed (Aaron, Lambrew, & Healy, 2008). A particular problem with the prescription drug bill is that the government is not allowed to negotiate for lower costs with pharmaceutical companies; therefore, costs are markedly higher than they otherwise would be (Cassel, 2005).

Medicare also began supporting hospice care in 1983 (Noe, Smith, & Younis, 2012). In 1988, a catastrophic coverage program was included in Medicare, although this program was repealed after a short duration because of displeasure by Medicare recipients about a number of implementation issues, including its high cost (Aaron et al., 2008; Lawlor, 2003) and partial coverage. Because Medicare—even with the supplemental and prescription drug coverage—still only partially provides for the medical needs of many elderly people, the majority of recipients use private Medigap insurance to supplement Medicare (Oberlander, 2008).

An important component of the Part D drug benefit is the "donut hole." Because of the way that reimbursement for drug costs was designed, there are different out-of-pocket costs based on how much a recipient spends on drugs annually. The donut hole involved a gap in coverage between $2,830 and $6,440, whereupon the complete costs were the burden of the consumer (Cassel, 2005; Kaplan, 2011). With the 2010 passage of the Patient Protection and Affordable Care Act (ACA, also referred to as the "Affordable Care Act" or "Obamacare") (P.L. 111-148) under the President Barack Obama administration, a gradual reduction in the donut hole has occurred over a 10-year period. During this time, the government has taken on an increasing amount of responsibility for covering these costs (Kaplan, 2011).

Effectiveness

Medicare has been successful in a number of important ways. First, the elderly poverty level has dramatically decreased since passage of the program in 1965. According to Oberlander (2008), the poverty rate declined "from 28.5% in 1966 to 12.2% in 1990" (p. 62). Certainly, this change is attributable not only to Medicare (because Social Security and other policies have also played a role) but also to health coverage, which has been a major factor in the decline. It is much less likely for elderly Americans to be thrust into poverty because of medical costs. Another area in which Medicare has been successful is in keeping down its overhead costs (Ball, 1998; Woolhandler & Himmelstein, 2011). Although the program has experienced dramatic cost increases, those increases are largely because of medical advances and the rising costs of medical care rather than the expense of running the program. One of the major arguments in favor of universal health coverage in the United States is that Medicare operates with much lower overhead costs than private insurers, although total costs continue to increase because of the overall increase in health care costs.

The major challenge surrounding Medicare relates to these dramatic cost increases over time and problems with building in controls to reduce these increases. One of the most important efforts to restrict costs was the development, in 1984, of the prospective payment system, which included diagnostic-related groups (Ball, 1998; Lawlor, 2003; Noe et al., 2012). This system provided a set cost, with some variation for geographic cost of living, for every procedure covered by Medicare. Physicians could bill more than this amount but would only be reimbursed at the set rate. Of course, as funding for services becomes more limited, physicians are increasingly wary of treating Medicare clients at all. This has always been an issue of concern; Rubin (2008), for example, wrote that a 2008 survey found that 60 percent of responding physicians were limiting or completely refusing to treat Medicare patients. In addition, as costs have risen and the government has attempted to hold down these costs, recipient out-of-pocket payments have expanded (Ball, 1998). Moniz and Gorin (2007) noted that, in 2003, Medicare covered less than half of the health services received by beneficiaries. Another major concern with the program, as with Medicaid, is large-scale fraud because many providers and scammers have found ways to illegally attain money from the system (Olson, 2003).

Some of the major recommendations for revising the Medicare system to maintain viability into the future parallel those made regarding Social Security reform. These include increasing payments by current workers and their employers, increasing the age at which benefits can be accessed, and providing additional taxes or disincentives to upper-income recipients who use benefits. The problems with these suggestions are largely the same as with Social Security: They would require increased money to be put into the system and decreased benefits on receipt, and they would lead to questions about intergenerational equity. Additional recommendations include increasing the use of managed care provisions and further limiting certain medical procedures (Moon, 1993).

As discussed, too, in the following chapter on Medicaid, some form of rationing will have to be developed in relation to major governmental health programs as well as health care provision in general in the United States. One particularly controversial recommendation for ensuring the continued viability of Medicare relates to what Cassel (2005) referred to as "age-based allocation." As she noted, we need to consider the extent to which providing certain expensive procedures to older individuals makes sense. Although this recommendation might sound callous, this practice has always been done to an extent.

As the population ages, funding issues are becoming more of a concern for both Social Security and Medicare. Certainly, the strength of the elderly voting population is important in ensuring that major changes are not made to these programs, but, as Lawlor (2003) wrote, one of the additional reasons there is little movement in a positive direction relates to the quick election cycle, especially for U.S. House of Representatives members, who must run every two years. Thus, they are incentivized to focus on short-term piecemeal changes rather than to attempt to stabilize the program on a long-term basis.

CHAPTER 17

Medicaid

◖1965◗

Historical Overview and Nature of the Social Problem

Over the course of the past century, a number of attempts have been made to secure a single-payer universal health plan for the United States similar to what every other industrialized nation has. These attempts began in earnest with President Franklin D. Roosevelt floating the idea as an element of his New Deal program, and they have continued with failed efforts by Presidents Harry S. Truman, Lyndon B. Johnson, and Bill Clinton. Aside from concerns that such programs would advance socialism within the country, large corporate and professional interests, led by the American Medical Association, have engaged in large-scale public relations activities to thwart these various plans (Moon, 1993).

Obviously, a major argument in support of universal health coverage is that a large portion of the American population, about 10 percent to 15 percent on average in any given year, is uninsured. Another significant group of Americans has minimal coverage that does not provide necessary support or that requires high out-of-pocket costs. Before Medicaid, the vast majority of those living in poverty, including children, were not covered. In part, this was because most adults worked in entry-level jobs in the secondary labor market, which did not provide company insurance, and because these families were so financially limited, they could not afford their own insurance. Even where individual workers may have been covered, family coverage often fell to the worker and was too expensive to purchase.

In addition to not being able to afford medical procedures, many of these families could not provide much in the way of preventative medicine, dental care, or psychiatric treatment. Unemployed and working poor families generally had to use emergency room services or charity provision by hospitals, the costs of which were (and still are, for those not on Medicaid) passed on to other consumers. Moreover, because either urban or rural poverty tends to be tied to various geographic locales, a small number of hospitals, providers, and clinics have always had to carry the lion's share of the burden in caring for such patients.

Policy Overview

Both John F. Kennedy and Lyndon B. Johnson understood the problems related to health care and insurance provision in the United States, but both also realized the difficulties of attempting to develop a universal system. Coming on the heels of the McCarthy era, opposition cries of socialism struck a responsive chord with the public. Johnson studied the possibility of a larger insurance proposal but realized that the necessary political support was not present. As a result, he put forward two smaller plans that pertained to the most pressing populations without health care: Medicare for elderly Americans and Medicaid for those living in poverty (especially families), elderly people, and disabled people.

Although Medicare was designed as a federal program, Medicaid involves a partnership between the federal and state governments. Medicare sets basic standards about minimal coverage and provides financial assistance, but the states have a degree of autonomy in deciding eligibility, additional coverage areas, and other elements of policy implementation in regard to Medicaid. As Boyd (1998) noted, a number of both positive and negative aspects are related to state as opposed to federal control. States presumably know the health needs of their poor population better and can therefore design more specific programs. On the other hand, states may attempt to dramatically limit coverage, especially in difficult economic times, such as during recessions. Although the federal government may also decrease funding in tough times, it may more easily spread costs especially because some economic problems can hit certain regions of the country more so than others. Because the federal government does set basic eligibility and coverage standards, the states can only go so far in limiting funding or access. The federal government has developed a formula for making expenditures to states. This formula, referred to as the Federal Medical Assistance Percentage, provides more support to states that have a higher percentage of people living in poverty (Boyd, 1998; Holahan & Cohen, 1986; McEldowney & Jenkins, 2005).

Medicaid primarily covers families on TANF (or, before 1996, AFDC) as well as elderly and disabled people who live under or close to the poverty line. However, as Moniz and Gorin (2007) noted, Medicaid does not automatically provide for families on TANF, as was the case with AFDC, and remains in the purview of states. Elderly and disabled poor individuals use the majority of Medicaid funding, and many also receive SSI (see chapter 20) (McEldowney & Jenkins, 2005). States can decide how far they want to extend coverage relative to the poverty line. Some older poor individuals may receive both Medicare and Medicaid, with each program covering specific services. Importantly, Medicaid provides some coverage for nursing home care, although recipients must meet income requirements. The issue of elderly people "spending down" by hiding assets or passing them along to their children so they can become eligible for such care has been an issue of controversy for much of Medicaid's existence.

Although Medicaid has undergone major changes over time, one change that needs to be highlighted was the 1997 development of the State Children's Health Insurance Program (SCHIP) (Patel & Rushefsky, 2006; Weil & Hill, 2003). When it was clear that the Clinton administration could not develop its larger health program, it focused on one aspect of that program that had particularly strong political support: increasing coverage to poor children. SCHIP provided states with support to increase the number of children who could access insurance. In some cases, this included expanding Medicaid, whereas in others, it helped these families get low-cost private insurance using a sliding scale that required higher-income families to pay a larger percentage of premium cost.

Effectiveness

Medicaid certainly has provided necessary medical assistance for a large number of poor people. The major concern with Medicaid, as with Medicare and private insurance, relates to the cost of care. For decades, costs for medical care have increased well beyond inflationary levels (Boyd, 1998). Although managed care elements have been added to both Medicare and Medicaid, they only help so much. The core problem with the U.S. system is that we pay much more per person for medical care, but we neither cover everyone nor see increased life expectancy over nations that pay less (Reid, 2010). After rising sharply for the first few decades of its existence, Medicaid spending stagnated during the 1980s as the result of policies reducing benefits and of cutbacks in certain population categories, such as women receiving AFDC (Boyd, 1998; Holahan & Cohen, 1986). After a few years, however, dramatic cost increases returned.

Another major problem with Medicaid is that it does not help everyone living below the poverty line (L. D. Brown, 1990; Moniz & Gorin, 2007; Monheit & Short, 1989). Many working poor families may still be unable to acquire Medicaid and also cannot afford private insurance. Medicaid may serve to provide a disincentive to finding employment for the working poor because they may be worse off with minimal income but have to pay for health care. The SCHIP program was designed largely to reach the children in these families because public coverage for children is more socially accepted than for poor adults. The children in these families, however, may suffer in various ways if their parents cannot attend to their own medical needs.

An additional problem with Medicaid relates to funding issues: both the level of funding for services and the gap between service delivery and payment (Holahan & Weil, 2007). Especially in difficult economic times or when efforts are made to control expenses, services may not be reimbursed at an amount that physicians and other providers feel is adequate (Patel & Rushefsky, 2006). At other times, the lag between when the treatment is provided and when payment finally arrives may be a lengthy period, which is problematic from a cash flow standpoint. As a result of these problems, medical providers frequently limit the number of Medicaid patients they will cover. A related problem is the movement of medical providers out of high poverty areas in large part because of an unwillingness to treat a large Medicaid population. As with Medicare, a difficult quandary related to Medicaid pertains to the proper balance between spending controls and physician or provider payment. Because spending controls are built into the system, providers will be reimbursed less, and more physicians will refuse to take on Medicaid patients.

Analysis Element: Vertical versus Horizontal Coverage

Given that we do not have the resources to give everything to everybody, politicians and bureaucrats often have to make difficult decisions about how to best distribute services. Many policy analysts have discussed vertical versus horizontal delivery—and in a variety of different ways. The description used here is as follows: One can imagine a simple graph with the potential number of service recipients on the horizontal line and the degree or number of services or payment per recipient on the vertical line. Boyd (1998) discussed this in terms of depth versus breadth of coverage. Given a specific amount of money, the payment per recipient will rise or fall based on how many people are covered. Looking at Medicaid, we can choose to provide a large number of services to a smaller population or expand the population served by limiting coverage and spread the money out more. States do have some autonomy related to these coverage issues, so when states want to even go beyond the standard level of care, they may apply to the federal government for a waiver, which would allow them to "experiment" in a certain direction (McEldowney & Jenkins, 2005).

One of the more important of the various Medicaid waiver experiments took place in Oregon in the early 1990s (Menzel, 1992; Wood, 1991). At that time, officials in the state decided to cover a larger number of poor people under their Medicaid policy, but they needed to reduce the level of benefits provided to make the expansion affordable. The state reviewed all medical treatments and decided which ones could realistically be cut. It focused on dropping those treatments that were not crucial to life extension or independence but might potentially increase the comfort level or reduce chronic pain for certain recipients. The policy served to dramatically reduce the number of uninsured people in the state, but one could argue that it increased the number of underinsured people because coverage was more limited. The policy was also criticized by disability groups for basing some health care decisions on quality-of-life indicators, which presumably would detrimentally affect people with various disability conditions (Menzel, 1992).

Although concerns about rationing arise when health reform is discussed, one might contend that we always ration services unless we want to be completely swamped by medical costs. As health costs continue to rise relative to inflation, families are spending a larger percentage of their income on insurance and out-of-pocket costs as well as pulling money from other areas of their budget. Problems certainly may occur, however, if rationing schemes are implemented in such a way that they primarily harm poor and marginalized groups.

CHAPTER 18

Older Americans Act

◖1965◗

Historical Overview and Nature of the Social Problem

It would certainly be inappropriate to make presumptions about a person's capabilities or needs based on their age status, yet as people age, they are more apt to face certain burdens. Elderly people may experience economic challenges if they live beyond their savings; they may become more socially isolated if they are unable to drive or ambulate easily; and they may experience "rolelessness" or depression as they stop working or if spouses, friends, or significant others pass away or children move away. The increasing potential for health problems or caregiving requirements adds to these potential burdens because elderly people are much more likely to experience a disability condition (Bachman & Gonyea, 2012). In addition, older people may also be targets for financial or other forms of exploitation or abuse.

Although older individuals were greatly assisted by the Social Security Act of 1935 (P.L. 74-271), until the 1960s, they remained in poverty out of proportion to the rest of society. A large percentage of those who were poor before 1965 were in dire economic straits in part because of the unaffordability of needed medical care and pharmaceuticals. Medicare, passed in the same year as the 1965 Older Americans Act (OAA) (P.L. 89-73) has helped with these costs. Moreover, the problems that elderly individuals as a group experience have expanded in conjunction with the aging of the population. Although the elderly population in general is increasing, with those in the baby boomer generation reaching or approaching retirement, we are likely to see the largest percentage increase with those who are among the oldest of this cohort. Takamura (1999) wrote that, according to U.S. Census Bureau estimates, the number of people who are 100 or older (centenarians) is expected to increase about 10-fold between 1990 and 2050.

Policy Overview

The OAA was signed into law in 1965 by President Lyndon B. Johnson to provide a range of services to support the economic, social, nutritional, employment, and health and long-term care needs of elderly people. The act included 10 objectives related to these areas, and the 1973 amendments to the policy established regional Area Agencies on Aging designed to coordinate the provision of services (FallCreek & Gilbert, 1981; *Older Americans Act: A Staff Summary*, 1979). The federal government provides funding to the states based largely on the number of people who are 65 or older in that state (Nofz, 1986). Most of the requirements of the policy are targeted at those elderly people who have the greatest financial and other needs.

Among other revisions to the act, the Older Americans Act Amendments of 2000 (P.L. 106-501) created the National Family Caregiver Support Program (Novak, 2006). Programs such as this provide supportive alternatives to facility-based, long-term care and allow elderly people to remain in their own homes or with family—at least for a while longer than they otherwise would (Kero & Ernst, 2019; Takamura, 2000). Nutritional support programs, such as Meals on Wheels, are important because many urban or rural elderly people live in food deserts (Lloyd, 2019) or cannot drive and have difficulty getting to stores or accessing nutritious food (Vieira, Vaccaro, Zarini, & Huffman, 2017). Lieberman (2013) added that many meal programs have lengthy waiting lists, especially when the economy is doing poorly. Meals served at congregate sites, such as senior centers, provide not only nutrition but also socialization activities and, at least at many, health screening (Naleppa & Reid, 2003; Wellman & Kamp, 2004). Colello wrote in 2011 that the "elderly nutrition services program" is the largest OAA program, accounting for "over one-third . . . of the Act's total funding" (p. 35). Many elderly individuals are eligible to receive SNAP benefits; however, a majority of those who are eligible do not apply (Wellman & Kamp, 2004)

The OAA supported employment opportunities for elderly people who wanted to continue working, but it did not include a nondiscrimination component. There was some effort to include age as a "suspect class" along with race, sex, and religion, in the Civil Rights Act of 1964 (P.L. 88-352), passed the year before the OAA. Legislators were concerned about this provision for several reasons, including the potential diminishment in certain abilities that may arise with increasing age. These matters were discussed over the next few years, and, in 1967, ADEA (P.L. 90-202) was passed, providing a measure of protection from age discrimination. In addition to presumptions (many false) about their capabilities to perform job tasks, older applicants frequently have not been hired for jobs because of employer concerns about high health insurance costs or other reasons.

Even though it does not include a nondiscrimination component, the OAA does include Title V, which provides job opportunities for retired individuals whose income is "below 125% of the federal poverty level" (Washko, Schack, Goff, & Pudlin, 2011, p. 184). These positions are generally part-time minimum wage jobs designed to augment Social Security or other retirement income and keep elderly people from falling into poverty.

An area that has garnered increased focus over time is financial exploitation of elderly people (DeLiema, Navarro, Enguidanos, & Wilber, 2015). This has become a greater concern in large part because of the spread of computer-based fraud and identity theft. According to Burnes et al. (2017), approximately 5 percent of all "cognitively intact older adults living in the community are victims of financial fraud or scams each year in the United States" (p. e13), and one estimate is that "one in five Americans older than 65 [has] been defrauded" (Kohl, Sanders, & Blumenthal, 2012, p. 106). Financial exploitation is particularly problematic because older people are targeted more frequently than others, some experience cognitive decline that makes them vulnerable, and many who are not in poverty are barely above the poverty line.

Netting, Huber, Paton, and Kautz (1995) noted that among amendments to the OAA in 1992 was a move to combine several programs that pertained to abuse or financial exploitation into one title, called "Vulnerable Elder Rights Protection Activities" (p. 351). More recently, the Elder Justice Act of 2009, passed in 2010 as part of the ACA (P.L. 111-148), created an oversight council to coordinate elder protection issues (Kohl et al., 2012; Petruy & Dalin, 2020).

Among other programs related to abuse prevention, the ombudsman program has the specific goal of "protecting the rights of residents of nursing homes and other long-term care facilities" (*Older Americans Act: A Staff*

Summary, 1979, p. 8). Self-neglect is a particular area of focus for abuse and neglect policies as well as caregiver abuse and the prevention of elderly suicide.

Effectiveness

The OAA has certainly aided elderly people in the United States, particularly those who have been impoverished or vulnerable to isolation and abuse. In conjunction with Social Security and Medicare, it has been instrumental in improving the quality of life for millions of older Americans. The percentage of elderly people who live in poverty has decreased; however, many in this age group survive barely above the poverty line, and given high out-of-pocket medical, pharmaceutical, or other expenses, they could easily fall back below the poverty line.

An issue related to elderly individuals that is particularly important for social workers is abuse and neglect. As Nerenberg (2008) noted, accurately defining abuse and neglect as they relate to elderly people has been problematic over the years and "impedes our ability to develop comprehensive responses" (p. 19). One area of some controversy relates to mandated reporting of presumptive elderly abuse or neglect. Although it seems obvious to many that social workers and others who work with older individuals should be mandated reporters, one argument in opposition to mandated reporting is that it is patronizing to assume that others need to stand in to protect elderly people, especially if dementia, Alzheimer's, or another cognitive problem is not present. Social work emphasizes self-determination, so at what point is mandated reporting an infringement on one's ability to make their own decisions? A related question pertains to self-neglect and whether the inability to properly care for oneself requires another person or authority to take control over aspects of a person's life (Nerenberg, 2008).

A final issue to discuss in terms of elderly concerns relates to the recent coronavirus pandemic. Stigmatization and even dehumanization of elderly people are unfortunately common themes in the public view of older people. Too often, elderly people have been thought of as useless and perhaps even as expendable, or at least less valuable, people. The pandemic affected older Americans to a much greater degree than other age groups, yet the large loss of life was not enough for everyone to take precautionary measures. For many, the balance swung in favor of jobs, "freedom," and the economy, even if the elderly and other vulnerable members of society paid the ultimate price. This part of our recent history, therefore, provides an excellent example of how dehumanization plays itself out, particularly during a time of national crisis. The many implications of the coronavirus pandemic are not yet known, but in addition to the health consequences for elderly people, it has served to further isolate them from their families, friends, and the rest of the community. This itself undoubtedly will affect mortality and both their physical and mental health.

CHAPTER 19

National Environmental Policy Act

◖1970◗

Historical Overview and Nature of the Social Problem

To a certain extent, fears about the adverse effects of humans on the environment arose with the onset of the industrial revolution and urbanization in the 19th century. Concerns related to the expanding populations within cities, combined with sanitation and other public health problems, and a rapid increase in the release of industrial toxins, drew attention to the effects of humans on the environment. During the early 20th century, progressive reformers added health and environmental problems, especially within congested urban areas, to their list of reform initiatives. Jane Addams, for example, became involved in improving sanitation and waste disposal as a garbage inspector in Chicago (Wise, 1935).

The contemporary environmental movement can be traced to the early 1960s with the release of Rachel Carson's (1962) book *Silent Spring*, which focused on the harmful effects of chemicals such as DDT on the environment (Lindstrom & Smith, 2001). Both then and now, issues related to pollution and toxicity have been particularly important for social work professionals because such problems primarily affect poor and marginalized populations, including people of color (Bullard, 2002; Faber & O'Connor, 2002). Such populations are much more likely to live in areas of high toxicity and smog, have difficulty accessing safe drinking water, and take up residence in older apartments and houses with lead paint and other contaminants (Taylor, 2014). The issue of high lead paint levels especially affects young children, most often those living in poor families or minority families, or both (Bullard, 2002). In addition, vulnerable populations also are much more likely to work in environmentally unhealthy jobs, such as the mining industry and factories (Bullard, 2002; Faber & O'Connor, 2002).

Even within Western nations, such as the United States, ecological damage can have profound negative effects on aboriginal groups and populations that have generational ties to their land, especially when these groups have non-Western views of resource development and land ownership. Many Native American and other ethnic populations in the United States have a strong connection to the land that can be threatened by displacement or ecological changes imposed on them (Peña, 2002). One pervasive ecological issue affecting Native Americans relates to water and fishing rights and protection of their land from mining (Gedicks, 2005).

Jennifer McKinnon (2008) wrote that social work as a profession has been too apt to view the "environment" in a clinical sense. Although social workers understand that an individual, child, or family's particular environment can greatly affect their functioning and development, she noted that the profession needs to consider more broadly the importance of the overall environment in terms of the goals of the profession. P. Jones (2010), too, contended that social work and related professions need to take more responsibility for adding environmental concern and sustainability as an important feature of the profession. Sustainability is often discussed to some degree in community organization classes; however, as these and other writers have contended, such discussions need to be more extensive and cut across all areas of social work education.

Policy Overview

The first major environmental policies passed in the United States were the Federal Water Pollution Control Act of 1948 (P.L. 80-845) and the Air Pollution Control Act of 1955 (P.L. 84-159) (referred to in later reauthorizations as the Clean Air Act). Although these policies placed some controls and regulatory authority over companies that emitted industrial pollutants, they were not highly effective (Lindstrom & Smith, 2001). As Lindstrom and Smith (2001) noted, a crisis or series of related crises is often a requirement for policymakers to focus on an issue of concern. This point was discussed in chapter 4 in relation to trigger events and the development of workers' compensation policies, and it is apropos here especially because of a great degree of overlap between workers' compensation and environmental protection policies. During the 1960s and 1970s, a number of major environmental calamities served to draw attention to the need for a strong federal environmental protection policy. First, during the late 1960s, the Cuyahoga River near Cleveland caught fire several times, producing major damage and spewing toxic pollution into the air. Now, of course, rivers are not supposed to catch fire because they are, well, rivers. As one might assume, however, this river received an enormous amount of toxic waste from surrounding industries, and thus became quite flammable. As a result of this and other environmental disasters, the National Environmental Policy Act of 1969 (NEPA) (P.L. 91-190) was passed and signed into law by President Richard M. Nixon on the first day of 1970 (Lindstrom & Smith, 2001). That same year, the Environmental Protection Agency (EPA) was developed and several other important environmental policies were enacted, including a major revision of the Air Pollution Control Act of 1955 (P.L. 84-159) and the Occupational Health and Safety Act of 1970 (P.L. 91-596) (Faber & O'Connor, 2002).

Among other requirements, NEPA mandated the development of environmental impact statements related to "major federal actions significantly affecting the human environment" (Z. A. Smith, 2000, p. 57). These statements are to be circulated among government agencies and the general public, and they are subject to public discussion related to planned projects. According to Bevington (2009), the first Earth Day celebration in 1970, the same year as NEPA implementation, also played an important role in drawing public attention to environmental activism.

Another important catastrophe from the 1970s that served to strengthen the requirements of NEPA arose in Love Canal, New York, a community close to Niagara Falls. This massive toxic waste dump required the relocation of a large number of nearby residents and led to the development of the Superfund policy (also known as the Comprehensive Environmental Response, Compensation, and Liability Act of 1980, P.L. 96-510) under the EPA. Superfund was designed to provide massive cleanup efforts at such sites and attempt to hold those companies that created the pollution responsible for supporting cleanup costs (Lindstrom & Smith, 2001).

A large degree of overlap exists between environmental protection policies and both natural disaster and national defense and anti-terrorism policies. Natural or industrial-based disasters may seriously harm the environment and require federal relief, and both environmental protection and domestic defense require a form of large-scale national response that may cut across a large number of public and private providers. In addition, anti-terrorism policies include protection from the purposeful spread of weapons of destruction that may harm the environment, such as contaminants like smallpox and anthrax (Mackelprang, Mackelprang, & Thirkill, 2005).

As a result of the connection between environmental/natural disasters and national defense preparedness, the federal government has gone back and forth over the years in regard to the utility of a *dual-use strategy*, whereby the same oversight and planning body is responsible for both natural disaster and anti-terrorism procedures and operation (Sylves, 2008). As further discussed in chapter 39, these areas were connected with the development of the Homeland Security Act of 2002 (P.L. 107-296), whereby the Federal Emergency Management Agency (FEMA) was brought under the umbrella of the U.S. Department of Homeland Security following the 9/11 attacks (Sylves, 2008).

Effectiveness

The effectiveness of NEPA and other environmental policies has been hotly debated. NEPA provides a mechanism for ensuring that companies maintain emissions within acceptable limits and that the federal projects go through an environmental impact review, yet many would argue that NEPA often fails to follow its own procedures, especially during presidential administrations or congressional periods that are less environmentally friendly. Environmental groups have frequently sued the EPA for not following their own policies. Bevington (2009) has argued that one of the reasons that much environmental regulation is not adequately enforced is because of the establishment nature of major environmental advocacy groups. To maintain funding from major contributors and ensure continued support from important political players, Bevington contended that these groups, such as the Sierra Club and Audubon Society, are often too willing to agree to weak compromises. He argued that the development of Earth First! and other more radical advocacy organizations was largely the result of this "insider approach" taken by established groups.

On the other side of the coin, a particular quandary related to environmental protection is that such measures do indeed add to the costs for industry, and these costs are pushed onto the consumer as higher prices (Faber & O'Connor, 2002). In addition, businesses that feel hamstrung by such regulations may seek the most receptive economic environment for establishing factories and other business operations. This is particularly disconcerting when it means that toxic waste and pollutants simply are moved to especially poor countries. "Environmental degradation and [their resulting] health problems," Faber and O'Connor (2002) wrote, are often exported "to the Third World" (p. 20).

Analysis Element: International Policy Concerns

Although this text looks at policies developed within the United States, it is important to understand the various ways that internationalization comes into play in both the assessment and the handling of large-scale social problems across borders—as well as the effect that other nations have on the implementation of U.S. policy, and vice versa. Environmental policy has to take an international approach because Earth is an ecosystem that we all share. Environmental toxins and pollutants do not know national boundaries and, as noted, U.S. industries have a long history of setting up shop in poor countries that desperately need money and are willing to waive environmental protections to attract such industries or that simply have weak protections in the first place.

Moreover, poor nations "are plagued by battles over the control of resources, which might include water, diamonds, gold or oil" (Schmitz, Matyók, Sloan, & James, 2012, p. 280). People who live in poverty or are oppressed reap few of the benefits of these resources and are often forced from their land when those resources are extracted. Many of the refugee crises in various countries have environmental degradation as an important causative feature (McKinnon, 2008). Many of these resources are exported to the United States and other Western nations, and, therefore, Americans play a role in supporting any human rights or environmental problems that result. In addition, a massive number of people in poor nations, many of them children, suffer from deadly but easily preventable diseases (such as those that cause diarrhea) simply because they do not have access to clean drinking water or arable land that might support crop development (Pink, 2012). In many situations, these resources are available but are controlled by powerful economic, political, or military interests.

Importantly, a major concern related to effectiveness in environmental policy is that many relevant issues, such as climate change, require an international response, and nations frequently have difficulty working together on such issues because they are so intensely focused on national interests. To a certain extent, this concern applies to the United States, too. Regions or states that are likely to be affected the most and the earliest by climate change may be more interested in dealing with that issue than other states that would see economic problems arising from policies that hurt oil production, automobile manufacturing, factory production, and so forth (J. [James] H. Williams, 2015).

CHAPTER 20

Supplemental Security Income

◖1972◗

Historical Overview and Nature of the Social Problem

In the continuing discussion of what groups constitute the "worthy poor"—that is, those people who should "rightly" be provided with some degree of governmental assistance—most would agree that a few groups fall into this category. These groups include people with disabilities whose condition is readily apparent and limits their ability to work; poor families with at least one working adult, especially those families with a child with a disability; and elderly individuals living in poverty. Even when it comes to these groups, though, "deservedness" arguments remain. How disabled should such a person be? Should the definition of disability also relate to mental and emotional as well as physical impairments? How much money or support should be given to such people? Should government support be provided to poor elderly individuals who have well-off children or nonliquid assets (for example, a farm or other property)?

Over the past century, the federal government has provided certain forms of support for people in these categories, although these forms have generally been relatively small programs that offer low levels of support. The Social Security Act of 1935 (P.L. 74-271) (see chapter 7), for example, included an old age assistance program (Older Americans Act, 1965, P.L. 89-73; see chapter 18) and several small disability-related programs, but all were fairly minor aspects of the larger policy, and all were limited in scope. These policies also were implemented in "an extremely fragmented, uncoordinated fashion" by the various states (Applebaum & Payne, 2005, p. 27).

Families that live in poverty and include either disabled or elderly individuals have particular difficulty in moving above the poverty line. Because elderly and disabled people are frequently discriminated against in the job market, they may have little opportunity to attain a job. Many have impairments that preclude their employment, and employers may presume such people to be potential liabilities to the business. Elderly people who have one or more disability conditions are particularly limited in their earning potential and also may require extensive medical support, which many employers will not want to provide. Even though some medical support may be covered by Medicare or Medicaid, or both, additional out-of-pocket expenses are often required, and government programs can stand as a disincentive to employment because, to continue to receive their benefits, eligible people often are not allowed to earn above a specific amount of money. In addition, elderly individuals who are poor and people with long-term disabilities are less likely than most to have retirement income other than Social Security, such as pensions or 401(k) accounts. Furthermore, families with a child or parent who is disabled or partially incapacitated frequently must provide caregiving duties, which impedes the ability of at least one parent/guardian to attain full-time employment.

Policy Overview

The SSI program was developed in 1972 to bring together a number of public assistance programs that had previously operated independent of one another (Dolgoff & Feldstein, 2007; Ozawa, 2002), and provided a uniform monthly payment to eligible recipients. The majority of SSI recipients (about 60 percent) have a long-term disability, and the rest is almost evenly split between children who are disabled and poor elderly people (Applebaum & Payne, 2005). Many states provide their own supplemental benefits in addition to the base federal provision, and many automatically qualify SSI recipients for Medicaid (Perrin & Stein, 1991). Benefits are not generous, and, in many cases, recipient families remain in poverty (Parish, 2013). Eligibility applications include information on income and assets, and only those with financial need are eligible for the program. People who live in Medicaid-supported facilities do not receive the full SSI benefits but, rather, a small monthly allotment to cover personal expenses (Dolgoff & Feldstein, 2007).

Over time, major concerns regarding SSI have arisen related to benefits to two major recipient groups: (1) people with a history of drug or alcohol addiction, or both; and (2) children with disabilities. Regarding the first group, a basic question that is important not only for SSI but also for the Americans with Disabilities Act of 1990 (ADA) (P.L. 101-336) and other disability-related policies is whether substance abuse is to be considered a disability that should qualify one for policy coverage (Hogan, Speiglman, & Norris, 2010). On the one hand, like other disabilities, such abuse may impair one's ability to work or harm other major life-functioning areas. Unlike other disabilities, however, substance abuse can be considered to be the result of individual behavior or choice. As noted in chapter 32, however, attempting to distinguish how much choice plays a role in any condition opens a hornet's nest and subjects potential recipients to judgments by others.

Regardless of one's position on this problematic issue, during the 1990s, legislators began to decry the fact that many people who were actively using addictive substances were receiving SSI benefits. As a result, the eligibility policy was changed in 1997 to make it more difficult for active users to receive the benefits. According to Hogan et al. (2010), more than 150,000 former recipients lost their SSI benefits and their Medicaid support. An issue that makes this question more problematic is that there always is a complex relationship between mental health conditions and alcohol or drug addiction, especially because many of those who become addicted began substance use either by self-medicating or by using prescription drugs to treat a mental health or disease condition.

Regarding children with disabilities, until the 1990 *Sullivan v. Zebley* decision by the U.S. Supreme Court, many potentially eligible children were not approved for SSI benefits (Boyd, 1998; Burkhauser & Daly, 2017; Ford & Schwamm, 1992). Because the ability to work has been a hallmark of determining the extent of a disability condition, it has been problematic when taking into account children—who do not work. With various forms of mental illness and physical disabilities, comparability between children and adults in terms of diagnostics, effect, services, and so forth can be difficult to gauge. Because children are still moving through a maturation stage, moreover, it is difficult to determine how a condition will eventually play itself out in relation to an individual's physical, mental, and emotional development. According to Roberts-DeGennaro (2001), between 1986—before the *Sullivan v. Zebley* decision—and 1993—following that decision—the number of children who were eligible for SSI tripled. However, recipient numbers decreased somewhat when the Personal Responsibility and Work Opportunity Reconciliation Act of 1996 (P.L. 104-193), which produced the TANF program, was passed and included a "more rigorous disability definition for children under age 18" (Dolgoff & Feldstein, 2007, p. 219).

Because of their similarities, the SSI and Social Security Disability Insurance (SSDI) are often confused. Although both programs are operated by the Social Security Administration, SSDI recipients need to have "sufficient, recent work history of paying FICA [Federal Insurance Contributions Act (1954)] taxes into the Social Security system" to be eligible, or they must be a dependent of someone who has done so (Lang, 2019–2020, p. 18). Unlike for SSI, there is no means test for SSDI, but, as for SSI, people need to have a disability condition to apply for SSDI (Lang, 2019–2020).

Effectiveness

SSI has assisted many individuals to meet their basic living needs, yet many of these recipients continue to struggle financially. Those receiving benefits are allowed to work, often part time, although their salary diminishes the amount of SSI they receive. State differences related not only to the basic provision but also to the effect of income on benefits mean that, as with many social welfare programs, where one lives affects that person's ability to meet basic needs. Burkhauser and Daly (2017) argued that when supporting children and adolescents, the SSI program has too often set them up for lifelong government dependency because the program provides disincentives for a later work career. Although many recipients have extensive disabling conditions that preclude full-time employment, these authors contended that the program needs to do more to help transition young adults to college and a career.

Many policymakers and other stakeholders have expressed concern about the increase, over time, in the number of recipients along with the "recovery rate" for recipients (Ozawa, 2002). To qualify for benefits, the disabling condition should be of a severity level that the person would not be expected to work for at least a year (Ozawa, 2002). Even though it is assumed that a number of recipients will eventually recover and return to full-time work, this seldom happens. Another problem is that applications often take a long time to move through the process—sometimes as long as several years. This is especially true if recipients are judged to not be qualified and, therefore, must go through an appeals process (Ozawa, 2002).

CHAPTER 21

Women, Infants, and Children Program

1972

Historical Overview and Nature of the Social Problem

Hunger is one of the most pressing social problems because it relates directly to a basic human need. As noted in chapter 15, hunger or food insecurity in a nation such as the United States, particularly for children, seems especially difficult to comprehend. We live in a wealthy, food-producing nation that seems to have more than enough sustenance for our entire population. A nation that spends more than $15 billion each year to feed its pets ("U.S. Sales of Dog and Cat Food," 2009) would be hard-pressed to sufficiently rationalize any child or pregnant mother going hungry.

Hunger is problematic not only in relation to the physical and intellectual development of children but also for proper fetal development. This is an especially important consideration that led to development of the WIC program. Developing fetuses who do not receive sufficient nourishment because their mothers either cannot afford or cannot access healthy food are likely to develop a broad range of physiological and mental/intellectual problems as well as to have impaired immune systems that make them vulnerable to infections (Seipel, 1999). Many are also likely to die in utero or to be born premature and underweight. Low birth-weight babies often have multiple health complications that require intensive medical intervention following their birth. Many of those children who do survive experience long-term complications that require continuing medical support or even some form of out-of-home institutional care along with ongoing government support, such as SSI, Medicaid payments, and other disability-related expenditures. Infant mortality is a particularly important problem that the WIC program was designed to diminish. Both infant mortality and premature births, moreover, occur more frequently with African American as opposed to White women, and use of WIC services will hopefully close this "racial gap" (Khanani et al., 2010).

Policy Overview

Although the Food Stamp program was initiated approximately a decade before WIC, it was clear to many advocates and legislators that additional provisions needed to be made for pregnant mothers and young children. The National School Lunch Program (initiated in 1946) and, later, the School Breakfast Program provided nutritional support for children in school, but younger children and developing fetuses were seen as particularly vulnerable to hunger because of the importance of early development (Rossi, 1998). In addition, even pregnant mothers and young children who were "food secure" did not necessarily eat highly nutritious meals often because of a lack of access to such food. The WIC program also encourages breastfeeding, and the nutritional benefits to the mother are important because, for breastfed infants, what the mother eats, the infant does also.

Rossi (1998) wrote that WIC was in large part a response to the "1969 White House Conference on Food, Nutrition, and Health [that] . . . claimed that the nutritional deficiencies found among low-income women and children constituted a threat to the nation and led to high medical care costs" (p. 45). WIC was developed as a pilot program in 1972 and was extended to a national program three years later (DiNitto, 2005). The program was supported by U.S. Senator Hubert Humphrey of Minnesota (Morrissey, 2016), who earlier had served as vice president under President Lyndon B. Johnson.

Unlike SNAP, WIC is restrictive in terms of what food, prenatal supplements, and other benefits can be purchased. Conservative legislators especially are more apt to support programs such as WIC that have high control over benefits than they are to support programs like SNAP. The income requirements for program eligibility are also more generous than many other support programs, both because the costs are generally lower per person and because of the potential cost savings (Morrissey, 2016). Whaley et al. noted in 2012 that approximately half of all newborns received WIC benefits. A number of food packages are available, and on intake, the package that is the best fit for the mother, based on both preferences and dietary needs, is determined (Morrissey, 2016).

Effectiveness

WIC seems to be one of the most widely embraced public assistance policies available in the United States. It is generally the case that liberal legislators and stakeholders often support public assistance programs, whereas conservatives do not. However, there is a greater degree of uniform acknowledgment of the importance of WIC than with SNAP, TANF, or most other support programs. A major reason centers around the financial benefits of the program, which I describe shortly. Also, however, WIC benefits are time limited; that is, WIC only provides assistance until a child is five years old. Unlike more open-ended programs, such as SNAP, WIC can be seen as a temporary assistance program that will be removed, thus mitigating dependency. Of course, many families will move from WIC to school breakfast or lunch programs, or SNAP, but that is another issue.

An additional reason that many conservative legislators who are generally wary of public assistance programs often support WIC is that it constitutes the only public assistance program that directly supports fetuses and fetal development. Because most conservative legislators are "pro-life" and want to see fetuses brought to term, one would certainly expect them to embrace a policy designed to support the nutritional intake of fetuses. Moreover, the supportive information and services apart from food that are included within WIC and are provided to pregnant mothers also benefit the developing fetus and thus may provide emotional support to expectant mothers as well, encouraging their decision to bring their child to term. According to a 2004 study, long-term involvement in WIC was successful in leading to increased gestational periods and increased birth weights (Lazariu-Bauer, Stratton, Pruzek, & Woelfel, 2004).

In discussing their support for WIC, many legislators and other stakeholders have noted studies that show that for every dollar paid into the program, $3 is saved in eventual health care or other costs that relate to the ill effects of premature birth or the adverse effects of poor nutrition on the developing fetus (Carlson & Senauer, 2003; Morrissey, 2016). Greenstein (2001) contended that this financial benefit pertains to the "prenatal component of WIC" rather than the benefits provided after the child is born (p. 111). Because the majority of mothers receiving WIC benefits are on Medicaid, much of the cost savings are on lower Medicaid costs, especially during an infant's first few months (Carlson & Senauer, 2003; Lee et al., 2004).

The services provided by WIC assist developing fetuses and young children during the most vulnerable developmental period of their lives, yet many of those who received these services continue to live in households that are food insecure and require further support during their early educational years through the school breakfast and lunch programs (Ryu & Bartfeld, 2012) as well as SNAP. The ability to continue on a positive health and developmental trajectory and succeed in school is contingent in part on having access to proper nutrition.

CHAPTER 22

Child Abuse Prevention and Treatment Act

1974

Historical Overview and Nature of the Social Problem

Of all of the problems that affect society, surely child abuse and neglect are among the most disconcerting. It is difficult for us to understand why anyone would harm or fail to care for a child. Many behaviors that currently might be considered abuse (for example, corporal punishment, various forms of child labor) were often viewed as more permissible in the past. As is the case with many public issues, the perception that certain forms of child abuse or neglect constitute societal problems might be referred to as a social construct: accepted more in certain cultures and times than others. Before the past few centuries, children were often viewed more as parental property than as people with their own rights, and they also were much less likely to survive childhood because of the lack of medical care and the poor environments within which they lived. High childhood mortality rates may have had the effect at various times of ensuring that parents would be wary of developing a particularly close attachment to their children. Many Western religious traditions have also embraced a "spare the rod and spoil the child" form of child rearing, accepting a degree of corporal punishment that, at some point, may grade over into physical abuse.

What is true is that there has not always been a formalized means of protecting abused children. In addition, like a large number of social problems, before urbanization during the latter half of the 19th century, child abuse was less likely to be viewed as a problem in need of a governmental solution. Child abuse and neglect as well as the need for outplacement of victimized children or orphans came to be viewed as large-scale problems during the last quarter of the 19th century and became a central concern of progressives over the next few decades. According to M. Kahan (2006), the first adoption act was passed in Massachusetts in 1851, and Charles Loring Brace's famous Orphan Train Movement began shortly afterward, followed quickly by other private foster care and adoptive programs. Brace's efforts to remove children from the "corrupting influence" of large congested areas of New York and other large urban areas to rural farms have been criticized for a number of reasons, not the least because many of his "orphans" had living parents, and many of the "adoptive" families treated the children more like hired farmhands than members of the family (O'Connor, 2001).

Spurred by such issues as child labor, especially in rural, poor, and immigrant families, coupled with neglect that left many children in poor families to fend for themselves on the streets of large cities, as well as famous early examples of abuse, such as the Mary Ellen Wilson case (Paulson & Blake, 1969; Sealander, 2003), social workers, judges, and others began to look for a formalized way of categorizing and responding to abuse and neglect. The Children's Bureau, formed in 1912 in large part to deal with these problems, constituted one of the first government agencies to directly address social welfare needs. The Children's Bureau was originally headed by Julia Lathrop, one of the more well-known social workers of the day and an early leader in the effort to protect children (Lathrop, 1912). Also in 1912, James Garfield, son of the late President James A. Garfield, called for the creation of a "children's protective society" in the *Proceedings of the National Conference of Charities and Correction* (Garfield, 1912).

From the initiation of the Children's Bureau until the 1970s, each state developed its own method of investigating and responding to cases of abuse or neglect. For the most part, child abuse and neglect was not a major area of policy discussion between the Progressive Era and the 1960s (Lindsey, 1994). It was with Henry Kempe's writings in the 1960s (Kempe & Helfer, 1972), however, that "battered child syndrome," as he referred to it, would again become perceived to be a social problem of pressing national importance (Lindsey, 1994; Sealander, 2003). A pediatrician, Kempe wrote of the large number of children who were being seen in hospitals, clinics, and other health care facilities who were victims of abuse or neglect (Helfer, 1985; Kempe & Helfer, 1972). He contended that this was a widespread problem that most medical officials were aware of but had not received much public attention for a variety of reasons. In 1963, shortly after Kempe began to write about the issue, the federal government developed a "model child abuse reporting statute," and within a few years, every state had some form of child abuse reporting (Erickson, 2000).

Policy Overview

Although each state had developed its own child welfare system, each state differed widely in regard to its definitions of abuse and neglect as well as investigatory procedures and the specific aspects of mandated reporting. During testimony on the 1974 Child Abuse Prevention and Treatment Act (CAPTA) (P.L. 93-247), professor and social worker David Gil spoke before the Senate Subcommittee of the importance of uniform national standards (*Child Abuse Prevention Act, 1973: Hearings*, 1973). He also contended that there existed no clear agreed-on definition of "abuse" or "neglect." In addition, there was little communication between states, and, therefore, people who had been accused or convicted of abuse or neglect could change their state of residency without being tracked.

CAPTA, passed in 1974, was designed in large measure to provide uniformity in the standards related to abuse and neglect investigations, response, and treatment. It created the National Center on Child Abuse and Neglect, formalized mandated reporting requirements, established child abuse hot lines, set forth standards for the investigation of alleged cases of maltreatment, and supported the development of educational materials related to child abuse and neglect (Sealander, 2003). The 1974 act also provided a forum for initiating discussions of child sexual abuse and its prevention. Although this form of abuse was widely known, it was so sensitive that it was generally not subject to widespread public discussion.

Changes in the policy over the years would include an increased focus on early intervention (for children up to age three years), the provision of supportive services to children aging out of the foster care system, and the interrelationship between child protective services and the Individuals with Disabilities Education Act of 1990 (IDEA) (P.L. 101-476) (Herman, 2007). This connection between child protective services and IDEA is especially important because a disproportionate number of children with disabilities are subject to abuse and neglect investigations. There has also been an increasing emphasis on *kinship care*, that is, allowing children stay with relatives instead of foster care provided by nonrelatives (Hegar & Scannapieco, 1995).

Effectiveness

It is not surprising that with this increased attention on the problem of child abuse and neglect, the number of children removed from their homes dramatically increased following implementation of CAPTA. From 1975 until 1981, reports quadrupled from slightly under 300,000 to more than 1.2 million (Lindsey, 1994). Although the policy was highly effective in supporting investigations, it was problematic on three related fronts.

First, in many cases, child abuse investigators were overly disposed to removal of children from their homes. Second, the huge influx of cases, especially following the establishment of hot lines, swamped already overworked investigators (Sealander, 2003). Third, the tendency to remove children from their homes led to a flood of children into out-of-home placements. Unable to be adopted, the large majority of these children went into foster care or into alternative settings, such as group homes or orphanages. Often, the environments that children were placed into were not much of an improvement (if at all) from their original homes, and it was difficult for states to find enough quality foster care placements, particularly for hard-to-place children, such as those with disabilities or older or minority children, or those who displayed problematic behaviors. The result was *foster care drift* in which many children were moved around frequently from placement to placement (Erickson, 2000). Some states even had difficulty tracking where all children in the system were at any given time.

Analysis Element: Prevention Disincentives

Ironically, although the subject of "prevention" was notable in the title of CAPTA, as with many social welfare policies, one could argue that intervention, and particularly punitive measures, such as the threatened removal of children from the home or social stigma, had diminished the ability of social workers and related professionals to help prevent abuse or neglect. In any area of social work that overlaps with criminal justice or other areas of state control, punitive measures may serve to drive the problem underground, so to speak, because individuals and, in this case, parents, may be fearful of seeking assistance at an early stage because of concerns that the child welfare system will become involved in their lives. It becomes extremely difficult for child welfare authorities to develop a supportive relationship with potentially abusive or neglectful parents when the possibility of child separation looms, especially if these workers may be the ones instigating such separation.

These concerns become even more palpable when important racial, ethnic, or social class differences exist between child welfare authorities and caregivers. Roberts (2002) argued that in the eyes of many parents who have been investigated for potential abuse or neglect, authorities are viewed as assessing their situation from a White, middle-class perspective related to child rearing and the preferred home environment. This perspective is laden with moral judgment because single-parent families, more likely to be Black, may be viewed as less capable of adequately caring for their children. Poorer parents also are less likely to have legal representation and to live in urban neighborhoods where environmental hazards (for example, vermin, lead paint, toxins, crime) may adversely affect the family. Roberts (2002) noted that between 1982 and 1999, the number of African American children in foster care doubled from 262,000 to 568,000. As child welfare authorities became increasingly involved in the lives of those in the Black community, a contentious relationship was fostered. Roberts argued that African American parents are given fewer opportunities to keep their children in the home as opposed to White parents, even for similar abuse or neglect issues.

This contentious relationship serves to adversely affect the degree to which authorities, and particularly social workers, can effectively engage with such parents before the time when serious issues may arise. Even when different individuals or agencies may work on the prevention side as opposed to the penalty side of the issue, parents are likely to have concerns regarding confidentiality and what can be shared in a nonmandated counseling, mentoring, and parent training context.

CHAPTER 23

Housing and Community Development Act

1974

Historical Overview and Nature of the Social Problem

As a basic necessity of life, public support for available housing has long been considered, although albeit not by everyone, to be a proper area of government involvement. Of course, as with any other provisions related to such necessities, numerous questions surround how much support to provide, to whom, and for what length of time. The need for housing provisions and whether to provide low-interest or matching loans to support homeownership, rental support, public housing developments, or temporary housing to stave off homelessness are among the most pressing issues to consider during poor economic times. Housing policy is based not only on the simple fact that people need shelter but also on the realization that a degree of residential stability is a vital element in community-building and the maintenance of a well-functioning neighborhood or community. This residential stability in turn affects the locating of businesses within the community and the attainment of the tax revenue and jobs that such businesses provide. This chapter briefly reviews public housing policies; homelessness will be taken up in chapter 29.

An important issue in public housing policy is the deconcentration of poverty, an issue that is impossible to disentangle from racial demographics and race prejudice in relation to where people, especially African Americans, may reside (Vose, 1959). *Deconcentration* pertains to efforts to disperse "poverty households" over a large section of a community based largely on the assumption that if poor families are congested in a confined area, this section of the community will become stigmatized, and people who do not live in or approach the poverty threshold will refuse to reside in (or even visit) such neighborhoods (Goetz, 2003). Moreover, businesses may refuse to locate in or may flee such areas, leading to a lack of jobs and smaller tax base. Many housing experts have argued that such congestion supports a "culture of poverty" among its residents and that individuals who live in such isolated pockets of poverty, especially children, often develop a degree of disempowerment and hopelessness about future opportunities.

An obvious method of deconcentrating poverty is to support the movement of poor families into diverse middle-class neighborhoods, and many public housing policies, such as U.S. Department of Housing and Urban Development (HUD) Section 8 funding, have taken this approach. As one might suppose, these efforts have frequently been fought by homeowners concerned about a decline in their housing values or fearing increased crime. A variety of restrictive zoning laws, NIMBY (*n*ot *i*n *m*y *b*ack*y*ard) movements, "White flight," and the development of "community protection" policies and organizations are just a few ways that residents have combined their efforts to fight public housing in their communities (Dreier, Mollenkopf, & Swanstrom, 2004; Duke, 2010).

As discussed in greater depth in chapter 19, in addition to high poverty and frequently crime, few decent jobs, and outdated schools, those who live in areas marked by high poverty often must deal with high toxicity, including such issues as lead paint, poor sewage systems and drinking water, and the runoff from highly toxic industries (Taylor, 2014). Inner-city areas in particular are also adversely affected by media presentations and movie/TV depictions that highlight and expand on their problems as well as exploit public fear of the city for entertainment purposes (Macek, 2006). Fear of the city augments fear of city-based public housing and of those who live there.

Policy Overview

It should come as no surprise that the interest of federal legislators in housing policy arose during the Great Depression. This was a period when massive need existed, and providing support for home and other property investments was deemed an important precursor to stabilizing impoverished neighborhoods and the overall economy. The Federal Housing Administration was created under President Franklin D. Roosevelt as a component of the 1934 National Housing Act (P.L. 73-479) (Jacobs, Harney, Edson, & Lane, 1986).

This, along with a similar act three years later, provided some federal support for public housing and low-interest loans to home buyers. Bratt (1994), however, noted that, like many of the New Deal programs, these were short-lived policies designed to provide a degree of stability during this difficult period. These programs also served to reinforce racial segregation. As further delineated in chapter 11, the 1944 G.I. Bill also provided housing assistance to returning veterans from World War II, leading to the mass movement of families out of large urban cities.

Federal housing policy began in earnest with the Housing Act of 1949 (P.L. 171-338), which focused on "slum clearance" and the development of large public housing projects in major cities. It also supported suburban sprawl through the provision of Farmers Home Administration and other low-interest loans as well as highway development and government support for suburban development (Dreier et al., 2004). HUD was created by President Lyndon B. Johnson in 1968 largely to deal with problems that had arisen because of racial segregation in housing, the deterioration of housing projects, and as part of his larger War on Poverty agenda (Jacobs et al., 1986).

The Housing and Community Development Act of 1974 (P.L. 93-383) included a number of programs designed specially to improve inner-city areas but is perhaps most well known for its development of Section 8 housing vouchers, which are designed to allow some families living in high-poverty areas to move. Over the past half century, deconcentration of poverty has been a major goal of federal housing policy. Along with programs related to deconcentration, the government has supported gentrification and other community redevelopment efforts designed to entice middle- and upper-class families to move back into the cities.

Perhaps the most concerted federal effort to reform public housing is the HOPE VI (Housing Opportunities for People Everywhere) program, which began in 1992. This program called for demolishing many large-scale public housing complexes and providing vouchers to allow many of those who were displaced to other areas of the community, again with the deconcentration of poverty being a principal goal (Greenbaum, Hathaway, Rodriguez, Spalding, & Ward, 2008). To reach this goal, this and other public efforts have focused on "mixed-use" or "mixed-income" housing, supporting the development of larger, more "attractive" units that integrate people of multiple income classes

(Duke, 2010) in an effort to encourage people to move back to the city. In many of these facilities, rent is decided on a sliding scale based on family income.

Another important trend in public housing has been a move away from public ownership of facilities and in the direction of privately owned, government-subsidized projects. According to Edgar Olsen (2017), in 2013, the majority of rental assistance from HUD was for private project units. Many of these developments are supported through Low-Income Housing Tax Credits.

Efforts to redesign areas often include eminent domain projects that allow the federal or state government to forcibly take over large areas of a "blighted" community for public purposes (Main, 2007). Eminent domain is particularly controversial when the land is given over to private developers or other corporate interests, often with the excuse that this will increase job opportunities in an area that has a dearth of employment options. As many readers are undoubtedly aware, gentrification and eminent domain are also controversial because those people who are forced out of an area that is being redeveloped may have limited alternative residential options.

Effectiveness

Although many have supported large-scale community redevelopment efforts in the high-poverty areas of large cities, these efforts have also courted controversy, especially when those who are displaced by gentrification or the removal of housing projects are unable to be relocated within those areas. As John Arena (2012) wrote, nonprofit organizations and indigenous community leaders are often co-opted by those in power to support such redevelopment efforts. Greenbaum et al. (2008) noted a number of concerns related to programs that support the movement of poor families outside areas of high poverty concentration. Having to move often forces them away from support systems and extended family, social activities, schools where children may feel comfortable, more accessible transportation, and so on. Although programs like HOPE VI focus on Moving to Opportunity for Fair Housing, the job options in the areas that accept vouchers, especially "inner-ring suburbs," may be just as limited as in the original area.

Obviously, an underlying issue that relates to the effectiveness of housing policy designed to minimize poverty deconcentration is racism. Those areas targeted for redevelopment and "dispersal," as one might guess, have a highly disproportional number of African Americans and other minorities. Even though the Fair Housing Act of 1968 (P.L. 90-284) "prohibited discrimination in housing including racial steering, redlining, and blockbusting, . . . it did not promote racial integration in middle-income areas" (Dreier et al., 2004, p. 124). As they and other authors have pointed out, suburban communities can continue to build in a large number of zoning restrictions that serve as backdoor methods to discriminate—if not based directly on race, income, and family structure—and thus ensure continued community "homogeneity."

Again, because many of these families are required to move into areas that will accept them, this means pushing them to inner-ring suburbs that may have poverty concentration not far removed from the inner city. Greenbaum et al. (2008) wrote that many communities have taken steps to limit the movement of displaced families into their communities and that a majority of those who are required to move are less pleased with their new living arrangements. Despite the investment in poverty deconcentration over the past few decades, Ann Owens (2015) contended that, from 1980 to 2009, these programs "only modestly reduced metropolitan-area poverty concentration" (p. 326).

CHAPTER 24

Juvenile Justice and Delinquency Prevention Act

◖1974◗

Historical Overview and Nature of the Social Problem

Although crime of all types is viewed as an important social problem deserving of public policy initiatives, juvenile crime is accorded particular attention. Adolescents and young adults, especially males, are considered to be responsible for crimes that are senseless (for example, random vandalism) as well as frequently violent. Importantly, if the juvenile justice system does not respond effectively to early indicators of criminality, the fear is that youths will enter a life of crime. Juvenile justice is also a matter of policy interest because of concerns related to labeling—that once youths begin to engage in criminal activities, they will be identified by others as a "delinquent," which may lead them to self-identify in this way, particularly if they see few positive alterative options open to them.

Juvenile crime has long been viewed as a specific area of criminal justice, and, in 1899, the first juvenile court was established in Chicago (Jensen & Rojek, 1998). Shortly thereafter, in 1909, President Theodore Roosevelt convened the first White House Conference on Children and Youth (Abrams, 2003; Olson-Raymer, 1983) for which juvenile delinquency was a key area of focus. By 1925, nearly every state had developed a juvenile court (Bowman, 2018). According to McCarter and Bridges (2011), a separate juvenile court system was established because juveniles were perceived as more vulnerable within the justice system and "more amenable to rehabilitation and treatment" than adults (pp. 168–169). Abrams (2003) noted that during its early decades, the Missouri juvenile justice system attempted to move away from a criminal justice model. It replaced crime-related terminology with alternative, less stigmatizing descriptors, and it often framed the descriptors from a nationally recognized medical and disease standpoint because delinquents were frequently seen as "morally sick" rather than criminalistic (pp. 57–61).

The response to juvenile offenders has swung back and forth over the years between a focus on harsh punishment to supportive treatment as the best deterrent to juvenile crime (Goshe, 2013). Diversion and work programs, military-style boot camps, mentoring, and community or victim restitution programs (van Wormer, 2006) have been only a few of the alternative forms of treatment used over the years in response to at-risk youths. According to Howell (2003), many of the most well-known prevention programs for juveniles, such as the DARE (Drug Abuse Resistance Education) drug abuse program, zero-tolerance policies, and Scared Straight, have little if any proven effectiveness in diminishing juvenile delinquency. Chamberlain and Moore (2000) contended that one program that has demonstrated effective results, especially for children in foster care who have a history of delinquent behaviors, is a specialized form of foster care that includes highly trained caregivers.

In 1967, the Supreme Court ruled in the *In re Gault* decision that juvenile courts needed to become more uniform and follow a more formal means of responding to juvenile crime (Bowman, 2018; Kuanliang & Sorenson, 2007). Jensen and Rojek (1998) wrote that the *Gault* decision came about because the alleged perpetrator, a 15-year-old boy named Gerald Gault, was not afforded legal counsel, and there was not even a transcript of the hearing. Although a more informal process of dealing with juvenile cases was intended in large part to destigmatize juveniles, it also infringed on their constitutional rights to defend themselves. Jensen and Rojek also noted that the punishment of Gault was much worse than the maximum penalty had he been tried as an adult. This court decision would inform the 1974 policy (see next section) because it made clear that federal guidelines for juvenile cases were needed.

Policy Overview

The Juvenile Justice and Delinquency Prevention Act of 1974 (JJDPA) (P.L. 93-415) was designed in part to ensure separate treatment of in the criminal justice system of juveniles. Those who developed the policy believed that if youths were directed away from adult prisons and provided an opportunity to rehabilitate themselves, many would not become career criminals. A primary goal of the policy, therefore, was to hold most young offenders in juvenile facilities or grant them probation. Diversion from detention facilities was particularly emphasized in the case of youths whose only crime was a status offense, such as drinking or truancy (McCarter & Bridges, 2011; Shubik & Kendall, 2007). In cases in which placement in a juvenile facility was unfeasible, youths who served time in adult prisons were to be placed in a separate area (referred to as "sight and sound separation" from adult prisoners; McCarter, 2011).

As has been true of the adult criminal population, over the course of the past few decades, the disproportional number of minority youths, and especially African Americans, has become a pressing juvenile justice concern (McCarter, 2011). Disproportionate minority confinement (DMC) "was officially recognized by the federal government in the 1988 amendments" to the JJDPA (Mooradian, 2007, p. 100). Controlling for other factors (for example, crime severity, previous convictions, family structure), race is an important factor in the response to particular juvenile offenses (McCarter, 2011). As a result, amendments to the JJDPA require states to track and reduce DMC (McCarter, 2011). Nicki Cole (2021), like a number of other authors, also pointed out that zero-tolerance policies in schools have been used disproportionately against minority youths and thus play an important role in the school-to-prison pipeline.

Kolivoski, Goodkind, and Shook (2017) noted issues of concern related to what they referred to as *crossover youths* who are involved in both the child welfare and juvenile justice systems. These youths also include a disproportionate percentage of African American children, which is not surprising because these children are found in larger numbers relative to their population in each of these two systems. These authors noted that because the child welfare and juvenile justice systems serve different ends with differing values, they may not communicate or interconnect well with one another. Certainly, that setup has its benefits, especially because we would not want to presume unlawful behavior from youths in foster care or further stigmatize them.

Effectiveness

As with many policy issues, presumptions of policy effectiveness in controlling juvenile delinquency largely depend on one's political leanings. As with other areas within the field of corrections, those embracing more conservative values will generally support get-tough measures. DMC continues to be an area of particular emphasis within the juvenile justice system. Mooradian (2007) contended that not only are minority youths disproportionally mistreated in the system but these differences expand as the youths move through the system to the sentencing phase. He also noted the results of experiments on implicit racial bias held by those involved in the process, including social workers. As in other areas of research, those studies demonstrate the veracity of claims for such bias.

In part, as a result of DMC, many courts have made concerted efforts to provide options to the traditional juvenile system. Perhaps the most important of these efforts, and one that is especially focused on social work interests, is restorative justice. Of the several forms that restorative justice may take, all provide a more informal approach to alleged crimes than the traditional formal juvenile court. The victim(s) and potentially close friends or family members and the juvenile are brought together with a trained mediator or coordinator who runs the sessions. In many cases, select community members are also involved, especially because crimes may be viewed as targeting not only specific victims but also the larger community, which is particularly the case when a specific community subgroup may have been targeted (for example, a hate crime).

All forms of restorative justice involve the juvenile's not only admitting the crime but providing an explanation for the action. The victim or victim's friends or relatives share the effect on themselves, and everyone discusses ways of repairing the damage. Restoration by the juvenile may be in the form of community service; actions on behalf of the victim(s); or other means of acknowledging, through physical actions, the need to make up for the crime. As one might assume, restorative justice is much more in keeping with the values of social work than the traditional system because it requires juveniles to take responsibility within the context of a less stigmatizing process (van Wormer, 2006).

CHAPTER 25

Education for All Handicapped Children Act

◖1975◗

Historical Overview and Nature of the Social Problem

One could certainly argue that not allowing a particular group to have access to education is among the most egregious forms of discrimination, thus impeding an individual's future development. We make a demoralizing statement about a child's future potential when we tell them (overtly or covertly) that they are not likely to progress much and therefore should not attend school (Shapiro, 1993). Although some may argue that this was not the message that was sent to children with disabilities and their families before the 1970s, there certainly exists ample evidence to the contrary.

For much of the 20th century, when compulsory education was generally in force throughout the country, educational access for students with disabilities was thwarted for a variety of reasons. Students with severe or mild cognitive disabilities were thought to be largely uneducable (Altshuler, 2007; Keogh & Barkett, 1978), those with mobility issues or who could not access regular modes of transportation simply could not get to or maneuver around many schools, and many students with physical or emotional impairments were subject to harassment. In addition, many individuals with learning disabilities and other difficult-to-diagnose conditions simply dropped out because of the struggles they faced in a conventional educational setting.

To a great extent, educational opportunities for children with disabilities were expanded as a result of the 1954 *Brown v. Board of Education* decision. When the U.S. Supreme Court supported integrated education for African Americans and other minorities, it also opened the door for education for students with disabilities. As Turnbull (1993) wrote,

> In *Brown* it was proven that although the U.S. Constitution never once refers to a public education, its principles of equal protection and due process under the Fifth and Fourteenth Amendments [U.S. Const. amends. V and XIV, respectively] have a significant effect on public education. (p. 8).

The policy was also fostered by growing advocacy among parents of children with disabilities during the 1960s and 1970s.

By the 1970s, a number of important court cases had been brought that demanded a free appropriate public education for children with disabilities. The most important of these cases were the Pennsylvania Association for Retarded Children (*P.A.R.C. v. Commonwealth of Pennsylvania*, 1972) and the Mills (*Mills v. Board of Education*, 1972) cases, both decided by district courts in 1972 (Boyle & Weishaar, 2001). These and other cases were brought on behalf of children who were excluded from attaining a public education, were not provided with education in the regular educational environment because of their disability, did not have a sound plan of education that took their disability into account, or did not have parental input into or due process protections related to their educational placement or plan (Boyle & Weishaar, 2001; Underwood & Mead, 1995). These legal cases forced the hand of the federal government to pass the Education for All Handicapped Children Act of 1975 (EAHCA) (P.L. 94-142).

Policy Overview

Efforts to pass the EAHCA took place at a time of heightened awareness of disability rights in the United States (Shapiro, 1993). In 1973, the first major civil rights legislation related to people with disabilities, Section 504 of the Rehabilitation Act of 1973 (P.L. 93-112), became law (Scotch, 2001). This brief but powerful legislative statement outlawed discrimination against people with disabilities by the federal government and any businesses that contracted with it. Importantly, the government's refusal to implement this section of the law also energized people with disabilities to develop their own civil rights movement (Scotch, 2001). Parent advocacy groups had already developed by this time and were also instrumental in pressuring Congress to pass various forms of disability-related legislation.

Legislators generally supported the idea of educational rights for children with disabilities, but the costs associated with accommodating such children, particularly those with serious or multiple disabilities, were a grave concern. Because, traditionally, local communities had primarily provided education costs, the issue of what level of government was going to pay for such accommodations needed to be decided. For the federal government to require services without supporting them would be considered an unfunded mandate.

The EAHCA was signed into law in 1975 and included six major principles. These were (1) zero reject: that no children with disabilities would be excluded from attaining an education because of their disability; (2) nondiscriminatory evaluation: efforts to ensure that assessment tests leading to a disability determination were fair, accurate, and not culturally biased; (3) the development by an interdisciplinary team of an individualized education plan (IEP) that was appropriate to each particular student; (4) provision of education in the student's least restrictive environment; (5) due process provisions for parents and guardians who disagreed with the plan or process related to their student; and (6) meaningful parental participation in IEP development and implementation (Turnbull, 1993).

The policy set forth requirements for testing and assessment of students who might have one or more recognized disability conditions (Keogh & Barkett, 1978); allowed for input by specialists (for example, speech, hearing, occupational therapists); and the development, with parental involvement, of an IEP that clearly spells out the form of education provided along with measurable education goals and time lines. An important element of the policy is the development of due process guidelines for parents or guardians who disagree with IEP team decisions (Underwood & Mead, 1995).

Even though the policy requires schools to provide accommodations for students with disabilities to assist in their education, schools do not have to provide the specific accommodations requested by parents or others. In this way, the policy is similar to the ADA (1990) (P.L. 101-336) requirement for "reasonable" accommodations. As Yell, Katsiyannis, and Hazelkorn (2007) noted, the *Rowley* case, heard by the U.S. Supreme Court in 1982, spelled out what schools needed to provide to abide by the policy (*Board of Education of the Hendrick Hudson Central School District v. Rowley*, 1982). The Court held that the school was required to afford an educational option that allowed for "educational benefits" but that questions remain about how extensive these benefits must be or how much educational progress a particular student is to demonstrate. This is especially important, these authors noted, in light of the recent movement in education to focus on results more so than process.

In 1990, a major reauthorization of the EAHCA was completed that included a change in the title of the policy to IDEA (1990) (P.L. 101-476). Changes in the policy included an expansion of recognized categories of disability from 11 to 13 (Altshuler, 2007) as well as increased emphasis on services to children younger than five years old, stronger parental participation requirements, and an expanded focus on students preparing to transition from high school to college or the workforce. The transition issue focuses on increased attention to the future of students once they leave the school setting, which may include preparation for independent living or higher education, or both, or learning a trade (E. W. Carter, Brock, & Trainor, 2014; Certo et al., 2008).

Effectiveness

Certainly, EAHCA/IDEA has dramatically improved access to education for students with disabilities. Questions remain, however, about a number of issues, such as the most appropriate educational environment for children and adolescents with specific disabilities; the effectiveness of the due process procedures; the various options schools have in response to students with behavior problems or who engage in bullying and the extent to which behavioral problems constitute a disability (Kelly, 2016; Raines, 2006); issues related to minority populations (for example, cultural aspects of testing and assessment, implicit bias in education, possible overdiagnosis); and controversy over hard-to-diagnose disabilities, such as various learning disabilities (Colker, 2013).

Some would argue that the zero-reject element of the policy is problematic and that, especially in the case of students with multiple severe disabilities, the funds would be better served providing other forms of support. Although most would argue that IDEA is successful in the main, discrepancies always arise when considering the best interests of individual children. Social workers, who frequently are the leaders of or at least heavily involved in IEP teams, often feel caught in the middle between various team members with differing opinions of a treatment plan. Unfortunately, such disagreements often pit parents against school personnel. In addition to the grievance policies accorded to parents, it is in the best interests of the team that parents are engaged in a real sense as integral members. Along with other reasons, parents or caregivers will need to generalize IEP elements to the home environment to ensure consistency. They are more likely to do so if they have had true input into the plan.

Analysis Element: Social Costs and Benefits

Issues of costs and benefits loom large in an analysis of EAHCA/IDEA, and this includes not only financial costs and benefits but also social ones. Social costs and benefits are much more difficult to delineate quantitatively or to accurately measure than economic costs and benefits, and they rest largely on subjective interpretation and individual values. Because they are frequently extremely important in the passage of policies (or the opposition to passage), however, they must be included within problem and policy analysis. Furthermore, social costs/benefits may bleed into economic costs/benefits. If, for example, a social benefit of IDEA is to enhance the educational potential and knowledge of a student with a disability (a social benefit), this has numerous secondary benefits, including potentially a better job or chance at higher education, both of which can be an economic benefit for the individual.

One problem that many policy advocates often face relates to the fact that the benefits for one group are said to carry with them a cost to other groups. The presumption, therefore, is that there is a zero-sum relationship similar to what we see with affirmative action policy (yes, members of the other group get the job, but members of my group who are just as qualified do not get the job). IDEA was fought by many parent groups on the grounds that their own children would not get a high-quality education (a social cost) if students with disabilities were disruptive, taking the teachers' attention, or if the teacher was "teaching down" to the class because of students with disabilities. Interestingly, some parents/caregivers for children with disabilities often have the opposite concern: that their child will not get a good education in the regular classroom because the teacher may not provide the attention the child would receive in a separate room or school.

Obviously, there are other important potential social costs or benefits that specifically relate to those students who receive services. For example, will the child be bullied or be a source of embarrassment? Will there be more acceptance of the child if there is a diagnostic label attached to their behaviors, or might the child not be blamed so much for "acting out"? Will the label be attached to the child even into adulthood, possibly negatively affecting their ability to gain insurance or get a job?

Social costs and benefits need to be delineated as they relate to the student, family, and others who might be affected by the policy. Often, perceived costs will be in the form of unfounded fears. Even these, however, can have an important effect on the passage or implementation of a policy and need to be taken into account.

CHAPTER 26

Earned Income Tax Credit Act

1975

Historical Overview and Nature of the Social Problem

Starting in the 1950s, AFDC and other federal public assistance programs (including those that were initiated after the 1950s) saw rather dramatic increases in enrollment and the total amount of federal money paid out, although it is also true that the presumption of large increases in support payments per recipient or family is largely inaccurate. As noted in chapter 36 and elsewhere within this book, these increases led to a major public backlash against such programs (Ventry, 2001). This backlash was partly based on well-publicized myths related to beneficiaries (for example, the "welfare queen") and misconceptions about the actual percentage of the federal budget such programs entail (Zucchino, 1999). Therefore, the savings that many assumed would be realized if these programs were dramatically cut was vastly overestimated.

This issue of "work or welfare" also relates to the concept of "less eligibility," which has been a central feature of arguments surrounding public support (Ozawa, 1995). Even when it has not always been described using this term, less eligibility has been an inherent element of the public debate over welfare spending for centuries. The concept is that people who are assumed to be capable of work but are receiving welfare payments (the "unworthy poor") should never be in a better financial situation than the lowest wage earners among the working class. In other words, those poor individuals who can work should never have a financial incentive for choosing not to work. Conservative critics of "welfare," such as Charles Murray (1984), argued that the system of support in the United States during the 1970s was such that poor families were better off not working and receiving benefits from AFDC, Medicaid, SNAP, and other government programs.

The movement to pass the EITC arose largely as a means of incentivizing employment among poor individuals who either were living in poverty or barely above the poverty line and, simultaneously, to make public assistance a less attractive option. Although EITC is not generally a policy that social workers have a strong interest in, it can be extremely important to those with financial needs because it has served to keep many poor families above the poverty line. Meyer (2017) noted that EITC is currently the "largest antipoverty program for the non-aged in the United States" (p. 1).

Policy Overview

The EITC (P.L. 94-12) passed in 1975, was signed into law by President Richard M. Nixon, and, in 1986, the credit was indexed for inflation (Beverly, 2002; Mendenhall, 2006). Nixon had first presented the Family Assistance Plan, which would have provided a small guaranteed income to families in poverty (Burke, 1974; Handler & Hasenfeld, 2007; Ventry, 2001). A number of states, Mendenhall (2006) wrote, have passed a policy to provide supplemental state benefits over and above the federal minimum. In 1993, the federal benefits were increased by President Bill Clinton as one effort in fulfilling his promise to diminish the extent of welfare provisions (Ozawa, 1995). Although Clinton's TANF proposal did not pass until 1996, expanding the EITC was important for those whose TANF benefits would be time limited and those who would require employment.

The EITC has been referred to as a negative income tax in that it provides tax benefits to poor families based on their income and family structure (Handler & Hasenfeld, 2007). A small portion of the funds are provided to childless individuals or couples; however, the vast majority goes to families with children, and the allotment is increased based on the number of children. Unlike most other social welfare policies, the policy, being tax related, is administered by the Internal Revenue Service (IRS) (Delavega, 2016). To receive the benefit, applicants must complete a supplemental form to their regular tax statement (Delavega, 2016; Meyer, 2017). Because many recipients would already have no tax liability, providing benefits rather than decreasing the tax liability was the feasible option (Ventry, 2001).

In addition to its primary goals of encouraging work over "welfare" and pulling families above the poverty line, a secondary goal of the program is to incentivize consumption, which benefits the national economy (Mendenhall,

2006). Certainly, if the government wants to incentivize purchasing, it makes the most sense to provide funding to those who most need to purchase: the poorest working families. Moreover, because many of those who receive the benefit reside in high-poverty areas, this consumption, one might assume, secondarily assists the businesses and employees who work in these geographic areas.

The policy includes a *phase-in range*, that is, a graduated increase in reimbursement based on income and the number of children; a *plateau range* for those eligible for the maximum amount; and a *phase-out range* for those with higher incomes but who are still poor (Mendenhall, 2006). The graduated phase-in range encourages people at the lowest income levels to increase their income (Lim, DeJohn, & Murray, 2012). As Dolgoff and Feldstein (2007) pointed out, one problem with the phase-out range is the possibility of work disincentives. In other words, if families will likely have less EITC reimbursement—or not make much more—from working more hours, from receiving a promotion, or from working a second, part-time job, it may not be worthwhile for them to have the increased income (Beverly, 2002). Therefore, as Ozawa (1995) wrote, the program may have countereffects as a work incentive (for example, working more hours or earning more) based on whether a family is at the phase-in or phase-out stage.

Effectiveness

The EITC is generally considered to be highly effective. As of 2009, it was "estimated to lift 6.6 million people out of poverty annually, roughly half of whom are children" (Lim et al., 2012, p. 177). Meyer (2017) claimed that Social Security is the only federal program to raise more people out of poverty. It is likely, however, that the combination of Social Security and Medicare have had this effect. Similar to WIC, EITC is an anti-poverty program that politicians from across the political spectrum generally support (Beverly, 2002; Handler & Hasenfeld, 2007; Ventry, 2001). The EITC not only provides support to poor families, and particularly children, but does so in a way that is less stigmatizing than TANF and other "welfare" programs (Delavega, 2016). Yet another reason that the program has broad-based support is because it costs relatively little to operate, especially when compared to other public assistance programs (Ventry, 2001).

A major concern related to EITC is that many eligible poor families are taken advantage of by shady tax preparation companies that consume "a nontrivial portion of an EITC refund and adds financial burdens" that "[reduce] the effectiveness of the EITC" (Lim et al., 2012, p. 178). Fraud is also a problem with the program (Mendenhall, 2006; Meyer, 2017), especially related to single parents claiming children who did not live with them full time (Handler & Hasenfeld, 2007). In many cases, such a claim is not purposeful because it can be confusing whether to deduct for a child when the parents share custody. This being the case, the vast majority of those families eligible for the support do receive it, although, among the poorest working families, fewer people are aware of their eligibility (Handler & Hasenfeld, 2007). Social workers who work with poor families need to be aware of eligibility and ensure that their clients receive the benefit (Delavega, 2016). Furthermore, a number of nonprofit agencies exist to assist those who are eligible to attain the support (Lim et al., 2012). The IRS, noted Beverly (2002), sends "a notice to nonclaimants who appear to be eligible encouraging them to file an amended return" (pp. 260–261).

Of all governmental policies, the EITC is one that is most in accordance with the values of the social work profession. It supports poor people, particularly children, in a way that is largely nonstigmatizing; it encourages self-sufficiency; and it benefits the overall economy in a way that secondarily helps those in struggling communities.

CHAPTER 27

Indian Child Welfare Act

1978

Historical Overview and Nature of the Social Problem

To say that Native Americans have been maltreated is a vast understatement. As was the case with many aboriginal cultures, conquering Western nations subjected Native Americans in the United States to a wide array of purposeful (for example, removal, murder, broken treaties) and largely accidental (for example, disease spread) forms of subjugation and abuse. Many Native American tribes were decimated over the years, and most were forced to live in unfamiliar barren land that was often far removed from that of their ancestors. The government frequently broke promises it had made with Native Americans. At the same time they were being killed off, they were stereotyped as bloodthirsty savages who were a threat to innocent settlers. A central theme in any large-scale oppression is the rationalization of self-defense on the part of oppressors, and this is clear in considering this history.

For decades before the passage, in 1978, of the Indian Child Welfare Act (ICWA) (P.L. 95-608), the United States had been forcibly removing Native American children to educate them in non-Native schools (S. L. Cross, 2006; Graham, 2009). As Graham (2009) wrote, as "early as 1867 the U.S. Commissioner of Indian Affairs was advocating for the forcible removal of Indian children from their tribal nations as 'the only successful way to deal with the 'Indian problem'" (p. 51). The ironic process of forced "Americanization" of the most native Americans was designed to assimilate these children into Western culture and to physically as well as emotionally remove them from reservations and Indian society. According to Linda Herzberg (2013), child placement outside the tribe was "legitimized in the Indian Adoption Project established by the Bureau of Indian Affairs and the Child Welfare League of America in 1958" (p. 477). Many Native American advocacy organizations referred to this as a form of cultural genocide because the forced removal of many of their children had the effect of destabilizing not only families but entire tribes.

Into the 1970s, these placements were actively supported by child welfare organizations (Graham, 2009), and, according to B. J. Jones, Tilden, and Gaines-Stoner (2008), "in states with large Native American populations an incredible 25 percent to 35 percent of all Native American children were removed from their homes and placed in foster or adoptive homes at one time in their lives" (p. 2, also see B. J. Jones, 2009). Because of these and other historical events, one might well assume that many Native Americans would not trust the decisions made by government representatives, including child welfare authorities (Barnes, Constantine Brown, & McCarty-Caplan, 2019).

The Native American population in the nation also began to organize for their own rights during the 1960s and 1970s. Groups staged a series of protests that included a highly publicized takeover of the abandoned Alcatraz prison and an incident in 1973 at Wounded Knee, the site of a massacre in the late 1800s. The primary group responsible for these incidents was the American Indian Movement, which sought self-determination for Native Americans and retribution for past government offenses.

The ICWA was also influenced to some degree by the controversy over cross-racial adoption in the African American community (Jennings, 2006). During the 1970s, the National Association of Black Social Workers and related groups attempted to stem the tide of large numbers of African American children being adopted into White families. They argued that this was inappropriate for a variety of reasons, including that such children would then be removed from their racial heritage, and many would suffer a loss of racial identity or experience identity confusion and self-esteem issues.

Policy Overview

The ICWA was designed for two primary purposes. The first was an effort to redress prior harms imposed on Native Americans specifically related to child removal and related issues. The second rationale was reestablishing Native American children into their tribe as a means of supporting the survival of these groups, many of which were rapidly dying out, but also to reacquaint these children with their heritage (Hunter, 2009; Limb & Brown, 2008).

The policy was preceded by the Indian Self-Determination and Education Assistance Act of 1975 (P.L. 93-638), which provided for "tribal self-governance" (S. L. Cross, 2006). Mannes (1995) noted that at the end of the 1960s, the Devil Lakes Sioux Tribe of North Dakota was particularly interested in advocating for self-determination in child placements. They and other tribes developed and advocated for passage of the ICWA, and the policy was passed and signed into law in 1978 by President Jimmy Carter. The policy basically gave decisions regarding child custody to the tribe when the child was identified as a member of that specific tribe. The policy pertained primarily to adoption and foster care rather than divorce cases (B. J. Jones et al., 2008).

Because the extended family system is an important social unit in many tribes, the act prioritizes the placement of children, when they are unable to stay with their birth parents, in foster care in kinship care or with extended tribal family members (S. L. Cross, 2006). The majority of tribes "operate a tribal child welfare program as well as a tribal court" that are supposed to have authority over placements (Leake, Potter, Lucero, Gardner, & Deserly, 2012, p. 48).

Effectiveness

The ICWA has provided a degree of increased autonomy to tribes, yet, as Bussey and Lucero (2013) have contended, "American Indian children continue to be disproportionally represented in public child welfare systems across the United States" (p. 394). One area of some confusion, as B. J. Jones (2009) pointed out, is how the ICWA interrelates with other child welfare policies, especially the Adoption and Safe Families Act of 1997 (P.L. 105-89). It is somewhat unclear which of these policies supersedes the other when their goals do not coincide. Limb and Brown (2008) added that data collection is problematic; thus, it is difficult to say the degree to which states are properly implementing the act or whether they are interpreting it uniformly.

As with any policy that provides services or benefits to a select group of people based on race or ethnicity, identification as Native American is an important concern of the ICWA (S. L. Cross, 2006). The question arises as to how much Indian heritage a child must have for the policy to be in effect and how to determine tribal membership in cases where this is problematic

(Bussey & Lucero, 2013). In addition, if a child has never lived with an Indian family or has few ties to a tribe, questions surround whether the policy should relate to that child. B. J. Jones et al. (2008) referred to this issue as the " 'existing Indian family' exception" (p. 37). In addition, in some locales, it is difficult for child welfare authorities to recruit Indian foster homes (B. J. Jones et al., 2008).

One concern put forth about prioritizing Native American homes, especially within reservations, is that many have disproportionally high rates of poverty, alcoholism, domestic violence, and other social problems that lead to "greater vulnerability to poor health outcomes" for children (Barnes et al., 2019, p. 222). As further discussed in the following section, this brings up the question of what the proper balance is between what is best for the child and what is best for the tribe.

Analysis Element: Reparations

A number of social policies that pertain to past government offenses focus to some degree on the concept of *reparations*, that is, the provision of some form of benefit or atonement as a result of harms perpetrated by the government. Examples include the provision of monetary or other benefits related to Japanese internment, allowances given to the surviving victims of the Tuskegee syphilis study, and recommendations that the African American community be provided with reparations for slavery or other abuses (Brooks, 2004; Brophy, 2006). At times, reparations relate to state policies rather than federal government policies, such as when the victims of state involuntary sterilization laws call for reparation (Begos, Deaver, Railey, & Sexton, 2012). At other times, even corporations may be sued for knowingly profiting from various forms of oppression or exploitation (Brooks, 2004). Unfortunately, in many cases, such as Tuskegee, by the time reparations are provided, few victims of these abuses are still alive. Difficulties arise also when considering reparations for past abuses that might be provided not to those who were directly harmed (for example, by slavery) but to their descendants. Often when the provision of benefits for past injustices, such as slavery, are discussed, recommendations relate to provisions to the larger class of individuals (for example, funding for the National Association for the Advancement of Colored People, historically Black colleges) rather than to specific individuals.

To a certain extent, the ICWA stands as one form of reparation as an effort to provide some redress for the past removal of Native American children from their families and for government policies that severely damaged the sustainability of various tribes. Other forms of redress have been provided at various times to Native Americans, such as the Alaska Native Claims Settlement Act of 1971 (P.L. 92-203), which awarded $1 billion and the return of a large outlay of land (Brophy, 2006). Nevertheless, these provisions have certainly not come close to adequately providing atonement for past abuses.

One of the issues that makes the ICWA as a form of reparation controversial is that it so intimately involves the future of children. Child welfare authorities may experience a quandary when following the ICWA in those cases in which the policy seems to run counter to the best interests of the child (B. J. Jones et al., 2008). This issue may arise in any situation in which culture, race, or ethnicity is an important factor in placement. Given the alternative options for placement and the relative benefits of each, how important should these factors be in the decision?

CHAPTER 28

Adoption Assistance and Child Welfare Act

◀ 1980 ▶

Historical Overview and Nature of the Social Problem

To a large degree, the historical precursors of the Adoption Assistance and Child Welfare Act of 1980 (AACWA) (P.L. 96-272) were the same as its predecessor, CAPTA (1974) (P.L. 93-247), the subject of chapter 22. Problematic elements of the 1974 act or its implementation paved the way for the AACWA. Following the earlier policy, child abuse and neglect became an important topic of discussion in social welfare, and states began to take harsh measures against abusers. Children were removed from their homes in large numbers, and there were not enough foster home placements to meet the demand for placement. CAPTA focused extensively on protecting children, but little focus was on the provision of necessary services to keep families together (R. Alexander & Alexander, 1995) or to ensure long-term stability for children placed outside the home. Parents often believed that they were given little opportunity to maintain their children within the family or to work on parenting issues.

In addition, many of these children experienced *foster care drift*; that is, they were moved frequently from placement to placement (Samantrai, 1992). As one might guess, this had an adverse effect on their ability to bond and to develop self-esteem. This movement also had a negative effect on their schooling because it necessitated a frequent change in schools. Many states were also overwhelmed, with the large number of children being moved into foster care, which led to minimal contact between foster parents and caseworkers. Furthermore, some states even had difficulty tracking or locating many foster children (Chipungu, 2003).

Policy Overview

The AACWA was passed in 1980 primarily as an effort to correct for the unintended consequences of CAPTA. Its primary focus was on *permanency planning*, ensuring that children were in the safest permanent placement possible. A range of placement options from most to least preferable was conceived of, and permanency and safety were the two primary factors in deciding on the relative preferability of the placement. The best possible option was coordination with the child's parent(s) or caregiver(s) to work through whatever problems existed to allow the child to remain in that setting. Barring that possibility, adoption was the preference because it is a more permanent option than foster care or other forms of outplacement. Because adoption chances diminish with the age of the child, one element of the AACWA was to provide the parent(s) or caregiver(s) a limited amount of time to reach treatment goals to retain custody of the child. It was thought to be unfair for the child to keep their status up in the air any longer than necessary.

The policy also increased financial incentives for adopting children, especially those who would potentially be hard to place because of age, race, disability status, or other reasons (Stein, 2007; Waldinger, 1982). Under the AACWA, nonpermanent placements, such as foster care and congregate care (for example, orphanages, group homes) settings, were seen as the least preferable options. Even in the case of foster care, however, efforts were made to ensure a good match and to support permanency regardless of the option. In many cases, kinship care was a preferred option because the child would remain with extended family and would often continue in their community/school (Hegar & Scannapieco, 1995).

The policy mandated that all states were to engage in "reasonable efforts" to retain or, in the case of emergency outplacement, return children to their natural home setting. Services, such as drug or alcohol counseling, therapy, parenting training, and domestic violence intervention, were to be provided, and child welfare authorities were to give "evidence of sustained activity with and on behalf of the parents to engage and maintain them in relevant services" (Seaberg, 1986, p. 474). Specific services were to be delineated within a treatment plan, and parents signed that they agreed to the services and target deadlines. Failure on the part of parents to meet requirements could be used in court to support outplacement of the child (Seaberg, 1986). Many families received a highly intense short-term treatment, such as family preservation services, designed to focus on the broad range of family and parenting needs (Hartman, 1993).

Effectiveness

As CAPTA and the AACWA illustrate, ever since the early Orphan Train Movement, there have been shifts in the social services and policy response to child welfare from support for preserving families to child placement outside the home (McWey, Henderson, & Tice, 2006). As Samantrai (1992) noted, one criticism of the AACWA is that it has focused much more on "preplacement and reunification" services as opposed to "primary prevention services" (p. 298). Child welfare authorities traditionally have difficulty carrying out prevention services both because fewer resources are directed toward those services and because, as discussed in chapter 22, they are widely viewed as an arm of law enforcement and thus are not trusted by many caregivers as supportive partners in preventing abuse. This is important because a "shift of protective services for children from an adversarial criminal focus after children have been damaged to a preventative focus would reduce the need for extensive interventions years later" (Westman, 1996, p. 50).

Transracial adoptions also became an increasing area of emphasis within the AACWA. Groups such as the National Association of Black Social Workers began decrying the adoption of African American children by White families in the 1970s (M. Kahan, 2006; McRoy & Griffin, 2012; Phillips & Mann, 2013). They argued that such adoption placements deprived these children of an important aspect of their heritage and would adversely affect the child's identification as a Black person (Jennings, 2006). In her 2002 book *Shattered Bonds*, Dorothy Roberts was particularly critical that child welfare workers viewed parenting from a middle-class White perspective, which harmed the ability of Black parents to retain their children. The backlash against transracial adoptions was an important reason why kinship care expanded as an outplacement option. Efforts are to be made to ensure same-race placements, but controversy may exist where a same-race but temporary placement option (foster care) and a cross-racial but more permanent option (adoption) both exist for a given child.

Child welfare policy underwent several more major changes following the AACWA. Two major revisions were the Multiethnic Placement Act of 1994 (MEPA) (P.L. 103-382) and the Adoption and Safe Families Act of 1997 (ASFA) (P.L. 105-89). MEPA encouraged same-race placements but stated that placement of a child could not be delayed because of the desire for a same-race match (Jennings, 2006). It also demanded states to "recruit a diverse population of foster and adoptive parents" (McRoy & Griffin, 2012, p. 42). The ASFA "reduced the time allowed to resolve cases of child maltreatment from 18 to 12 months" (Phillips & Mann, 2013, p. 865), again in an effort to give children a better chance of being adopted or at least figuring out what their placement option would be. This policy also enhanced the incentives given to states to increase the number of adoptions and supported the adoption of children by their foster parents (Lercara, 2016). Thus, many states saw large increases in adoptions at the end of the 1990s. Given cutbacks in support and concerns that the incentives were harming the chances of family reunification, though, these increases were generally short lived (Edwards & Few-Demo, 2014; Lercara, 2016). The ASFA also included concurrent planning, which requires both a plan for family reunification as well as the alternative long-term option (Lercara, 2016). The assumption here is that the state should not wait to see if unification is possible before working on out-placement alternatives. Although shorter timelines may be viewed as being in the best interests of the child, they make it difficult for many parents to reach goals, especially when mental health or substance abuse treatment is involved.

Analysis Element: Court Involvement

An important aspect of social welfare policies is the interplay between the political system and the state and federal courts. The judicial system may affect policy at a variety of levels up to and including the U.S. Supreme Court. Among other things, court decisions may set the stage for policy development—as with the right to education claims paving the way for EAHCA (1975) (P.L. 94-142)/IDEA (1990) (P.L. 101-476); they may require major revisions to or decide on the constitutionality of policies—as has been the case with the ACA (P.L. 111-148); or they may serve to affect claims related to social justice or discrimination—as with the Defense of Marriage Act of 1996 (DOMA)

(P.L. 104-199). While I purposefully focus on legislative policies throughout this book, Pollack and Kleinman's (2016) *Social Work and the Courts: A Casebook* provides an instructive overview of important court cases that have affected the direction of social policy in areas of interest to the profession.

In regard to child welfare policy specifically, local family courts are heavily engaged in implementing child welfare policies. One of the key policy areas that has been reviewed by the higher courts has been the concept of reasonable efforts. The U.S. Supreme Court took on this issue with the 1992 Illinois *Suter v. Artist M.* case (Pollack & Kleinman, 2016). According to Kopels and Rycraft (1993), the AACWA was fairly vague in terms of what steps states were expected to take to ensure that reasonable efforts were made to allow parents to retain custody. These authors noted that the "Court concluded that the states were left with a great deal of discretion by Congress in how to provide reasonable efforts" (Kopels & Rycraft, 1993, p. 402).

The court system may be called on to decide on parental capacity or lack thereof. McWey et al. (2006) wrote that "studying court documents provides some insight into the process of decisions and legal reasons that [may lead] to the termination of parental rights" (p. 198). These authors specifically researched the mental health issues of parents and the feasibility that parents with various conditions could receive effective treatment within the AFSA time limits. They concluded that, in many cases, not only could effective treatment not be rendered within this time, but, frequently, therapists "lacked awareness of ASFA" (p. 206).

These are only a few examples of the ways that courts at both the local and higher levels may affect social policy. These examples support the contention that to fully understand the political process, we need to be aware of how judicial decisions may affect policy passage and implementation.

CHAPTER 29

McKinney-Vento Homeless Assistance Act

1987

Historical Overview and Nature of the Social Problem

Other than food and water, there are no necessities of life that are more important to people than a place to live. Although abject poverty and homelessness have been staples in American society, both are difficult social problems to measure because of the "hidden" nature of the population and the temporary aspect of many episodes of homelessness. Defining "homelessness" itself can be problematic because many people without a fixed address may periodically stay in a variety of places. As one would assume, high poverty areas are likely to have a larger percentage of homeless people, but it is also true that such areas attract people who are at risk for becoming homeless in part because of the placement of shelters and other services in such areas (Alexander-Eitzman, Pollio, & North, 2013). Just as with migration from nation to nation or region to region, there are push-and-pull factors that lead to the congregation of homeless people within specific areas, especially in large cities.

Homelessness came to be seen as a particular problem during the 1970s and 1980s for a number of interconnected reasons. The ranks of the homeless had been augmented over these decades by the large number of Vietnam Veterans who had returned from the war addicted or suffering from PTSD, or both, or suffering from other physical or mental war injuries. Deinstitutionalization and closure of many mental institutions led to people with long-term psychiatric conditions being remanded to the community often without the support required to maintain a job or home. A bad economy in the 1970s followed by Ronald Reagan–era cutbacks to many social services programs in the 1980s also served to dramatically increase the homeless population (Hoch & Slayton, 1989). Additional factors that added to the problem included gentrification and redevelopment in urban areas as well as a substantial decrease in affordable housing options in many cities and towns (E. A. Anderson & Koblinsky, 1995).

Because of historic problems with measuring homelessness, over the past several census dates, there has been a concerted effort to complete a "point-in-time" census of those who live without a fixed address (Donley & Wright, 2018; Wilkins, Mullins, Mahan, & Canfield, 2016). Social work agencies and higher education programs frequently volunteer to support these efforts, which includes going into areas where homeless people may be and attaining basic information about them.

Policy Overview

The McKinney-Vento Homeless Assistance Act (1987) (P.L. 100-77), named after its major legislative supporter, Stewart B. McKinney, was passed in 1987 in large measure as the result of the persistent advocacy efforts of such groups as the National Coalition for the Homeless and individuals like Mitch Snyder. Snyder was a longtime advocate who engaged in a highly publicized hunger strike to force the government to support the development of shelters (Hopper, 2003). The population of homeless has changed over the years partly because of to the aforementioned issues. As Katherine Miller (1996) wrote, the "new homeless of the late 20th century are more likely to include women, children, and intact families" than at earlier periods (p. 82; see also Fleary, Joseph, Zhang, & Quirion, 2019).

Among other provisions, the policy included a definition of homelessness, provided grant money to support shelters and other services (for example, drug abuse treatment and mental health counseling) for homeless individuals and families, expanded housing support provided under HUD (such as Section 8 allowances), expanded food stamps provisions for homeless people, and required that surplus federal property could be used by established agencies to develop new shelter space (National Coalition for the Homeless, 2008).

The 2001 reauthorization of the McKinney Act, titled the McKinney-Vento Homeless Education Assistance Improvements Act of 2001 (2002) (P.L. 107-110), provided, among other things, a range of services designed to support the education of children in homeless families (Crook, 2015;

Markward & Biros, 2001). This policy made it easier for families without a fixed address to access education enrollment for their children, supported connections between homeless shelters and other relevant agencies and the school system, and provided special services for such children in the schools. The provision of special services was important especially because children who have experienced homelessness or who move frequently from place to place are at risk for a range of emotional, behavioral, and physical problems because of a lack of health care (Jozefowisz-Simbeni & Israel, 2006). This aspect of the policy is important for social workers because many serve as liaisons for homeless children for the schools (Wilkins et al., 2016).

Services for children are also important because of the large number of runaway adolescents who have neither an intact family nor a permanent home and also because many foster children who age out of the system have nowhere to go (Donley & Wright, 2018). Crook (2015) noted that it "is estimated that anywhere between 1.6 and 2.8 million children run away" each year (p. 396). There also exists a strong connection between domestic violence and homelessness because many women, along with their children, may need to leave their homes temporarily following a violent incident.

Effectiveness

Among the challenges facing homelessness advocates are issues pertaining to the construction of shelters and safety within shelters as well as concerns related to shelter policies based on family structure. Regarding the construction of shelters, large, dormitory-style facilities have historically been used as a primary service option specifically for single males. These facilities, however, are not conducive to serving families, nor do they offer much in the way of privacy or safety. Many homeless individuals prefer sleeping on the streets as a better option and only visit such shelters in poor weather. Critics have argued that the focus of housing policies needs to be more on permanent housing as opposed to temporary makeshift solutions. It is often difficult for families to find adequate shelter space, especially because many do not allow adult (or, in some cases, even juvenile) males; thus, families often have to separate, at least temporarily, to find adequate shelter (E. A. Anderson & Koblinsky, 1995).

A number of cities have made efforts to diminish homelessness by establishing small apartments where homeless people can live while receiving services to assist them in various ways (for example, drug or alcohol treatment, mental health counseling, job training). Primary among these efforts is the Housing First program. Although traditional housing programs required residents to first go through substance abuse or mental health treatment, the advocates of the Housing First model contend that individuals can more successfully get treatment if they first have a permanent residence (Donley & Wright, 2018; Tsai, Lee, Byrne, Pietrzak, & Southwick, 2017). Another goal of Housing First is to help prevent medical problems, which are endemic in those who are homeless and are especially problematic because many homeless people do not get treatment until a medical issue has reached a crisis point. Studies show that the "costs of delivering supporting housing are offset in large part by reduction in the uses of crisis services" ("Does Housing First Work?" 2020). Housing First has led to a fairly substantive decrease in homelessness over the past few decades (Henwood, Matejkowski, Stefancic, & Lukens, 2014).

Crook (2015) contended that the educational aspects of McKinney-Vento are inadequate and that states have little incentive to follow federal guidelines. Jozefowicz-Simbeni and Israel (2006) added that more attention needs to be given to preschool services for young children who are homeless. Shelter space is also an issue because many of them are not designed or do not have policies in place to take in families, many rural communities have no shelter options, and older male children often cannot access family shelters.

Analysis Element: Social Problem Etiology

With any major social problem, effectively developing public policies to deal with the issue necessitates clearly understanding what has caused it in the first place or allowed it to spread. Just as medicine treats symptoms of disease, medical researchers also focus on attempting to understand what leads to the disease so that it can be prevented and treated at its source. To simply see a reduction in symptoms does little good if they or related manifestations of the disease may reappear. To take the medical analogy a step further, etiology can be difficult to pin down because there are a number of physical, social, nutritional, and environmental issues that interact in unique ways for each person. Nonetheless, the closer we can get to knowledge of cause, the better individual treatment and public health measures can be applied. The same holds true with social policy.

When deciding how best to develop policies to mitigate homelessness, therefore, we need to have a handle on the primary cause(s) of the problem. This has always been somewhat difficult because interrelated factors include some combination of poverty, unemployment, substance abuse, domestic violence, mental illness, housing access, and so forth. Historically, conservative politicians and stakeholders have generally been more likely to contend that homelessness is primarily a factor of individual irresponsibility, is caused largely by drug or alcohol abuse, or results from an inability to maintain employment. Miller (1996) noted that President Ronald Reagan believed that homelessness was largely an individual choice. Even when homelessness is caused by addiction, conservatives are more likely to contend that even this situation was largely under control of the individual.

Liberals for their part tend to focus more on the environmental issues, including economic downturns, domestic violence, and mental illness. Presumptions of responsibility may also relate to various personal or demographic factors. The increase in homelessness among veterans during and following the Vietnam War and the recent decline in inner-city housing options (Macek, 2006) may serve to affect not only the image that the public has of homeless people but also perceptions of etiology. Tsai et al. (2017) contended that, over the past few decades, public attitudes toward those who are homeless have become more supportive of government support, and the authors attribute this shift largely to the changing homeless population.

CHAPTER 30

Anti-Drug Abuse Act

◖1988◗

Historical Overview and Nature of the Social Problem

Substance abuse is responsible for a myriad of individual, familial, and societal problems. For the purpose of this policy, I primarily focus on those aspects of drug dependency or sale that carry with them criminal penalties and result in the need for punishment, rehabilitation, or other forms of substance abuse treatment. Drawing a firm line between "legal" and "illegal" drugs, however, is a bit difficult, especially because some illegal drugs may be prescribed for certain conditions, and some of the societal problems that pertain to drugs in the United States include the improper use of legally prescribed substances.

Drug abuse has been a long-term problem in the United States. An early example of societal anxiety related to drugs was the fear on the West Coast of opium dens. Such dens were supposedly run by Chinese immigrants, and one of their major goals was said to be luring young White women into a life of addiction and prostitution. The panic that surrounded opium dens was an important rationale for efforts to end the immigration of Chinese people into the country, and it led to the Chinese Exclusion Act of 1882 (P.L. 47-126), the first U.S. anti-immigration policy directed at a specific nation or ethnicity (Kraut, 1994).

The earliest policy restricting drug development and sale was the 1906 Federal Food and Drugs Act (34 Stat. 768). This policy was an outgrowth of concerns related to the limited controls that were in place to restrict how both food and medications were developed as well as toxicity and effectiveness concerns related to medications. Early in the 20th century, fears turned to marijuana, cocaine, and other substances, and substance abuse was tied to gang warfare, especially during Prohibition. One of the earliest antidrug policies was the Harrison Narcotics Tax Act of 1914 (P.L. 63-223), which controlled marijuana possession. The Federal Bureau of Narcotics was developed in 1930 as the agency responsible for controlling drug development and sales (Bertram, Blachman, Sharpe, & Andreas, 1996).

The current War on Drugs had its origins in the 1960s and 1970s. LSD, marijuana, and other drugs became tied to various student movements (for example, antiwar, counterculture, hippies) Increasing crime rates, especially in the 1970s, were said to be largely caused by the need to support drug addiction. Furthermore, many soldiers returning from the war in Vietnam had become addicted to heroin and other drugs. The National Institute on Drug Abuse was created in 1973 to deal with these problems (Bertram et al., 1996), and increasingly punitive antidrug policies were passed throughout the next few decades.

Efforts to reduce the development, use, and sale of illegal drugs as well as addiction to them may take one of two complementary approaches: focusing on diminishing either supply or demand. Diminishing supply includes methods to stop such substances from entering the country or punitive action taken against those who create or grow those substances domestically. The diminishing demand approach includes educational programs designed to ensure that people will not start using such substances along with rehabilitation or treatment to end use. As discussed further shortly, during the course of the "drug war" in the United States, demand policies increasingly took a back seat to efforts at limiting supply.

Policy Overview

The Anti-Drug Abuse Act of 1988 (P.L. 100-960) was passed at the height of the "war against drugs." It had been preceded by a number of other major antidrug policies (for example, the Comprehensive Drug Abuse Prevention and Control Act of 1970, P.L. 91-513, and the 1986 Anti-Drug Abuse Act, P.L. 99-570), and it continued the movement to penalize drug users and suppliers as well as to support a criminal justice over education/rehabilitation approach to the issue (Bertram et al., 1996; Mosher & Akins, 2007). A related policy—the Drug-Free Workplace Act of 1988 (P.L. 100-690), passed in the same year—levied penalties against companies with federal contracts that had not developed policies restricting illegal substance abuse among employees (Petersen & Massengill, 1991).

One important component of the 1986 and 1988 policies was the focus on mandatory minimum sentencing. Because of the widespread assumption that drug penalties were not harsh enough and that judges frequently were too lenient in their rulings on drug cases, mandatory minimum sentencing enhanced the amount of time that perpetrators would spend in prison. More recently, policies have also focused on *civil forfeiture*, the ability of law enforcement authorities to seize the bank accounts and assets of presumed drug traffickers (Inciardi, 2008). Additional penalties for those involved in the drug trade include limitations on forms of governmental support (for example, SSI, HUD funding, student loans).

It was largely as a result of the harsh drug policies of the 1970s and 1980s that the prison population in the nation exploded. Mosher and Akins (2007) noted that "between 1980 and 2001, the number of people in state and federal prisons for drug offenses increased by approximately 1,300%" (p. 203). A large percentage of these people were not convicted of selling illegal drugs but of using or possessing marijuana.

Although some policies have focused on education or treatment, the funding for such programs has been minimal compared to law enforcement, interdiction, and prison funding. Moreover, a number of the most widely used education programs, such as DARE, have been criticized for lack of positive results. Inciardi (2008) contends that such programs may enhance student knowledge of drugs, but they have little if any positive effect on changing behaviors.

Effectiveness

Few politicians or analysts would argue that the War on Drugs has been highly effective. Even though increasing amounts of money have been directed toward law enforcement and other areas of criminal justice, drug use has not declined (Robinson & Scherlen, 2007). In 1996, the libertarian *National Review* published a lengthy editorial titled, "The War on Drugs is Lost" (1996), and little has occurred in the interim that counters this belief. To quote Judith Grant (2009), "The number of drug offenders in the United States under incarceration has grown tenfold since 1980, but there is strikingly little evidence that increased punishment has significantly reduced drug use" (p. 62).

Critics often charge that not only has the drug war failed to stem the tide of drug use, but it has also principally targeted minorities (M. Alexander,

2010; Mosher & Akins, 2007). As Robinson and Scherlen (2007) contended, "Drug laws at times are not really about drugs, but instead about who is using them" (p. 20). One specific issue that many critics have pointed to is the establishment, within mandatory minimum sentencing, of vastly differential penalties for crack versus powder cocaine. Because African Americans have been more likely to use the crack version of the drug, they have received harsher penalties than if they had used powder. A counterargument is that the crack version of the drug is much more potent, and therefore even the same amount should not be categorized similarly.

Many judges and even the prosecutors have joined the backlash against mandatory minimum sentencing (Bertram et al., 1996; Mosher & Atkins, 2007). In their analysis of data collected by the Office of National Drug Control Policy, Robinson and Scherlen (2007) contended that even the federal government itself can find little evidence of meeting the major goals it set forth regarding reduction in drug use. From a market perspective, attempting to limit supply is problematic as long as demand is maintained. As long as the need is there, someone will fill it. Supply side intervention also becomes more difficult when drugs are not imported but, rather, are produced within the country, as is much of the methamphetamine (also known as "meth") and marijuana that are used.

Over the past few decades, much of the concern related to illegal drugs has moved from the "drugs of choice" from the 1960s to the 1990s (heroin, marijuana, cocaine, LSD) to other options, especially meth and prescription drugs, such as opioids. These substances have caused a change in how the nation responds to addiction because meth is often produced within the country, therefore, interdiction is not feasible. In addition, many opioids are prescription drugs. As alluded to previously, we skirt the difference between "legal" and "illegal" drugs when we consider prescription drugs that are inappropriately used or are used by the wrong person, or when people engage in "doctor shopping" to attain additional drugs either for themselves or to sell on the black market.

Analysis Element: Social Constructionism

A key consideration in drug policy relates to the fundamental question of which substances are or are not considered to be inappropriate or illegal—and why this is true. What historical elements came to bear to foster such decisions? How do power and control issues play a role? Are such decisions based somewhat on overt or covert beliefs of users (for example, crack versus powder cocaine)? How do cultural aspects affect such decisions? To what degree does such categorization actually relate to harm threats? As Ellwood (1994) noted, rhetoric, metaphors, and the stories/images shared by stakeholders and the media hold much sway in how the public views various substances and those who use them.

In looking, for example, at power and control issues and actual harm, one might ask why marijuana has generally been illegal in the United States, whereas cigarettes have not. A large legal sector of the U.S. economy is devoted to tobacco production, and highly influential corporations benefit from such sales even though hundreds of thousands of Americans die each year from its use. Although one could point to self-determination and a libertarian mindset as supporting the use of tobacco, the same arguments could be weighed on the side of other substances.

The acceptability of certain drugs waxes and wanes over the course of time for many reasons. Not only is medical marijuana more often perceived as normal, but many states are now allowing the sale of marijuana for nonmedical uses, and it is thus becoming an acceptable way for "legitimate" suppliers to make money. As Bowen and Redmond (2016) observed, the United States seems to be gradually moving away from a criminal justice framing of drug use more to a medically oriented harm-reduction framing. Although many have suggested legalization that goes beyond marijuana, such a recommendation is not only highly controversial but also carries with it a large number of logistical problems that would make operationalization difficult.

The way that drug use and abuse are constructed and framed by the media and other stakeholders is instructive because we are a society that is heavily drug fueled. No nation on Earth has ever taken to drugs as we have, and although these are primarily legal and prescribed, and include alcohol and tobacco, it is difficult to convince young adults that they should not use drugs when they are such an ever-present aspect of our culture. This is one reason why DARE and other programs are ineffective; at some point, people realize that the reasons that some drugs are acceptable and others are not has little to do with actual risk assessment (Inciardi, 2008). Although we would like to believe that we are logical when it comes to risk assessment, this is far from the case. Many of us readily engage in activities that have a high potential for harm while we refrain from other activities that are very low risk. Risk assessment itself is highly related to social construction and inherent fears that we are only partly aware of.

CHAPTER 31

Americans with Disabilities Act

◖1990◗

Historical Overview and Nature of the Social Problem

The ADA (1990) (P.L. 101-336) was developed primarily as a result of increased self-advocacy on the part of individuals with disabilities. Over the previous decades, many disability rights groups had come to repudiate the medical model of disability and had replaced it with a minority group or social model. The medical framework viewed people with disabilities largely as passive victims of their circumstances, many of whom were unable to succeed—or even make an attempt at success—in certain spheres of living because of the problems imposed on them by their physical or mental impairments. The minority group model, however, focused heavily on the barriers to success that institutions and the nondisabled community at large placed in the path of people with disabilities (O'Brien, 2011). These barriers were not just physical obstructions that limited mobility but, as with other minority groups, also included inaccurate and demeaning stereotypes and misconceptions, a tendency to focus on the person's disability as a "master status" that served to identify the person as deficient in an essential way, and prejudice based on simple fear or discomfort (Drimmer, 1993; Shakespeare, 1994; Shapiro, 1993). Disability rights groups argued that they were victims of discrimination and prejudice comparable to other minority groups and that they deserved similar forms of protection from discrimination or support.

It is estimated that approximately 15 percent of the American population has a long-term disability condition. Having a disability, especially a severe one, may put an individual at risk educationally and in regard to their occupational potential. Such individuals may be presumed to be more adversely affected by their condition than is actually the case, and they are frequently treated with a high degree of pity and even contempt. This being the case, even the advocates of the minority-group model will agree that although social constructionism plays a role in how we view disability, there are conditions that carry with them important psychological and physical burdens requiring medical intervention.

Policy Overview

The ADA was passed and signed into law by President George H. W. Bush in 1990 following a failed attempt two years earlier (Mayerson, 1993). The act was informed by both the Civil Rights Act of 1964 (P.L. 88-352) and the Rehabilitation Act of 1973 (P.L. 93-112). The Rehabilitation Act protected people with disabilities from employment discrimination but only covered offices and contractors of the federal government (Scotch, 2001). Lobbyists for small businesses, which formed the primary opposition to the ADA, expressed concerns about a number of issues, including the potential cost of accommodations and the vagueness of the proposed definition of disability ("Sweeping Law for Rights of Disabled," 1990). Led by U.S. Senator Jesse Helms of North Carolina, many legislators also opposed the provision of antidiscrimination protection under the ADA to people with HIV/AIDS.

The policy was pushed through with support not only by people with disabilities and disability advocacy groups but also by numerous religious and nonprofit organizations. Importantly, many of the politicians who led the campaign to pass the bill were personally affected by disability. U.S. Senator Ted Kennedy of Massachusetts, for example, had a sister who was considered disabled and a son who had a leg amputated; Senator Tom Harkin of Iowa, the primary sponsor in the Senate, had a brother who was deaf; and the Republican leader, Senator Bob Dole of Kansas, himself had a disability resulting from a war wound (Shapiro, 1989).

The ADA includes five sections: Title I, the employment discrimination section; Title II, which prohibits discrimination in public or governmental services; Title III, which requires accommodations within community services; Title IV, which provides for telecommunication accommodations; and Title V, which includes miscellaneous provisions, such as limitations to coverage for drug/alcohol addiction. The major goals of the policy relate to Titles I and III, the provision of employment nondiscrimination and the provision of reasonable accommodations in public facilities, such as restaurants and stores.

The disability definitions included within the ADA remain subject to wide interpretation, and confusion over these definitions has led to debate about who falls within the classification of a "disabled" person. As Karger and Rose (2010) noted, this is especially true for those with "invisible" disabilities, that is, whose conditions are not readily apparent. According to *A Technical Assistance Manual on the Employment Provisions (Title I) of the Americans with Disabilities Act* (1992), prepared in 1992 by the Equal Employment Opportunity Commission (EEOC), a disabled person includes an individual who has

- a physical or mental impairment that substantially limits one or more major life activities;
- a record of such an impairment; or
- is regarded as having an impairment. (p. I–9)

The "record of such an impairment" definition was primarily included to protect people who have a history of or have been treated for a disability, such as cancer, and who could be subject to discrimination, especially in the provision of insurance coverage, by employers who assume that the condition may reappear. The "regarded as having an impairment" definition primarily relates to people with facial impairments and other stigmatizing conditions that do not adversely affect an area of major life functioning but could still lead to discrimination (McAdams, Moussavi, & Klassen, 1992).

Regarding the employment component of the ADA, individuals who, because of the nature of their condition, pose a direct threat to themselves or others in the workplace (for example, people with most forms of epilepsy who work around industrial equipment) are not protected by the policy. Importantly, however, in these cases, the threat must not be based on employer supposition but, rather, on substantiated medical facts (O'Brien & Maue, 2002). The policy does not require affirmative action measures, but it does require a degree of proof that the presumptive act of discrimination (for example, refusing to hire, not providing a promotion, discharge) was directly related to the disability. Lack of such proof is a principal reason that most claims of discrimination are unfounded (O'Brien & Ellegood, 2005).

The requirement to provide accommodations within the community primarily entails such structural elements as ramps, larger doorways, accommodations within restrooms, and space for maneuvering wheelchairs. It may also include such provisions as Braille menus and assistive auditory devices. Employment accommodations may include not only structural changes but also measures such as revised work schedules or opportunities to complete some work at home, although any such modifications must not be costly or highly disruptive to the operation of the workplace. Otherwise, they may be determined to be an "undue burden" on the business.

Effectiveness

In one sense, the ADA has been fairly effective. One of the primary reasons the policy was put into place was to counter misperceptions of disabilities. The policy, therefore, has had what one might refer to as a "PR [public relations]" motive. In sharing accurate information about people with disabilities, the policy has brought about greater recognition of the realities and myths surrounding disability. The other objective of the ADA that has been at least partially effective has been the requirement for public, business, and transportation accommodations. People with disabilities have more access to their communities because of these structural accommodations, and they are better able to socialize and use public facilities, although contentious issues remain regarding the scope of such accommodations.

The employment nondiscrimination objective, however, has only been minimally effective in opening the doors of the workplace to people with disabilities. Some evidence exists that it has not been at all effective and may even harm the occupational opportunities afforded to people with disabilities. One reason this could be true is that antidiscrimination laws can have a contrary effect because employers may be fearful of eventual lawsuits if a potential hire belonging to a "suspect class" (group protected by antidiscrimination policy) does not work out (Karger & Rose, 2010). One of the realities of employment discrimination against any group is that the most likely time for employers to get away with such discrimination is at the hiring stage, when any number of rationales can be put forth for hiring an alternative applicant. Employers who are concerned about the possibility of a lawsuit down the road may be less apt to take a chance on an employee with a disability if they question whether that person can effectively do the job.

Analysis Element: Target Efficiency

Target efficiency pertains largely to two related issues. First, it asks who the actual recipients or beneficiaries of a policy are, and second, how this relates to the class of individuals who the public and policymakers assumed would be served by the policy when it was passed. If it appears that policy benefits fall to a much different group than that originally intended, this could pose a problem for continuation of the policy. Importantly, presumptions of who the policy recipients are relates largely to mass media depictions because this is where large sectors of the population receive their information about policies and recipient populations. As noted in chapter 36, for example, much was written about public perception regarding those receiving AFDC benefits in the 1980s and 1990s and that many of these perceptions could best be described as social myths. Although false, these myths were still a driving force for policy restrictions within TANF. Target efficiency is similar to questions about horizontal versus vertical service provision, discussed in chapter 17, because both pertain to questions about the wisest use of policy resources and whether they are provided to those who most need them.

When the ADA passed in 1990, many politicians assumed that policy benefits would primarily go to specific groups of disabled people, including those with mobility impairments who are wheelchair users, individuals with visual and hearing impairments, and those with other noticeable physical disabilities. As the policy was implemented, however, questions increasingly were raised about the legitimacy of the class of people benefiting from the policy (Shapiro, 1998). These included people with conditions that were difficult to accurately diagnose, such as back injuries, individuals with various forms of mental illness or different types of learning disabilities, and people with HIV.

Importantly, as is often the case, more questionable or "odd" conditions were often the ones that naturally drew media attention, and the public was awash in diatribes about people with "shift work maladaptation syndrome" (Tucker, 2010), "chronic lateness syndrome," and similar conditions exploiting the law. In many such cases, claims were unfounded anyway and were not pursued by the EEOC. Although important, a person in a wheelchair who can finally eat in a neighborhood restaurant does not make for compelling TV viewing. An individual who wants to force their company to only share written communications over the computer because they have a phobia related to possible paper cuts, however, would make for must-watch TV (this one, by the way, is not an actual case). The desire for increased ratings or readership often necessitates anger- and fear-based reporting, particularly when it relates to use of tax dollars or perceptions of fairness in relation to social policy. These issues also tie into the current backlash against what is perceived to be a victim mentality in American culture. If these are the images that the public has of the ADA, the policy may be vulnerable to changes that may harm all potential recipients.

CHAPTER 32

Ryan White Comprehensive AIDS Resources Emergency Act

◀1990▶

Historical Overview and Nature of the Social Problem

The first decade of the HIV/AIDS epidemic in the United States has been well documented. Early in the 1980s, an odd assortment of diseases was causing the death of a disconcerting number of Americans, a large proportion of whom were gay males (thus the first acronym describing the virus, GRID, which stood for gay-related immune deficiency disease). As the numbers of infected individuals exploded, and gay rights groups and public health officials became increasingly alarmed, the President Ronald Reagan administration was surprisingly slow to respond, and Reagan himself was hesitant to recognize or even mention the disease (Shilts, 1988). The virus depletes the immune system response such that diseases, including fatal ones, can more easily take hold and expand in the body.

By the second half of the decade, the nature of transmission of the virus was well understood to researchers, and early efforts to provide support and services to infected people were initiated. However, the general public remained largely unaware of the research related to transmission or unconvinced of its veracity, and panic ensued in cases in which people with the virus were known (or rumored) to be present within communities, schools, occupational settings, or, ironically, hospitals or other health settings. Infected people were often treated like pariahs, and many tried to hide their infected status (or their membership in high-risk groups) as long as possible.

Knowledge that a second highly stigmatized group, intravenous drug users, was highly affected by the disease led to an exacerbation of the fear of HIV and a belief that the general population would not be harmed by the disease so long as people kept their distance from those individuals and groups perceived to be most at risk. Newspapers and other media sources frequently trumpeted how bad the disease might be if it made its way to the wider public. Because of the fear of the disease, employment, educational, housing, and other forms of discrimination against infected individuals were rampant (135 Cong. Rec., Pt. 14, September 7, 1989, p. S 10722). Indeed, Ryan White, the policy's namesake, was subject to such discrimination.

Importantly, early in its evolution, HIV infection leading to an eventual AIDS diagnosis was truly a death sentence. Individuals who tested positive for the virus fell into a fairly rapid physical deterioration that terminated in a debilitating, painful death. The image of thin, wasted patients undergoing great suffering rather than fostering compassion seemed to reinforce the stigma against the victims of the disease. Many members of gay communities in large urban areas highly affected by spread of the disease saw their friends die in large numbers. Fears of infection or exacerbation of the condition once it was attained along with the great loss of friends and lovers combined with public indifference to the crisis caused much fear, anger, and depression among those who were high risk. As a result, many became activists in support of treatment and funding.

Panic subsided slowly as the 1990s progressed and into the turn of the century. The general public gradually came to accept the means of transmission, pharmaceutical treatments gave a measure of hope to infected individuals, and the widespread use of safe sex and additional prevention measures limited the spread of HIV. Widespread HIV testing also allowed those infected to begin earlier treatment and provided some assurance regarding the potential that sexual partners would be infected. In addition, the victimization of beloved celebrities and athletes, such as actor Rock Hudson, Olympic diver Greg Louganis, and basketball star Earvin "Magic" Johnson, had some effect on fostering a more humane view of the disease.

Policy Overview

The Ryan White Comprehensive AIDS Resources Emergency Act (CARE Act) (P.L. 101-381) was passed in 1990 following a contentious debate over whether Congress should provide the same protection to those who received the virus presumably by engaging in risky behaviors (sexual intercourse among gay men and intravenous drug use) as it did to those taken to be "innocent" victims, such as White. The "innocent" victims group included those receiving infected blood through a transfusion, infected infants, and possibly women who became infected through sexual relations with a man whom they did not know was infected. White became the symbol of this group. A child with hemophilia, White was in grade school when he attained HIV as the result of a transfusion. When his condition became known, he was subject to derision and brutal treatment (including the burning of his home) in his hometown of Kokomo, Indiana. Supported by his mother Jeanne, White became involved in the fight for medical treatment, service provision, and destigmatization of people with the disease. Eventually, as I discuss further shortly, he became the most important symbol in the fight for a policy. He died shortly before the policy was approved.

A group of politicians led by Jesse Helms, a conservative U.S. senator from North Carolina, expressed a strong viewpoint that services and funding should be directed to people like White as opposed to gay males and intravenous drug users. When the ADA (1990) (P.L. 101-336) was passed in 1990, Helms also opposed protection from disability-based discrimination if it meant that HIV-positive individuals fell under such legislation. The ADA did end up offering some workplace protection to infected individuals (O'Brien & Koerkenmeier, 2001), although the status of people with HIV as "disabled" was an issue of contention for some time, especially for those people who were asymptomatic.

In addition to supporting funding for medications and treatment, the policy also funneled millions of dollars into the search for a cure and provided psychosocial support and food and housing assistance to those affected by it. The policy provided housing assistance and other forms of support for people with HIV who could no longer work because of their condition. Funding was primarily provided in those geographic areas where the problem was most acute; these areas were referred to as "eligible metropolitan areas" (Martin, Pollack & Paltiel, 2006). This did lead to some controversy over the lack of support to affected people in rural areas (Martin et al., 2006). Part D of the policy included efforts to identify pregnant mothers with HIV to prevent mother-to-child transmission during birth (Hernandez & Potocky, 2014). Minorities have been disproportionally affected by HIV (Hernandez & Potocky, 2014).

Medication regimens for those affected by HIV became increasingly effective, and between 1995 and 2010, the condition had largely been controlled for those who could access treatment. Although HIV was not "cured," it no longer always led to terminal illnesses. To a large extent, concern about spread and lack of treatment access has moved overseas, especially to sub-Saharan Africa, where the condition continues to be a leading cause of death. In the United States, areas in the Deep South are currently particularly hard hit (Cesnales, Thyer, & Albright, 2017).

Effectiveness

The CARE Act was highly effective in providing meaningful support for research and treatment as well as information on prevention, and it attempted to destigmatize the condition to a degree. During the first part of the crisis, the vast majority of government funding was directed toward medical research and prevention, but growing activism by such groups as ACT UP (AIDS Coalition to Unleash Power) led to increased support services for affected people (Sheridan, 1998). Some argued, however, that too much of the funding from this policy was still directed to medical research, and not enough went to support services—much of which social workers provide—for those with the disease (Sheridan, 1998).

Obviously, the issue of values weighs heavily on public policy related to HIV/AIDS and other contagious diseases. Much has been written about the stigma related to risk groups and the effect of this stigma on policymaking efforts. An important aspect of this discussion that has wide application to social policy relates to the behaviors attributed to these risk groups and the element of responsibility (or presumptions of responsibility) for one's condition for which policy-based services are rendered. Policymakers often argue that the taxpayers should not be required to foot the bill for services if they relate to preventable conditions that the individual developed from engaging in at-risk behaviors. Such arguments, however, can be used in relation to a number of medical issues. The United States can be considered to be a risk-taking nation. The recent coronavirus epidemic provides a good example of this because Americans were more likely than those in other nations to refuse to undertake basic prevention actions, using individual freedom as a rallying cry. It is a convoluted and morally troubling path we take when attempting to provide policy benefits based on individual responsibility.

Analysis Element: Policy Symbols

Symbols, usually individual people, are important in policy because, similar to trigger events (see chapter 4), they focus attention on a particular issue. Although statistics may not hold much interest for most of the public, and facts can be questioned, symbols may be used to present a human face to represent a cause. Critics, however, may question whether that symbol actually represents those affected by the issue. And, as was the case with the disability rights movement's criticism of "Jerry's Kids," who were highlighted in Labor Day telethons to raise money for muscular dystrophy, critics also may argue that such symbols are exploited for financial or policy gain.

Ryan White was a highly controversial symbol of the movement for an HIV/AIDS policy. This was not in any way because White himself was controversial but, rather, the opposite: According to Helms and some other conservative politicians and religious leaders, White was an innocent victim of the disease who was being exploited by movement leaders to present a more acceptable face of AIDS. Helms said just this in the *Congressional Record*:

> Let [me] be candid, the homosexual lobby of America knew the Ryan White story was too good to pass up. Therefore, his struggle and his death could be used to frighten the American public into believing that AIDS is waiting to happen to everyone, even if they do not engage in illegal and /or immoral activity. So, Ryan White was portrayed as a typical victim, not the exception that he was. And the AIDS propaganda machine churned out the demand for special treatment and privileges for the kind of people who caused Ryan White's death. (142 Cong. Rec., 1990, p. S 6126)

The symbols who come to be the face of a lobbying movement are important figures in the response the public has to that social problem. Support for various issues tends to increase when a famous person becomes affected by it or when the public rallies around a symbol. Poindexter (1999) wrote that for this policy to pass, it was important that AIDS was "seen as affecting all segments of society" (p. 38). Helms and others contended that Ryan White as a symbol allowed activists to present this case.

Rock Hudson was also important as a symbol in contextualizing the nature of HIV/AIDS for many Americans. Most were surprised and even shocked when it became known that Hudson had contracted the disease and that he had hidden for many years that he was gay. To many, Hudson was the epitome of rugged masculinity and a heterosexual sex symbol. This, coupled with the fact that he had to hide this important aspect of who he was to maintain his career, forced many to rethink the stereotypes they carried with them about homosexuality.

CHAPTER 33

Family and Medical Leave Act

◀ 1993 ▶

Historical Overview and Nature of the Social Problem

Balancing the demands of work and family is often problematic, and employees often are forced to choose between their jobs and attending to their own health concerns or those of family members. This issue has historically been highly gendered (Gerstel & McGonagle, 1999) because (1) it has traditionally been women who have served as caregivers in society; (2) women have often been the "secondary earners" in two-parent or partner families and, therefore, often have fewer benefits than their male counterparts; (3) women experience pregnancy and often stay at home with infants, at least for short periods; and (4) women who are single parents need to be the sole caregiver in their immediate family.

In the past, many workers, and particularly women, were forced to give up jobs or scale down their career goals to engage in self-care or provide support for themselves or family members (Roog, Knight, Koob, & Kraus, 2004). Having to return to work following a medical emergency either because of financial necessity or fear of losing one's job could potentially harm recovery and cause more severe medical issues down the road. Frustration with attempting to properly balance financial security with caregiving responsibilities also could lead to increased stress and thus adversely affect one's own mental health (Gerstel & McGonagle, 1999).

Even though the United States is the among the wealthiest nations in the world, as with other areas of social support, it has historically fallen well behind most other developed nations in the provision of medical leave policies and particularly paid leave. Kornfeld (2018) wrote that among the most industrialized nations, only the United States and Australia "do not provide paid maternity leave" (p. 167). The Family and Medical Leave Act of 1993 (FMLA) (P.L. 103-3) was preceded by (mostly unpaid) leave laws in a majority of states (Fine, 2006; Wisensale, 2006). Many of these state laws are fairly specific in designating what they are to be used for, such as maternity leave (Wisensale, 2006). Although many companies included paid or unpaid medical leave as a benefit, those workers to whom such benefits accrued were generally more highly paid workers.

Policy Overview

According to Gowan and Zimmermann (1996), the FMLA was "the first bill introduced in the 103rd Congress" in 1993 (p. 57). It was preceded by a previous version of the bill that was vetoed by President George H. W. Bush (P. A. Monroe, Garand, & Teeters, 1995). Primary opposition to the policy came from small businesses, which argued that it was difficult with a small workforce to provide the necessary accommodations for employees going on leave. The FMLA was signed into law by President Bill Clinton and provides up to 12 weeks of unpaid leave to many working Americans.

Not all employees were covered by the FMLA, however, because only employers with 50 or more employees are required to provide leave under the policy, and potential beneficiaries of the policy have to have worked for an employer for at least a year. Leave may be taken for personal health reasons, such as surgical recovery or treatment, to care for a close relative, or following the birth or adoption of a child. Employers have the right to require documentation supporting the need for FMLA leave (Gitnik, 1996). Unless the reason for the leave is an unforeseen emergency, employees are required to give 30 days' notice to allow employers to cover the position (Gowan & Zimmermann, 1996).

Employees who are granted leave under the FMLA are entitled to reinstatement in either their former position or an equivalent one with the company (Jasper, 2005). Because leave is unpaid, many employees refuse to take it, or, for leave that is anticipated, such as the birth of a child, employees try to save up vacation or other paid leave time instead (Roog et al., 2004). States have the option to go beyond the federal guidelines by requiring paid leave, expanding the time period, or covering additional workers. For those that do provide paid leave, payment is usually a certain percentage of the individual's salary. In 2002, California became the first state to provide paid family and medical leave (Wisensale, 2006).

The FMLA overlaps with the ADA (1990) (P.L. 101-336) in that both may allow for certain accommodations for disability conditions or serious health-related issues. As with the ADA requirement that employees be able to perform (perhaps with accommodations) the essential functions of a job, under the FMLA, employees may require that an employee "submit a medical certification that he or she is fit for duty and able to return to work" following a leave for personal health reasons (Jasper, 2005, p. 36). As Gitnik (1996) wrote, there is also a continuing legal question as to whether extended leave over and above what is allowed under the FMLA constitutes a "reasonable accommodation" under the ADA. Individuals who are ineligible for FMLA leave because they work for a smaller company might be able to attain some unpaid leave as an accommodation under the ADA. However, it is an open question whether this would be approved by the courts because the point of an accommodation is to allow the worker to perform the job in question. In any case, an employer who allows such an accommodation would be demonstrating a good faith effort to support their employees. There is also overlap between the FMLA and workers' compensation because one reason for personal leave may be a work-related injury (Bland, 1999).

Gerstel and McGonagle (1999) noted that the culture of many African Americans places a high value on kin relationship and the responsibility of Black women in particular to take responsibility for the care of family members. African Americans and Hispanics are more likely than Whites to work in low-wage jobs for which unpaid leave is not a viable option; thus, the FMLA disproportionally benefits White workers.

Effectiveness

The FMLA has been fairly successful in its limited goals of providing eligible employees with the ability to take leave without fear of losing their job. Such leave supports bonding with a newborn or adopted child, the availability of a caregiver may allow elderly parents to remain at home for a longer period, and leave allows for a more complete recovery from medical procedures, among other benefits. Because it is unpaid and only affects about 60 percent of workers (Wisensale, 2006), the policy does not place a heavy burden on employers, but it is underused because low-wage workers in particular cannot afford much time off without pay. Approximately half of those taking leave use it for their own health issues rather than maternity/birth or caring for someone else (Wisensale, 2006). Employers who are required to follow the policy are to develop procedures for carrying it out and share this with their employees.

Although federal policymakers have been unwilling to require that employers or the government support paid leave, such a program could have financial benefits not only for the family but in a more general sense, especially in relation to elder care. Given the substantial outlay of taxpayer money for Medicaid, alternatives to long-term care treatment, such as supporting those adult children who are willing to take leave to care for aging parents, has the potential of providing a financial benefit to all. As Roog et al. (2004) pointed out, the FMLA, although designed to assist working mothers who primarily serve as the caregivers within families, actually provides limited support. This is because women, especially single mothers, are often ineligible for benefits. In addition, because women are more likely to earn less, unpaid leave is not an attractive option.

CHAPTER 34

Brady Handgun Violence Prevention Act

◖1994◗

Historical Overview and Nature of the Social Problem

Gun crime is among the most pressing social problems that our nation faces. Based on population size, the United States has a much higher rate of gun deaths and injuries than other nations. Furthermore, these deaths and injuries fall most heavily on marginalized populations, including minority youths (Reiss & Roth, 2001) and those living at or close to the poverty line. Guns and other weapons are also frequently used in domestic disputes, and access to guns is an important factor in completed suicides.

Few would argue that gun crime is not a major problem in the United States. However, the proper response to the problem is highly contentious. Supporters of gun rights have argued that restricting ownership of such weapons not only runs counter to Amendment II to the U.S. Constitution (U.S. Const. amend. II) and individual rights but, moreover, would put people at increased risk because many people use guns for protection and self-defense (Kleck, 1997; Reiss & Roth, 2001). For example, a key argument in favor of concealed carry laws, which grant permits allowing citizens to carry handguns in public, is that this practice dissuades perpetrators from attempting criminal acts because those perpetrators would not know which potential victims or bystanders might have guns. Thus, the perpetrators would have to suspect that everyone is potentially armed.

Opponents have argued that the notion of "good guys with guns" versus "bad guys with guns" is oversimplifying what, in reality, is a highly complex issue. Some "good guys" may turn into "bad guys" when drinking or when angry, and others may not exercise the best judgment in using their weapons or may, even when acting with the best of intentions, harm bystanders. Supporters of gun control have generally argued that their goal is not to completely limit ownership and that doing so would be impossible anyway. Their primary goal, rather, is to track weapons and better control who can access them, enhance gun safety, and limit the use of certain types of weapons or ammunition, such as AK-47s.

The gun control debate originated in the 1930s in response to high-profile gangster violence (G. L. Carter, 1997) and the increased access to guns. Calls for control expanded during the 1960s following the assassination of President John F. Kennedy. When his successor, Lyndon B. Johnson, supported a gun control policy, the National Rifle Association (NRA) provided strident opposition (DeConde, 2001). The gun control movement picked up additional support following the 1968 assassinations of U.S. Senator Robert F. Kennedy, the former president's brother, and Martin Luther King, Jr. With every wave of support, however, the NRA and other gun rights groups expanded their involvement in the political arena. Eventually, President Johnson was able to pass a watered-down control policy, the Federal Gun Control Act of 1968 (P.L. 90-618), which limited the sale of certain weapons. The policy did little to diminish gun crime (Reiss & Roth, 2001) in part because it lacked a strong procedural method for enforcement of its objectives (G. L. Carter, 1997). Most of the components of the 1968 policy were discontinued with the passage of the Firearm Owners' Protection Act of 1986 (P.L. 99-308) (G. L. Carter, 1997), which was passed under President Ronald Reagan, a strong supporter of gun ownership.

Interestingly, even though the violent crime rate decreased beginning in the 1980s, gun-related homicides, especially against the most affected group—young adults in the inner cities, particularly minorities—did not decrease. According to Slovak (2002), "the risk of dying from a firearm injury more than doubled for youths ages 15 to 19 years between 1985 and 1994" (p. 104). It is also interesting that this reduction in crime did not appear to decrease the general public's fear of criminal activity. This fear seems to remain high regardless of actual crime statistics (Goss, 2006).

Policy Overview

The Brady Handgun Violence Prevention Act (1994) (P.L. 103-159), also known as the "Brady Bill," was named after James Brady, the Communications Secretary under President Ronald Reagan. Brady was badly wounded during the assassination attempt on Reagan and was left with permanent disabilities. As a result of this event, he and his wife, Sarah, became strong activists for gun control legislation and created the Brady Campaign to Prevent Gun Violence. Along with other advocates, they pushed for a feasible gun control measure. This bill included two major objectives: (1) stiffen the background check procedure to control who could legally purchase weapons and (2) ban the sale of certain guns that were designated to be assault weapons (DeConde, 2001). The background check proposal required a five-day waiting period, which would eventually become instant background checks once a system was in place to provide for them (DeConde, 2001). The assault weapons ban proposal included about 20 types of weapons deemed particularly dangerous.

The Brady Bill was passed and signed into law by President Bill Clinton in 1993 and was implemented early in 1994. The policy was a key component of the Violent Crime Control and Law Enforcement Act (P.L. 103-322) (Carter, 1997), which also included the 1994 Violence against Women Act (VAWA). As described further shortly, the measure resulted in a political backlash by the NRA and other gun rights supporters. The ban on assault weapons was allowed to expire and is no longer in force.

Shortly after the passage of the Brady Bill, the Republicans took over the U.S. House of Representatives in large numbers behind then–Speaker of the House Newt Gingrich and his "Contract with America." Although the Brady Bill was only one factor in this landslide victory, it did play an important role. Following the passage of the act, the NRA and other gun rights groups put a great deal of money and effort into defeating supporters of the policy, which primarily included Democratic politicians.

Effectiveness

Of the two major goals included as part of the Brady Bill, background checks seemed to be much more effective in safeguarding the public than the ban on assault weapons. Of course, because the assault weapon ban was later discontinued, what its long-term effect would be is uncertain. Checking to ensure that potential owners do not have felonies or fall into other "disallowed buyer" categories has kept a number of potentially dangerous people (including perpetrators of domestic abuse) from owning guns. However, a number of backdoor routes to ownership exist, the primary simply being purchase on the black market or through an informal transaction. Kwon, Scott, Safranski, and Bae (1997) contended that gun control laws need to be considered as only one of a number of interrelated factors in controlling gun violence. Other issues also play a role in this social problem, including unemployment, poverty, and drug and alcohol use, yet these issues were not important components of the Brady Bill.

An issue of controversy related to gun control that is particularly of interest to social services professionals pertains to the restriction of ownership by people with various forms of mental illness. Many have contended that people with severe forms of mental illness, especially paranoia and schizophrenia, are responsible for most of the large-scale massacres in the nation, such as the Sandy Hook Elementary School shooting in Newtown, Connecticut, and the Virginia Tech shooting in Blacksburg, Virginia. At Sandy Hook, 26 people, mostly young children, were killed, and 32 people were killed in the Virginia Tech shooting (Jenson, 2007). Such mass murders, however, are not representative of gun crimes as a whole, although they garner a great deal of media attention (Collier, 2013).

Major concerns about using mental illness as a rationale for not allowing someone to purchase a weapon include that the vast majority of people with mental illness do not pose a danger to others, and this type of policy would limit the constitutional rights of such people and provide a disincentive for receiving treatment or obtaining mental health treatment in the first place. As a result of these and related concerns, many states only disallow purchases if the individual has been involuntarily committed for treatment or has displayed particular behaviors that make gun ownership a viable concern. As with recent policies related to undocumented immigrants, this type of policy puts many social workers and other professionals in the problematic position of being "informers" or enhancing stigmatization of people who fall into certain diagnostic categories.

Another issue of importance related to control of guns surrounds questions of how dangerous particular weapons are. Although many argue that assault weapons or semiautomatic weapons need to be controlled to a greater degree than other guns, these are fairly nebulous categories (Kleck, 1997). The Brady Bill disallowed ownership of a number of weapons, yet others that were fairly similar remained on the market. Adding to this problem is that many gun owners are adept at modifying their weapons in certain ways, further blurring the lines between different types of guns. Some have argued that large magazine clips need to be controlled because these clips dictate how often a particular weapon can be fired within a certain amount of time.

The Brady Bill provides a good example of the difference between "soft" and "hard" support for various policies. Support for gun ownership constitutes hard support; that is, NRA members are likely to vote in relation to a politician's stance on gun ownership, and, thus, it is considered a highly salient issue. This side of the debate includes a much more vocal support group and a much larger number of single-issue voters who are focused primarily on the issue. On the other side, support for restriction generally waxes and wanes based on extent and number of publicized mass shootings. As Kleck (1997) noted, support for policies related to gun control diminishes rapidly once a major tragedy passes from the headlines. Although many people would count themselves as gun control advocates, many are not highly likely to vote based on this issue alone. Those supporting the Brady Bill found that even though many people expressed support for moderate forms of gun control, for the majority of these people, gun control was not their major issue (Goss, 2006). Again, many of the legislators supporting the bill were voted out of office because of their support of it, and a new generation of legislators has learned to be cautious of gun control legislation as a result (DeConde, 2001). Furthermore, many who support some form of gun control believe it is likely to have little positive effect on the extent of gun violence in the country (Goss, 2006).

Although groups, such as Handgun Control Incorporated, have developed as a countermovement to the NRA, gun control advocacy groups have had only a small portion of the membership or financial support that the NRA has had (G. L. Carter, 1997). Recently, because of financial and other problems, the NRA has experienced problems in attempting to continue operations (Hakim, 2021). Until gun control advocacy groups are able to pressure legislators to a similar degree that their opposition does, only the weakest gun control legislation will pass into law. One might even contend that such bills are largely symbolic in nature and are not designed to have a real effect on this issue.

CHAPTER 35

Violence Against Women Act

◖1994◗

Historical Overview and Nature of the Social Problem

In the United States as well as internationally, women have historically been subject to acts of violence and oppression for a number of reasons. Many cultures have traditionally emphasized the submissive role of women and girls as well as the right of men to exact a degree of economic, social, sexual, and other forms of control over their wives, daughters, and other women. The relatively poor economic standing of women compared to that of men, fostered in part by the historical barriers to educational and job opportunities and the ability to control their finances as well as other restrictive measures, has served over time to support the financial and thus social dependence of women on men. In addition, many of the institutions that have traditionally served to counteract violence in society (for example, police and other law enforcement authorities, justice system officials, politicians) have been operated largely or even exclusively by males, and thus these systems as well as the policies they create and the practices they follow often do not speak to issues related to the discriminatory treatment of women.

As is frequently discussed, gendered patterns are maintained through a number of subtle and obvious messages that males and females learn throughout their lives, and many of these messages that girls and young women receive, either overtly or in subtle ways, support male domination over them. Importantly, both boys and girls are strongly influenced by the adult role models in their lives, and when violence occurs in the home, children may view this pattern as the accepted way of dealing with troubling issues (McHugh & Frieze, 2006). This may be particularly true when domestic violence occurs in conjunction with child abuse (McKay, 1994).

Although violence against women primarily relates to abuse by significant others, women may encounter a broad range of criminal behaviors, including stalking, even by men they do not know well or have not even met (for example, cyberstalking, cyberbullying), and "date rape" (Chisholm, 2006; Logan, Cole, Shannon, & Walker, 2006). Women remain at risk even after a relationship with an abusive partner has ended, and often they, along with their children, must seek temporary shelter outside the home and counseling and other support services to protect themselves. Thus, partner violence overlaps with homelessness and housing support policies.

Policy Overview

VAWA was passed in 1994 as part of the Violent Crime Control and Law Enforcement Act (P.L. 103-322) and was signed into law by Bill Clinton (Adelman & Morgan, 2006). The following year, the Office on Violence Against Women was created administratively under the U.S. Department of Justice to administer federal grants authorized under VAWA (Sacco, 2013). Among its other goals, VAWA and its later amendments require the training of law enforcement officers on domestic violence, the tracking of perpetrators and the ability to attain orders of protection against them, the creation of a domestic violence hotline, and a measure of protection for women against stalking and cyberstalking. In sexual assault cases, the policy also provides some restrictions regarding what details can be shared in court about a victim's sexual history. The policy includes programs to track sex offenders; provides stiffer penalties for rape and sexual abuse; and supports funding for shelters, counseling, and other services (Tiefenthaler, Farmer, & Sambira, 2005). Regarding counseling, intimate partner violence can lead to PTSD and other long-term psychological problems that may require assistance from social workers or other mental health specialists.

A particularly controversial issue related to violence against women pertains to the limitations on gun ownership by people who have been convicted of crimes against women. This is especially important in relation to law enforcement personnel, who must carry a weapon in the line of duty. The Lautenberg Amendment to VAWA, officially called the Domestic Violence Offender Gun Ban (P.L. 104-208), was passed in 1996 and limits the ability of law enforcement officers (as well as others) to maintain ownership of a weapon after a domestic violence conviction (Adelman & Morgan, 2006).

As one might guess, this is a particularly contentious policy area for several reasons. First, law enforcement officers may be required to deal with complaints against members of their own force, and if officers lose their weapon (and perhaps their job), that can have a detrimental economic effect on both the victim and the alleged perpetrator. For these and other reasons, such cases may be vastly underreported, even compared to other domestic violence cases (Erwin, Gershon, Tiburzi, & Lin, 2005).

One controversial element of VAWA has been mandatory arrest policies, whereby a perpetrator (or in some cases a victim, or both) must be arrested whenever police investigate a domestic violence call (Eigenberg, 2001). Even though these laws are in place in many jurisdictions, often an arrest is not made. As Messing, Ward-Lasher, Thaller, and Bagwell-Gray (2015) noted, such policies have increased the chance that both partners will be arrested and perhaps prosecuted. They added that in some geographic areas, domestic violence courts similar to mental health or drug courts have been developed specifically to review these cases.

The policy also supports services directed at children who have been affected by intimate partner violence (McNeal & Amato, 1998). These services include counseling, support for children while in shelters, and liaisons to assist with educational needs especially while families are homeless (Chanmugam, Kemter, & Goodwin, 2015). Funding also may be used to support counseling, anger management, substance abuse treatment, or intervention programs for perpetrators (Bennett, 1995; Messing et al., 2015).

Effectiveness

In looking at long-term violence reports from the U.S. Department of Justice, one might think that VAWA has been quite successful given that incidents of rape, murder, and other violent crimes against women dropped following its passage (Sacco, 2013). According to Meyer-Emerick (2001), the rate of partner violence diminished markedly during the five-year period after the policy was signed. However, nearly all types of crime decreased during this span of time, so it is difficult to tell the degree to which VAWA may have been responsible for the decline in crimes against women. As with any policy though, the public awareness that surrounds the issues surely had a positive effect. Largely because many couples are no longer traditional male–female dyads, the issue of violence against women has more recently been termed "intimate partner violence." Women, though, are frequently subject to violence or abuse by people who are not "intimate partners"; therefore, protections need to be broader.

As with other policies that relate to both physical and psychological harm, psychological harm is more problematic from a diagnostic perspective. It is more difficult to discern the emotional or psychological effects of cyberstalking, for example, as opposed to violence that leaves traceable marks on a body (Logan et al., 2006). This is especially the case if incidents of emotional or psychological abuse were not preceded by an order of protection or other form of cease-and-desist notice.

According to Tiefenthaler et al. (2005), one criticism of VAWA is that services and funding are not provided equitably: Rural communities or those communities with a high percentage of poor and minority residents receive few services. These authors noted that in 2000, "58% of counties had no [VAWA] services whatsoever" (Tiefenthaler et al., 2005, p. 576). Shelter access is particularly problematic in many areas. The past few reauthorizations of the policy have been fraught with controversy related to issues surrounding protection for undocumented immigrant women and individuals who are transgender or identify as LGBTQ (Messing et al., 2015). Recent authorizations have also sought to enhance the protection of Native American women ("The Pros and Cons of Reauthorizing," 2019) and have focused extensively on protecting the victims of human trafficking (Sacco, 2013).

Given the messages that children receive about power and control issues, decreasing the degree of physical and emotional abuse that women are subject to begins early in the life of children with a reconsideration and alteration of these messages. In what subtle or obvious ways are we modeling—including through TV, music, and other media—negative interpersonal behaviors to children, not only in relation to intimate partners but to the interaction between individuals with a differential degree of power?

CHAPTER 36

Temporary Assistance for Needy Families

◖1996◗

Historical Overview and Nature of the Social Problem

As alluded to in chapter 1, several recurring themes have wound their way through the history of poor support in the United States. Among the most obvious is this question: What individuals/groups are "deserving" of such assistance and how we are to delineate and respond to "deserving" versus "undeserving" populations? Although different terms today may be used to discuss this issue, the theme has been prevalent through the history of public support to families in poverty from its inception more than a century ago as Mother's Pensions to the push for "welfare reform" in the 1990s and beyond.

Mother's Pensions were initiated in the early 1900s as small-scale, state-based payments to poor single mothers with children (Abbott & Breckinridge, 1921; Davis, 1930). Most of these women were widowed, although, in some cases, support might be provided to families in which the husband had deserted the family or had become disabled. Mother's Pensions were often given to the wives of soldiers who had lost their lives or became disabled in World War I or other military conflicts or who died or had become disabled as a result of industrial accidents, which were highly common in the years before work safety regulations and unionization efforts.

A version of Mother's Pensions was provided by the federal government with the development within the larger Social Security Act of 1935 (P.L. 74-271) of Aid to Dependent Children, which would eventually become AFDC. Like the state programs, the target population for assistance primarily consisted of poor women with children who were widowed or had been deserted by their husbands. Desertion by husbands was particularly prevalent during the Great Depression. Over the course of the program, however, and especially beginning in the 1950s and 1960s, the recipient class would change dramatically because an increasing percentage of divorced or never-married women began to apply for benefits.

The push for "welfare reform" began in earnest during these decades. As early as 1951, for example, *The Saturday Evening Post* published an article titled, "The Relief Chiselers Are Stealing Us Blind" (Molloy, 1951), and many similar writings followed. Reform advocates argued that AFDC and other forms of government support were creating a class of dependent citizens who chose not to work. By the 1970s and 1980s, conservative and libertarian writers, such as Charles Murray and Lawrence Mead, were calling for an end to all forms of federal public assistance to those who were capable of working (Goldberg & Collins, 2001; Murray, 1984), and their plea was echoed by many legislators and a large percentage of the general public. By the late 1980s, it was obvious to many politicians that some major change needed to be made in AFDC, which had become the primary target for calls to reform the "welfare" system.

Policy Overview

The TANF program was preceded by the 1988 Family Support Act (P.L. 100-485), which included some of the elements of the former policy in a much smaller package (Mead, 2000). During the 1990s, many states were engaged in AFDC "experiments" designed primarily to limit benefits or control recipients in various ways. One of the more well-known of these experiments was the New Jersey family cap. Through this policy, the state refused to increase benefits for recipients when they had additional children once they were on AFDC (Popenoe, 1996). Many of these experimental initiatives were taken up by states after TANF passed, especially because the new policy gave states more control over eligibility and benefits provision.

TANF was supported not only by nearly all Republicans in Congress but also by many moderate Democrats, including President Bill Clinton, who promised to decrease government expenditures on welfare. Many Progressive Democrats and other opponents of the bill, however, argued that the policy was too harsh and added that forms of government assistance, such as "corporate welfare," were not targeted by reform measures because their recipients were wealthy and had powerful connections and political pull (Goodgame, 1994). Many also argued that the policy was driven largely by emotion and unfair stereotypes of recipients (for example, the "welfare queen") rather than sound research on the issue (Piven & Cloward, 1971; Placek & Hendershot, 1974; Zucchino, 1999).

The policy passed fairly easily and provided time limits for most of those on the AFDC rolls. Time limits generally allowed families to continue to receive benefits for only two years at a time and five years total. These limits could be waived in certain cases, such as when a parent was caring for a child with a severe disability. Recipients were required to find employment or to engage in activities, such as drug or alcohol treatment or job training, that would position them to enter the workplace. Other requirements included placing limitations on teenage girls to disincentivize having children (for example, requiring them to stay in high school or live with their parents), expanding paternity testing and going after "deadbeat dads," and providing some support for child care and other relevant expenses.

States were given a good amount of autonomy to set eligibility policy limitations and requirements and were required to track progress related to policy goals and report results to the federal government ("Welfare Reform: Can the States Fly Solo?," 1996). States could also set more restrictive time limits than the federal limits (Hamilton, Wingrove, & Woodford, 2019). An especially problematic issue related to the interconnection between TANF and associated forms of public assistance (for example, Medicaid, SNAP or food stamps benefits, WIC support, EITC, HUD support, SSI, child care), involved questions about how TANF eligibility would affect eligibility for these other programs. To be effective, poor support programs need to be reviewed in the context of the broad range of support policies to truly assess their interactional effects.

Effectiveness

Very simply, TANF has been either extremely successful or woefully inadequate, depending on what one considers to be the primary goal of the policy. Most supporters would contend that its primary goal was to remove people from the welfare rolls, and it did indeed do this: The caseload went from more than four million families to slightly more than one million by 2016 (Oh, DiNitto, & Kim, 2018). Opponents of the policy, however, would counter that the goal of reform legislation should have been to move recipients out of poverty. On this count, TANF was largely ineffective.

Although the policy did well in its early years at moving beneficiaries into jobs and often above the poverty line, there are important caveats to these achievements. First, the economy of the late 1990s was fairly good, certainly compared to the first decade-and-a-half of the 21st century (Lens, 2002). When a recession hit approximately a decade after the policy was implemented, good jobs were hard to find. Second, many of those moving into the workforce early on were short-term recipients. In many cases, these individuals were experiencing a temporary setback and likely would have moved into employment positions regardless. Third, many of the long-term recipients of AFDC or TANF had multiple personal and environmental issues that precluded employment. These included various forms of substance abuse or mental illness, disability or health issues, illiteracy, and living in urban or rural communities where few employment opportunities were available (Shin & Choi, 2007). Because of these and additional reasons, the presumed success of TANF has been questioned.

A large percentage of those moving off the TANF rolls had little education and few marketable skills and thus wound up in low-wage jobs with little real possibility of advancement. Moreover, many of these positions provided few benefits, such as support for child care or health insurance. Many of those who used up their eligibility for TANF and moved into entry-level jobs found themselves in a worse economic situation than when they received public assistance. This relates to the concept of *less eligibility*, which holds that, to incentivize employment for those who are poor, the government should ensure that people who are employed in entry-level jobs are in better financial shape than those receiving public assistance. According to Abramovitz (2005), welfare reform also resulted in problems in the service delivery system itself because agencies were saddled with more requirements and paperwork and, simultaneously, had less autonomy to assist those in need.

At its most basic level, social policy is about the balance of rights and responsibilities. Any policy provides certain rights (for example, money, services, opportunities, protection) and delineates responsibilities (for example, tax payments, loss of privacy, control of behavior). When the mass of the population considers that they are gaining few rights from a policy but are saddled with the lion's share of responsibilities, the policy will likely be revised. Responsibilities may be willingly taken on by taxpayers when they believe the beneficiaries are truly in need of assistance; this was not the case with AFDC, at least in the view of much of the public.

When recipients are generally seen as falling within the "undeserving poor" category, those who are responsible for supporting such benefits require that recipients themselves accept certain responsibilities. Recipients may be subject to a degree of surveillance or oversight such that their privacy may be abrogated and their choices limited. One of the ironies of policies like TANF is that, although its supporters may contend that "get-tough" welfare policies constitute an important means of instilling responsibility in recipients, within the constraints of those policies, beneficiaries are often treated in a highly punitive, patronizing manner, which diminishes individual initiative and self-esteem.

Rights and responsibilities were central to TANF, as can be seen by the larger policy that TANF was included within: the Personal Responsibility and Work Opportunity Reconciliation Act of 1996 (P.L. 104-193). Although the rights of beneficiaries were radically curtailed by the time lines and decreased supporting services (for example, Medicaid, Food Stamp program/SNAP), their responsibilities under the policy were increased in many ways. For example, women were responsible for naming the father of their child, and men who tested positive for being the father were required to pay child support; unmarried teen mothers were required to stay in school, and, except in certain situations, remain in their parents' home (Wilson & Sylvester, 1996); and most recipients were responsible for attaining a job within a specific period.

Policies that take a get-tough approach, such as TANF, sex offender legislation, and various criminal and juvenile justice policies (for example, boot camps or Scared Straight programs) often feel like the right approach to various problems, but they generally are based much more on emotion as opposed to a sound research approach to the problems they target. As such, they often constitute knee-jerk responses that may not effectively deal with the problem. In some cases, they could indeed be counterproductive and feed the problem they are designed to solve.

CHAPTER 37

Sex Offender Registration and Notification Act

◖1996◗

Historical Overview and Nature of the Social Problem

If you asked Americans to populate Dante's circles of hell, for many of them, the innermost circle would be reserved for those who sexually abuse children. For many, there is no greater sin or crime than sexual abuse of a child. Although this has been known to be a social problem for much of our nation's history, it is still primarily a taboo subject; therefore, it could be thought of as a random anomaly that requires prosecution but not publicity or special policy attention. Even though state sex offender registration laws go back to the 1940s, community notification requirements only began in the 1990s (Fodor, 2001).

To a large extent, child sexual abuse became an issue of public discussion in conjunction with a number of highly publicized cases during the 1980s and 1990s. Adam Walsh, Jacob Wetterling, Polly Klaas, and Megan Kanka were the most well reported of these cases. The Adam Walsh case, in particular, was important in putting the issue before the public both because a movie was made of the case and because John Walsh, Adam's father, became a well-known leader in the fight against child sexual abuse. In addition to the sexual abuse, each of these children was murdered, and their cases paved the way for legislation designed to protect children. Unlike most types of policies, sex offender laws often progressed through the political system fairly rapidly partly because of the emotions involved combined with the lack of dissent. When it comes to child molestation, no politician wants to be portrayed as being soft.

In addition to these cases focusing on individual children, there were a number of very disturbing cases related to day care centers, with the most scandalous being the McMartin case (*Virginia McMartin et al. v. Children's Institute International* [1989]), which went to trial in the late 1980s (Beck,

2015; Sauer & Okerblom, 1993). These cases garnered media attention because of the harrowing nature of the allegations, which included secret torture rooms in the preschools and satanic rituals. In retrospect, many of these allegations were unproven, and at least some of the children involved were unknowingly guided to testify about the abuse. Also important in the continued focus on child sexual abuse were exposés of widespread abuse by priests, scoutmasters, and others who had been entrusted with the care of children.

Policy Overview

The 1994 Jacob Wetterling Crimes Against Children and Sexually Violent Offender Registration Act (P.L. 103-322) was the first of the federal notification policies passed (T. Thomas, 2011). The Wetterling Act was included within the Violent Crime Control and Law Enforcement Act, which also included the Brady Bill, VAWA, and "Megan's Law," named after Megan Kanka. The Wetterling Act required states to maintain a list of registered offenders made available to the public (Brannon, Levenson, Fortney, & Baker, 2007; Fodor, 2001). The Sex Offender Registration and Notification Act (2006) (P.L. 109-248), also known as the Adam Walsh Act, which passed in 2006, ensured that offenders would be tracked nationally through the U.S. Department of Justice (Jeglic, Mercado, & Levenson, 2012).

In addition to implementing tracking and increasing criminal sentences, a number of states in the 1990s began to develop civil commitment laws, which allow states to confine offenders in mental health facilities following the completion of their prison sentence if it is believed they remain a threat (T. Thomas, 2011). As R. Alexander (2000) noted, these policies are controversial because the individuals had completed serving their sentences. Numerous states and municipalities have also passed residency restriction laws whereby registered offenders cannot live within the proximity of parks, schools, bus stops, and the like. In many communities, such restrictions dramatically limit where people can reside (Skipp & Campo-Flores, 2009). As Levinson and Tewksbury (2009) noted, restrictive policies and stigma targeted at registered offenders adversely affect their families.

More recently, two important policy areas that pertain to this area are sex trafficking (Cacho & Saviano, 2014) and the use of the Internet in the course of sexual exploitation or trafficking. These areas bring up additional operational dilemmas related to policy, especially because they may be international in scope and thus require a broader policy approach.

Effectiveness

One concern that many have about these policies is that they could inadvertently increase repeated offenses among sex offenders. "Get tough" measures and heavy stigmatization of such offenses may drive offenders underground such that they may refuse to seek or remain in treatment because of shame (Comartin, Kernsmith, & Kernsmith, 2009). As Jeglic et al. (2012) wrote, "One of the key tenets of rehabilitation is reintegration back into the community. However, if such statutes increase or exacerbate stressors . . . that bear some relationship to recidivism, this legislation may become counterproductive and increase risk" (p. 56). Sex offender policies generally pass rapidly through legislatures on the strength of the emotions this issue entails, but one downside is that little research has been conducted on the best means of dealing with the problem (Ackerman & Furman, 2012). Brannon et al. (2007) noted, however, that a large percentage of the public supports community notification policies regardless of any research on its effectiveness.

Another problematic issue related to sex offender legislation is that media focus on the most sensational sex crimes leads to a public misunderstanding about the actual nature of is overall issue and, therefore, also leads to bad policy decisions (Ackerman & Furman, 2012). Public emotions run high when it comes to such offenses; it is difficult for many of us to engage in critical thinking relative to the problem. As is often noted, the "stranger danger" presumption is among the most inaccurate of these beliefs. The vast majority of offenders know their victims, and many are trusted adults or relatives (Ackerman & Furman, 2012; Berkowitz, 2010). It may be that the percentage of cases in which the offender is known to the family is actually much higher than reports indicate because parents may be wary of filing a complaint against relatives or friends (Ackerman & Furman, 2012). There also is little evidence that registration and notification laws serve to protect children (Levenson & Tewksbury, 2009). Indeed, such policies may provide parents and caregivers with a false sense of security. The general public also overestimates "the frequency of sexual recidivism when compared to published data" (Brannon et al., 2007).

One unintended consequence of community notification policies that was anticipated when the policy passed is that individuals and their family members would be subject to bullying and vigilante justice, including efforts to force them from their communities (Brannon et al., 2007). According to Levinson and Tewksbury (2009), that consequence has come to pass: Almost half of offenders or family members report that they have been threatened or harassed. In many communities, there are no places where offenders can live because of residency restrictions (Skipp & Campo-Flores, 2009). In addition, a large percentage of perpetrators have had suicidal ideations (Jeglic et al., 2012).

Many therapists, including those with experience working with sex offenders, believe that the policy is ineffective and fails to reduce both child sexual abuse and recidivism (Comartin et al., 2005). R. Alexander (2000) has cautioned against therapists using past criminal records as the basis for a *Diagnostic and Statistical Manual of Mental Disorders* (American Psychiatric Association, 2013) diagnosis. He argued that when mental facilities are used for civil commitment once an offender has completed their prison sentence, this makes such facilities an arm of the criminal justice system.

Because of the raw emotions that child sexual abuse gives rise to, especially those cases garnering a great deal of media attention, child sex abuse cases generate what Beck (2015) referred to as a moral panic. In such an atmosphere, our belief that those accused of a crime are innocent until proven guilty may go by the wayside, and alleged perpetrators may be tainted regardless of the facts of a case.

CHAPTER 38

Defense of Marriage Act

◖1996◗

Historical Overview and Nature of the Social Problem

The ability to marry has long been a central goal of the LGBTQ movement. Marriage is among the most basic of human rights. Not only is it an important way to demonstrate one's love and commitment to another person, but it also carries with it a number of benefits and privileges that heterosexual couples have long taken for granted. These benefits include a number of public policy and work-related partner benefits, shared custody rights in regard to children, and rights pertaining to having a say in relation to an incapacitated partner's medical care and end-of-life treatment. Marriage, in other words, is not simply a ceremony or statement of commitment to another. It is much more.

Same-sex marriage is one of a number of controversial issues advocated by members of the gay rights movement and fought by conservative politicians, religious leaders, and other "moral stakeholders" (Sullivan, 1997). Other issues include adoption and child custody; the Don't Ask, Don't Tell policy and the right to serve in the military; inclusion in hate crime legislation; and protection from housing and employment discrimination.

Parallels exist in the historic refusal to allow same-sex marriage and in the barriers to mixed-race marriages, especially in many southern states. Both have been viewed as being counter to Christian principles, harmful to children, and in opposition to what Nature intended. Many have viewed domestic partnerships, civil unions, or another quasi-marriage status as a preferable middle ground that allows some of the benefits of marriage; however, advocates have argued that this view is untenable and relegates same-sex partnerships to "second-class" status (Mucciaroni, 2008). One primary point of opposition expressed by a number of conservative voters and politicians to marriage is that it would naturally lead to an increased number of children being reared in same-sex households, which they contend would not be in the best interest of those children.

Policy Overview

DOMA (1996) (P.L. 104-199) was developed in response to same-sex marriage laws or attempts to develop such laws in Hawaii, Vermont, Massachusetts, and other states (Ritenhouse, 2011). Legislators representing other, generally more conservative states, argued that it was inappropriate for their states to be forced to recognize such marriages even if they were allowed elsewhere. Aside from the human rights issues, this view was problematic because, for the most part, state policies recognize marriages from outside their borders as legitimate based on the Full Faith and Credit clause of the U.S. Constitution (U.S. Const., art. IV, § 1). This clause effectively holds that contracts that are valid in one state are recognized as such in other states. A couple, for example, who marries in Massachusetts is accepted as married if they move to Colorado.

Many opponents of these state laws also argued that same-sex couples from other states would go to Hawaii or wherever else it would become legal to marry, and would return to their own state expecting their marriage to be recognized (Strasser, 2010). Those opposing DOMA argued that the federal government should not involve itself in marriage, which had traditionally been left to the states; however, "Congress has often found it convenient to use state-law marital status in federal laws and programs" (Whelan, 2012, p. 35). The policy specifically defined marriage—at least as recognized by the federal government—as being between one man and one woman (Strasser, 2010). Some states went so far as to include in their state constitutions that only "traditional" marriages would be legal (Mucciaroni, 2008).

As further described shortly, DOMA was discussed by federal legislators at the same time as the Employment Non-Discrimination Act of 1995 (ENDA) (H.R. 1863) was being considered. ENDA would have extended employment protections similar to the Civil Rights Act of 1964 (P.L. 88-352) protections to gays and lesbians ("ENDA Overview," 2013). Although a number of states have passed employment nondiscrimination bills, the federal government still has not. In those states without a policy, it is legal to fire or refuse to hire individuals because of their sexual orientation. It is also legal—at least as considered by the federal government—to discriminate against same-sex couples or anyone who identifies as LGBTQ in regard to housing.

DOMA passed both the U.S. House of Representatives and the U.S. Senate by fairly wide margins and was signed into law by President Bill Clinton. While Clinton was a Democrat, he could best be defined as a centrist on many issues, and his support for lesbian/gay civil rights legislation was decidedly lukewarm. ENDA failed by one vote in the Senate but likely would not have fared well in the Republican-majority House even if it had passed the Senate.

Effectiveness

Although DOMA passed and therefore allowed states to refuse to recognize same-sex marriages that were performed in other states, the benefits to conservatives were short lived. Two U.S. Supreme Court cases, the 2013 *United States v. Windsor* and the 2015 *Obergefell v. Hodges* rulings, held the policy to be unconstitutional (Brodyn, 2019; Pelts, 2014). As a result of these decisions, states were required to consider same-sex marriages legally valid.

The scenario of some states recognizing certain marriages to be legitimate but not others raised a number of difficult ancillary issues. Because marriage and divorce are directly related, what if a same-sex couple became divorced, said Strasser (2010), and one member of the dyad was displeased with the property settlement or spousal support? Perhaps the unhappy person could move to a state where the marriage (and thus the divorce) was not recognized as legal anyway. A host of similar questions related to raising children and custody are also tied to marriage, including taxation and other social and economic issues.

Analysis Element: Slippery Slopes

Slippery slope arguments are frequently used in policy debates to purposefully sabotage efforts to pass a particular proposal. If, opponents argue, the proposal is accepted, it will open the door to more radical proposals related to that social issue. Because policy is incremental, that is, it is built on previous ones, policies implemented may in the future be extended—for example, decriminalizing marijuana may lead to lax enforcement of stronger illegal drugs; if we allow abortion during the first few weeks of pregnancy, this period may be extended; any form of gun control will pave the way for greater restrictions.

Slippery slope arguments have a long history and are used particularly when there is a broad range of policy options that differs in terms of the policies' degree of public acceptability. With regard to gay rights legislation, policies that stand in opposition to housing or employment discrimination because of sexual preference and hate crime protection are generally supported by the public much more so than policies related to same-sex marriage or adoption (Mucciaroni, 2008). Opponents of those bills that have greater support will use the specter of less favored ones in their arguments. This indeed occurred within the context of the 1996 DOMA debate. As that policy was being discussed, ENDA was also up for debate. It was beneficial for those opposing ENDA that gay marriage was also on the agenda because it made the case for the slippery slope apparent (for example, "If we support nondiscrimination in employment, it will lead to marriage rights"). One might presume that, at that time, Republicans purposefully included ENDA in the policy mix to tarnish it by tying it to DOMA and therefore diminishing its support.

Opponents of same-sex marriage laws have used the slippery slope argument in another way, too. They often have argued that if we moved beyond a "one woman, one man" marriage, it would open the door for polygamy and even incestuous marriages (Rogozen, 2017). Yet another slippery slope consideration that frequently has come into play in relation to human rights issues related to those who identify as gay or lesbian is whether to include bisexuals or transgender individuals, or both groups, in such policies. Opponents of same-sex marriages or adoptions have argued that such a policy will eventually be revised to include those who identify as transgender. Those who support various rights-related legislation may face a quandary if they would like the group that is granted those rights to be as large as possible, but the inclusion of certain individuals may be used by opponents to negatively tarnish the entire group.

In looking at policies related to the gay and lesbian population from the perspective of the slippery slope, it is interesting to note that the right to marry "jumped the queue," so to speak, because it was legalized while ENDA remained in limbo. The more controversial measure went into effect first, although it did so based on judicial rather than legislative action.

CHAPTER 39

USA Patriot Act

◖2001◗

Historical Overview and Nature of the Social Problem

Fears surrounding a potential terrorist attack are long-standing. Such concerns were central to the Red Scare of 1919, which involved widespread anxiety over the possibility that Communists and anarchists in the nation were planning to incite terror through bombings and other violent acts. These fears often arise in conjunction with war; for example, the Japanese internment was supported because of concerns that potential sabotage in the United States would occur to assist the war aims of Japan (see chapter 10). Decades later, terrorism fears came to the fore in 1995 with the bombing of the Alfred P. Murrah Federal Building in Oklahoma City, and those fears were magnified with the coordinated 9/11 attacks on the twin towers of the World Trade Center in New York City, on the Pentagon, and with the crash of United Airlines Flight 93 in Pennsylvania. Following the 9/11 attacks, Congress acted quickly not only to support the war effort in Iraq and Afghanistan in response to Al Qaeda and other terrorist groups but also to set out a broad platform of anti-terrorism policies. These policies affected an array of areas, including immigration and refugee travel, personal (including computer) surveillance, airline and other travel policies, the tracking of students from outside the country, and the redistribution of law enforcement and military funding toward anti-terrorism efforts.

Policy Overview

According to Pitt (2011), "Patriot" in the name USA Patriot Act of 2001 (P.L. 107-56) is an acronym that "stands for Uniting and Strengthening America by Providing Appropriate Tools Required to Intercept and Obstruct Terrorism" (p. 54). Because of the emergency nature of the policy and the collective shock of the 9/11 attacks, the policy was passed only six weeks after the attacks with the understanding that it could be revised in the future.

In addition to providing funding to support surveillance activities within the nation and internationally, the policy increased requirements on the provision of visas and on immigration (Terwilliger, 2005), enhanced the ability of authorized federal investigators to access electronic and other communications (Dempsey & Kerr, 2005), and required colleges and universities to submit information to the federal government related to any of their enrolled international students and also visiting professors from abroad (Wong, 2007).

A central concern about the Patriot Act and similar policy responses for protecting citizens is this: Where do we draw the line between harm prevention and civil liberties? Many components of the Patriot Act, such as communication surveillance, body checks at airports and in other sensitive spaces, and racial profiling, have infringed on civil rights in various ways (I discuss this in more depth shortly). As Pitt (2011) wrote, the infringement on civil liberties is especially a concern because not only stigmatization and discrimination but also retributive violence may accompany racial and religious-based prejudice. One of the unintended consequences of the post-9/11 reaction was an increase in hate crimes against Muslims or those of (or believed to be of) Middle Eastern descent. Reports of the involvement of the National Security Agency (NSA) in surveillance regarding phone, e-mail, and other forms of communication raise the same concerns of the proper balance between government surveillance and control versus individual liberties.

Questions about the proper balance between privacy and security relate not only to "traditional" forms of terrorism that are rooted in criminal activities and are usually targeted at large numbers of people but also to concerns about the most appropriate governmental response to newer forms of potential terrorist threats, such as cyberterrorism (computer-based attacks) and bioterrorism (use of biological contaminates). Monitoring these potential threats, moreover, is particularly problematic because they can arise from outside the country; thus, strong international coordination is required to prevent them.

As noted in chapter 19, there is a degree of overlap between anti-terrorism and environmental policies. Both may require a large-scale coordinated response that includes a broad range of health, mental health, law enforcement, and other emergency first responders. As a result, good communication needs to exist among the various governmental agencies that may respond to either form of national emergency. Following the development of the U.S. Department of Homeland Security in 2002, this large federal body has been given control over FEMA, the primary federal bureau tasked with responding to natural disasters. Although having both natural disaster and terrorism response under the same umbrella agency makes some sense, there are concerns. For example, in responding to a natural disaster, such as Hurricane Katrina, many undocumented immigrants may be afraid of engaging with federal authorities, whom they may see as a law enforcement arm rather than as an agency providing support. In addition, the federal response to a large-scale natural disaster may be slow or otherwise adversely affected if it is led by a law enforcement body.

Effectiveness

As with most policies that focus primarily on prevention, one of the difficulties of assessing effectiveness with the Patriot Act is that there is no way of knowing what would have occurred had the policy not been in place. Although it seems that certain plans have been thwarted, there is no assurance that this would not have been the case anyway or that such plans would have led to action. This is similar to the response to COVID-19: There is no way of knowing how extensive the problem would have been without a large-scale quarantine effort.

As White (2002) noted, one of the key questions related to anti-terrorism policies is whether we consider such threats to be an act of war or a criminal enterprise. If a particular nation supported terrorism, it would fall more under the definition of a traditional war. But what if those supporting such efforts are a nebulous collection of people who cut across the boundaries of many nations and are unknowingly supported by these other countries? This is an important distinction because there are rules of war by which one must abide and also because taking action against "criminals" who reside in another nation is problematic. The United States might extradite individuals to another nation for criminal justice purposes, but there is a strict procedure we require other nations to follow. We would not, for example, take kindly to "foreign drones" taking people out within our borders for ostensibly anti-terrorism purposes and would likely consider this to be an act of war.

Another issue of controversy related to the policy and the anti-terrorist response in general is the degree to which the policy may be used as an excuse to close the borders to even legal immigration. If more barriers are placed in the way of immigrants or those seeking visas, they will be less able or willing to come to the United States. For example, universities that serve small numbers of foreign students may decide to not solicit such students because of the expense and red tape involved. Controversies also focus on interrogations, detention, and the due process rights that are afforded individuals.

Analysis Element: Policy Trade-Offs—Privacy and Security

On the face of it, it may appear that there is not much of a relationship among terrorism, the policy response to it, and social work practice. Yet, several important points intersect. First, any form of violence is a matter of interest for the profession, especially because a major focus of social work is the protection from harm. Social workers play a vital role in harm reduction and prevention activities. Second, social workers and related mental health and public health workers are becoming increasingly important as first responders in large-scale crisis situations, whether those relate to acts of terrorism or other catastrophic events. Third, although policies like the Patriot Act may offer a degree of protection from physical violence or other mass mayhem (for example, cyberterrorism), they also may limit individual freedom and privacy.

Having a stake in both public safety and individual rights, social workers should have input into the lines that are drawn related to these two concerns. This is particularly true when the restriction of rights may support the oppression of vulnerable populations or highly stigmatized groups, or may encourage racial profiling, or when such restrictions seem to be based more on mass hysteria and potentially invalid assumptions rather than sound research. Laws that require social workers and other professionals to share personal information about potentially undocumented immigrants to assist in deportation not only clash with our ethical code but also have a negative effect on our involvement in any surveillance activities even when true threats may emerge (Androff & Tavassoli, 2012).

Regarding the connection between anti-terrorism and oppression, one might contend that the fear of terrorism has been exploited by those wishing to develop harsh policies directed at "illegal immigrants" as well as other minorities (Padilla, Shapiro, Fernández-Castro, & Faulkner, 2008). One of the lessons of the past is that when the general public is highly fearful (regardless of whether the degree of fear is appropriate in light of the facts at hand or not), those who are potentially vulnerable to a restriction of rights are apt to be targeted even if they are innocent. In the face of fear, one cannot widen the circle of suspicion too far. As with Japanese internment, most will believe that it is better to ensure public safety at any cost. To not be above suspicion, "suspect" people need to prove that they are not a threat, which is a virtual impossibility for anyone.

Especially during the President Donald J. Trump administration, anti-immigrant and anti-refugee policies were often justified by the fight against terrorism. As has been well reported, these policies have negatively affected not only minors (many of whom are no longer minors) under the Deferred Action for Childhood Arrivals (DACA) program but also unaccompanied and undocumented children and, particularly disconcerting, those children who have been forcibly separated from their families (Hasson, Crea, McRoy & Lê, 2019).

Passed in 1988, the Robert T. Stafford Disaster Relief and Emergency Assistance Act (P.L. 93-288) included "provision for crisis counseling and training for public emergencies" (Patterson, 2009, p. 281). Social workers and other first responders need to work with individuals who may be suffering traumatic loss or distress from mass events and who, themselves, may also secondarily suffer from "PTSD overload," or what Pulido (2012) referred to as "Secondary Traumatic Stress . . . or Compassion Fatigue" (p. 307). Bliss and Meehan (2008) discussed a framework for disaster response in relation to Hurricane Katrina. As with the response to coronavirus, disaster responses include a form of triage and decision making about a hierarchy of need based on available resources and expertise.

CHAPTER 40

No Child Left Behind Act

◖2002◗

Historical Overview and Nature of the Social Problem

In a nutshell, the No Child Left Behind Act of 2001 (NCLB) (P.L. 197-110) was a reaction to the belief that children in the United States had been progressively falling behind those in other countries in the development of primary education goals, such as reading, math, and science. Over the course of the decades before the policy, studies had demonstrated that the average educational abilities of students in such areas were substandard compared to those in many other "developed" nations (Reese, 2005; West & Peterson, 2003). The Reagan-era report, *A Nation at Risk* (National Commission on Excellence in Education, 1983), was particularly influential in pointing to problems in the American educational system (Rudalevige, 2003). Moreover, the educational achievement gap between students in poorer and more wealthy districts and between minority and White children was not only maintained over time but was also potentially expanding.

The perception of general substandard education included a number of subthemes. First, lack of school accountability was a major concern. Because public schools took in children from a specified geographic area, the assumption was that because those schools did not have to compete with one another, they did not have to be highly accountable. Although private schools are a source of competition, many families cannot afford such an option. Second, many critics of public education contended that teachers' unions protected "poor" teachers and that the provision of tenure also served to allow such teachers to remain in their jobs. Third, social promotion and grade inflation presumably allowed students to progress even if they had not attained a requisite level of education. Stories of illiterate high school graduates became a typical feature of discussions related to education. In addition, many conservative stakeholders argued that schools had moved away from basic "three Rs" education—reading, (w)riting, and (a)rithmetic—and pointed to such areas as diversity, self-esteem, home economics, and other so-called "soft" programming as adding to student deficits in these basic areas. Some even implicated art and music as diverting from core educational goals.

In addition to an increased focus on school accountability, many stakeholders, including a large number of conservative politicians, supported school vouchers and other measures that would create competition for schools and presumably force "low-performing" schools to improve (Moe, 2003). Especially controversial was the question of whether such vouchers could be given for private or religious schools. Some critics of vouchers believe they are little more than a backdoor effort to break the teachers' unions and move the country away from public education (Kohn, 2004).

Like the 1990 IDEA law (P.L. 101-476) (see chapter 25), it is important for social work students to have a basic understanding of NCLB because social workers frequently are the professionals within schools who engage with teachers and administrators in implementing policies (Berzin & O'Connor, 2010). In addition, academic achievement, the primary goal of the policy, is greatly affected by issues that arise in a student's home and social life outside the school in which social workers are particularly involved (Lagana-Riordan & Aguilar, 2009). Even for social workers who do not directly work in schools, a basic awareness of school-based policy is important.

Policy Overview

Before 2001, the major federal policy related to public education was ESEA (1965) (P.L. 89-313), which was signed into law in 1965 by President Lyndon B. Johnson. This policy was an important component of Johnson's larger War on Poverty, and a primary goal was to provide federal funding for schools that served a large percentage of students from poor families (McDonnell, 2005; Palley, 2008; Reese, 2005; Rudalevige, 2003). Given that schools were largely funded through local taxes, children in areas that had few businesses and poor property values had much less money to support their education, which led to lower achievement, higher dropout rates, and related problems.

NCLB was enacted in 2002 with bipartisan support. The policy was a principal goal of President George W. Bush, who signed it into law. A similar proposal had previously been implemented in Texas when Bush was Governor (West & Peterson, 2003). The policy required annual testing of children across the country in certain grades as well as publication of the results. Schools were to demonstrate "adequate yearly progress," and "low-performing schools" whose students failed to reach goals on these tests could be punished (Koyama, 2015; Lagana-Riordan & Aguilar, 2009). Negative consequences could include allowing parents to place their student in a different school within the district or potentially even having the state take over control of the school (West & Peterson, 2003). The policy also included specific requirements to ensure that teachers were both qualified and held accountable for their students' progress (Adler-Greene, 2019).

Because the policy was designed to close the achievement gap between White and minority students, test results were to be categorized based on student race and subgroup totals were to be based on students with disabilities (Altshuler & Schmautz, 2006). One controversial issue that arose in relation to the students with disabilities group was whether they needed to take the standardized tests. Because the learning disability category is especially vague and can be interpreted in different ways by different states, there were particular concerns about the status of children with this designation being included in testing (Colker, 2013). The policy set strict limits on the number of children who could be waived from taking tests but did allow testing accommodations in certain circumstances for students with specific disabilities.

Effectiveness

An important failure of NCLB was that it held a simplistic view of academic achievement with a limited focus on the neighborhood, social, and familial factors that often negatively affect a child's ability to succeed in school (Lagana-Riordan & Aguilar, 2009). Although the "high-stakes" testing that NCLB required was tough on "underperforming" schools, little extra federal funding was provided to assist schools in reaching goals. Paschall, Gershoff, and Kuhfeld (2018) contended that even though Head Start and NCLB were designed in part to reduce the achievement gap "for both low-income . . . and Black children . . . research has demonstrated that these efforts have not reached their aims" (p. 1165). Indeed, NCLB was highly ineffective in reaching the overall educational gains that were sought by the policy. Many teachers and administrators also decried what they viewed as government micromanaging of education and felt that "teaching to the test" severely limited teacher creativity.

NCLB resulted in a serious backlash from teachers and administrators, and particularly teachers' unions, which argued they were being scapegoated for children not making sufficient progress and that many cultural and familial components were not being taken into account in framing educational policy. Many critics of the policy would agree with the contention that NCLB "attacks the symptoms, but not the causes, of the problems it seeks to solve" (Lagana-Riordan & Aguilar, 2009).

As a result of what many consider a failed policy, legislators, educational specialists, and other stakeholders have been considering how to move forward in the wake of NCLB (Leatherwood & Payne, 2016). In 2015, the President Barack Obama administration passed the Every Student Succeeds Act (P.L. 114-95) as its central education policy. This was a reauthorization and major revision of NCLB (Adler-Greene, 2019). The policy has maintained high-stakes testing; however, it also minimizes the importance of that testing and, instead, has brought other accountability factors into play. The policy also has lessened the harsh consequences included within NCLB and has focused more on incentives for success (Adler-Greene, 2019).

The Obama administration also introduced Common Core and Race to the Top. Common Core was highly criticized because of its vague guidelines and, like NCLB, what were seen as efforts to micromanage education, even using some methods that teachers themselves either were not highly knowledgeable of or did not feel were effective (Adler-Greene, 2019). Race to the Top focused on incentivizing educational success and emphasizing teacher evaluations (Aguilar & Richerme, 2014).

There continues to be a great deal of contention among lawmakers, parents, and other stakeholders over both the source of problems in the American educational system and the best policy solutions to deal with these issues. Most social workers would certainly like to see an approach that is more macro focused than NCLB and that involves attention to community issues, poverty, family struggles, and the various traumas that students may be facing.

CHAPTER 41

Patient Protection and Affordable Care Act

◖2010◗

Historical Overview and Nature of the Social Problem

The health care system in the United States has been the envy of the world in certain specific ways (for example, extent of technology and medical innovations, quality of care in top hospitals, physician training, pharmaceutical development), yet undoubtedly, many other aspects of our health care system, particularly related to health insurance and access, are highly problematic. Although many opponents of "Obamacare" (that is, the ACA) (P.L. 111-148) have argued that the United States has the "best health care system in the world," no nation has attempted to emulate our system, none likely will in the near future, and there are good reasons for this.

Many of the issues pertaining to our health system were delineated in the Medicare and Medicaid chapters (see chapters 16 and 17, respectively) and thus are only briefly reviewed in this chapter. Unlike other industrialized nations, the United States has a convoluted system of health care and insurance that includes various forms of government provision and payment of services (Veterans Hospitals), government payment systems with private providers (Medicare and Medicaid), a variety of managed care systems, and private insurance. On top of all of this, many people interrelate with multiple systems at any given time. Importantly, approximately 15 percent of the U.S. population traditionally is uninsured—some by choice and some because of a lack of finances or preexisting medical conditions that preclude affordable insurance; in addition, many more people are underinsured (Rivers & Rivers, 2012). The underinsured group may have high out-of-pocket (deductibles or copayments) expenses, or their coverage is limited in important ways. As Rosenbaum (2009) noted, an oddity of our health system is that insurance companies are incentivized for excluding as many sick or diseased people as possible.

Major health insurance changes have been considered every decade or two since the New Deal, yet any initiative that has approached universal coverage has been fought by the American Medical Association and other large interest groups (Maioni, 1998; Rivers & Rivers, 2012). These groups have referred to such plans as socialist measures that would reduce individual choice and lead to service rationing. Current private coverage, though, includes some form of managed care to control costs, and that coverage also limits choice and includes rationing. As Reid (2010) pointed out, the assumption that many Americans have that all nations providing universal coverage are examples of "socialist" medicine is inaccurate. Many of these nations have important policy elements that are more capitalistic than socialistic, but there also is strong governmental oversight and control even of these more capitalistic features.

As noted in the previous chapters on Medicare and Medicaid (see chapters 16 and 17, respectively), major problems with the U.S. health system have largely devolved from the rapid cost increases over the past 50-plus years. In most years, these increases have outdistanced inflation; therefore, health costs have risen more than other areas of both personal and governmental spending. Even though our country does not cover everyone, we pay a much larger percentage for health care than those nations that do have universal coverage. Japan, for example, pays almost half as much per person for health care (Rivers & Rivers, 2012), and its citizens, on average, have a longer life expectancy than in the United States.

There are a number of important reasons behind these cost increases. First and most importantly, other nations build cost controls into their systems more so than the United States. These controls can include, for example, negotiating with pharmaceutical companies for lower drug costs, limiting expensive machinery, and rationing services to a greater degree. Second, medical malpractice lawsuits not only lead to increased costs but also to "defensive medicine," whereby physicians and clinics order expensive tests to protect themselves against a possible claim (Reid, 2010). In addition, there are few disincentives in private insurance to keep people from using services, especially once they have paid their annual deductibles. We also engage in much more medical research and development than most other nations, and hospitals and providers pass along the cost of indigent care.

Policy Overview

Large-scale health reform was a major issue of debate during the 2008 Democratic presidential campaign. Hillary Clinton had been frustrated by the failure of the health package—which she had spearheaded—that was put forth by her husband, President Bill Clinton, and thus was intent on making health reform a central component of her campaign. Barack Obama, her Democratic rival, was equally interested in expanding health coverage. Even though they differed on the proper path it might take, both enthusiastically championed the cause of health reform. Once Obama won the election, plans for a health policy became a major priority of his administration.

The proposal that the Obama administration came up with, the ACA, was highly controversial and would continue to be contentious even after it was passed. A major area of debate surrounded the requirement that everyone attain some form of health insurance or otherwise pay a penalty. To a certain extent, this requirement was important because of the related mandate that insurance companies not refuse coverage because of preexisting medical conditions. If this health insurance coverage requirement had been passed without the preexisting medical conditions mandate, people could simply wait until they had a medical problem before getting insurance. As I revisit shortly, the requirement that everyone have insurance also can be supported by the fact that many uninsured people pass along large medical costs to the rest of society.

Following intense debate, the bill passed Congress and was signed into law. Because of the complexity of the policy, there is inadequate space here to provide great detail regarding its particular components. In brief, the policy goals include the following:

- Increase affordable coverage, especially for individuals who are poor but not eligible for Medicaid (Darnell, 2013).
- Expand to 26 the age at which older children can remain on a parent's insurance (Rivers & Rivers, 2012).

- Require uninsured people to attain insurance or be penalized.
- Allow people to gain entrance to an insurance pool through the development of state health insurance exchanges (Andrews, Darnell, McBride, & Gehlert, 2013; Gorin, 2011).
- Support preventative health services to ward off various problems early (Kaplan, 2011).
- Digitize all health records.
- Expand alternatives to nursing home care, such as the Community Living Assistance Services and Supports program (Shugarman & Whitenhill, 2011).

The policy had a staggered implementation (Copeland, 2012) so that various aspects of it went into effect at different times. Although this piecemeal approach was beneficial in allowing the government to focus on a few issues at a time, it was somewhat problematic in that the entire package could not be assessed until all major elements were in place. One important feature, the state health insurance exchanges, went into effect in October 2013. This rollout experienced grave problems because the system that was developed in many states either could not handle the large online traffic and a number of Web-related glitches hampered sign up.

Effectiveness

It is still a bit early to really say much about the effectiveness of the 2010 health policy because a number of policy features have either been revised by the courts or by the President Donald J. Trump administration and also because of the underfunding of other elements. Numerous efforts have been made by conservatives since passage of this law to diminish the scope of the bill or kill it altogether. Several important components of the policy, including the individual mandate, have gone before the U.S. Supreme Court. In the most recent decision, in 2020, the Court supported the constitutionality of the policy by a 5-4 ruling.

In one sense, at least the policy will likely be successful in allowing individuals with preexisting medical problems to attain insurance. However, it is still an open question as to how affordable this insurance will be. Regarding many of the major problems with health care in the country, especially its fragmented and convoluted means of delivery and increased costs, it is unlikely that the policy will be highly effective. One could certainly argue, however, that no policy that could have feasibly passed Congress would have solved these problems.

Analysis Element: Individualism versus Collectivism

The difference between the United States and other nations in regard to health policy largely pertains to differing value approaches and specifically to a focus on individualism or collectivism. The focus on individualism is often referred to as a "bootstrap" approach—as in the saying, "Pull yourself up by your own bootstraps." We are, individualists have argued, all responsible for ourselves and our own families, and the government should not intervene in people's lives any more than is necessary. Individualists have argued that the federal government especially has become too intrusive, and they frequently use the derogatory term "nanny state" to describe a collectivist approach to social policy. Collectivists, on the other hand, have contended that we have a shared responsibility to one another and that there are some areas of social policy in which a collectivist approach is warranted—for example, public education, in which our value system demands that all children be afforded a quality education.

In terms of health care policy, individualists have argued that people need to be responsible for their own health care and that they should be allowed to remain uninsured if they so choose. People presumably understand the consequences of this decision and should be able to make an informed choice. Collectivists, however, have contended that health care differs from most other areas of our lives because our need for health services is not primarily based on our personal decisions or behaviors but on matters largely beyond our control. It can be viewed as unfair to place extremely heavy costs on people because of their preexisting medical conditions. Many parents, for example, have had to endure bankruptcy to provide necessary medical care for themselves or their children. Even the most healthy and cautious people may develop a potentially fatal disease at any time and require extensive medical intervention. Those in this situation without health insurance are not likely to be capable of reimbursing for these services out-of-pocket and, therefore, will pass the costs along to others.

Collectivists may argue that it is at this point at which the individualist perspective breaks down. Even libertarians, who hold firm to the value of freedom, argue that we should allow people to make their own decisions so long as that does not harm other people. Passing large costs onto others can certainly be viewed as a form of economic harm. The libertarian or individualist perspective might be acceptable in regard to health care if people had control over their ability to remain healthy or those without insurance who became sick actually refused treatment—or at least any treatment that pushed costs onto others. Because neither is true, the collectivist approach to health care becomes more credible (O'Brien, 2019).

CHAPTER 42

Coronavirus Epidemic and Coronavirus Aid, Relief, and Economic Security Act

◖2020◗

Historical Overview and Nature of the Social Problem

Like the rest of the world, the United States has periodically been affected by widespread contagious diseases. Some of these epidemics have been of short duration and have exacted a small amount of damage, some have been catastrophic, and others have fallen in between the two (Krieg, 1992). It is particularly difficult to prepare for such events because we never know when they will arise, how extensive they will get, or what preventative or treatment approaches may be called for in response to any specific virus or disease. Moreover, as the coronavirus (COVID-19) pandemic has demonstrated, despite all our medical and technological advancements over the years, a major epidemic can even now be particularly difficult to effectively deal with.

The 1918 influenza pandemic is the historical precursor that is most often discussed in relation to COVID-19. That earlier pandemic killed between 50 and 100 million people throughout the world, and approximately one million in the United States (Krishnan, Ogunwole, & Cooper, 2020). As with coronavirus, the flu in 1918 took a disproportionate toll on minorities and those living in congested areas of cities. It, too, was also downplayed by some health professionals and members of the public until it became clear how bad the disease spread was (Krishnan et al., 2020). Although fears surrounding other potential epidemics (for example, swine flu, Ebola virus) have arisen every decade or two since, such pandemics have had relatively little effect on the United States.

Policy Overview

It is a bit of a challenge to complete a chapter on COVID-19 largely because the United States and the rest of the world are in the middle of the pandemic as I write these words (mid-2021). As of June 11, 2021, nearly 600,000 Americans have died from COVID-19, and more than 33 million have been infected (Centers for Disease Control and Prevention, n.d.). Although the federal government passed the Coronavirus Aid, Relief, and Economic Security Act (2020) (P.L. 116-136) to provide support to those families and businesses that were economically affected by the pandemic, debates raged over how the support was distributed. In March 2021, President Joseph R. Biden signed a $1.9 trillion COVID-19 relief package designed to stimulate the economy and provide support to those who had been adversely affected by the issue.

As most readers are well aware, and perhaps painfully so, the pandemic has led to much controversy over issues, including precautions like mask wearing and social distancing; closures of schools, businesses, and other areas; the efficacy and safety of vaccines; and a host of other concerns. These problematic issues played out in an especially chaotic time in the nation characterized by the George Floyd murder and BLM protests, two impeachment trials of President Donald J. Trump, an extraordinarily contentious national election, and a violent riot in Washington, DC, that reached into the halls and chambers of the Capitol building itself. In a decidedly strange and fearful time during which people were looking for answers, conspiracy theories ran amok, and many did not know what to believe about events. Among other issues, conspiracy theories centered around vaccine development and effects. It is likely true that many of the misconceptions over the years related to the connection between other vaccines and autism or other disabilities (Mnookin, 2011) gave credence to many that they should not trust the COVID-19 vaccine.

As with the rest of the nation, social workers have been greatly affected by the pandemic. Those who work in health care have fought to stave off infection while assisting first responders to deal with the onslaught of hospitalizations and deaths. Social workers employed in agencies serving the elderly and other vulnerable populations have needed to be extremely vigilant to protect their clients and continue to perform their jobs as well as possible. Clinicians have needed to rapidly learn how to transition into online counseling, which has been problematic both because many forms of clinical intervention are difficult to perform at a distance and because the trauma caused by the pandemic has led to a large increase in the number of people needing support (Chaney, 2020; Roy & Kaur, 2020). Students and instructors have also needed to quickly learn how to engage in online instruction, which has been especially challenging for students attempting to complete field practicum hours (E. L. Cross, 2020; Nissen, 2020). Zoom and other Web-based platforms have become essential for sharing information at a time when students and professionals are in dire need of learning how to adapt to the crisis (Peláez, Marcuello-Servós, de Mesa, & Kalixto, 2020). At a more macro level, many social justice and advocacy groups have needed to harness digital tools in an effort to build coalitions and engage in advocacy through social media platforms (Pinto & Gutelius, 2021).

Effectiveness

The effectiveness of government policies in stemming the expansion of COVID-19 will be hotly debated, and it will take some time for researchers and scientists to come to terms regarding how beneficial masks, social distancing, business closures, and other efforts have been at abatement. Unfortunately, the assumptions of effectiveness will likely be heavily politicized in the same way that following precautions and other aspects of the COVID-19 response have been. Only time will tell of the effectiveness of vaccines and whether the ones that have been developed will assist in providing protection against variant strains of the virus.

Much will be studied once the virus is under control, which will hopefully help not just the United States but other nations to better prepare for future epidemics. Indeed, one of the most problematic features of the pandemic is that it has demonstrated in clear terms that even the wealthiest and most scientifically advanced nations may be brought to their knees by a worldwide medical crisis. It is especially important that lessons are learned from the pandemic because we not only face the possibility of other "natural" epidemics but the specter of chemical or biological warfare or terrorism is always a concern (Mackelprang et al., 2005; White, 2002).

The pandemic has also "exposed existing inequalities . . . and [also] created new ones" given that African Americans, Native Americans, and other minority populations have been more apt to be killed or otherwise feel the adverse effects of the virus (Baird, 2020, p. 16; Chaney, 2020). Many of those classified as "essential workers" (for example, delivery drivers, grocery clerks, hospital housekeepers) have included people who have been paid poorly and provided few benefits (Chaney, 2020; Pinto & Gutelius, 2021). Many other low-wage workers have been left unemployed by business disruptions and closures because of COVID-19.

Some critics of "closing" have expressed the belief that the pandemic has been blown out of proportion; that the negative economic consequences of closures will seriously harm the nation; that most of the elderly and vulnerable people dying from the disease were close to death even before contracting COVID; or even that the cause of death was wrongly attributed to COVID for financial, political, or other reasons. The dehumanization of elderly people or people with disabilities has been a constant refrain in many pandemic discussions.

Analysis Element: Sphere of Authority

Although chapter 2 considered government involvement and questions about whether the private sector or government should respond to certain problems or needs, here, we are looking at which level of government should have authority over specific policy areas. Although the federal government has primary control over many of the policies described in this book, it is often required to work in conjunction with states, whereas some policies are primarily in the states' hands, and others, such as education funding and policy, require coordination among federal, state, and local governments.

The COVID-19 crisis has pointed to the fact that in regard to some issues, there is no clear delineation over who should have authority. Under President Trump, the federal government largely left decisions up to the states and local governments. One problem related to this is that an epidemic does not respect city, state, or regional boundaries. Therefore, lax policies in one area of the nation (or even one part of a region) may have had a detrimental effect on others. Nations could, and have, limited incoming travel because of the pandemic, but states and cities really cannot do that.

Over the course of the pandemic, many communities and counties have refused to follow their own state guidelines, often for partially politically motivated reasons, and many businesses have refused to follow either state- or citywide requirements. It has been unclear who has the ability to make decisions, and those who have had the authority have frequently been treated as if that authority were not sanctioned or lawful. Law enforcement authorities have been wary of becoming the "COVID police" and being called every time someone in a store refuses to wear a mask. Furthermore, because of a lack of enforcement, many regulations simply have not been followed. The rollout of the vaccine could best be described as uncoordinated and haphazard.

In short, poor planning, a lack of direction, politization, and controversy over the decisions made at multiple governmental levels have exacerbated the pandemic and added to the anxiety that it has caused. The full scope of the problems related to the COVID-19 response is still to be determined, although we can be certain that many books will be written with details about it. As often is the case, however, it has been those at the margins of society who have primarily paid the price for a lack of leadership and planning.

CHAPTER 43

Black Lives Matter Movement

◖2020◗

Historical Overview and Nature of the Social Problem

Although the BLM movement is not an actual policy, it certainly will have policy implications at multiple governmental levels, and its importance is such that including a chapter on it seems imperative. As with COVID-19, it is difficult at this point to speculate what the specific policy implications of this movement may be or even at what level of government these changes will come about. But we can make some educated guesses about the broad effects of the movement and the potential effect on social work education and practice.

Without wanting to be too flippant about something that is serious, perhaps an apt metaphor to describe BLM is the image of Russian nesting dolls. At its core, the movement is a reaction to police response, especially killings, of African Americans and of Black males, in particular. This is a part of a larger issue that includes the War on Drugs, mass incarceration of Black men, and racial discrimination within the criminal justice system (Alexander, 2010; Davis, 2018). At a broader level is the contemporary maltreatment of African Americans and other minorities, which takes into account both overt and implicit racism. Enclosing and giving additional contextual meaning to all of this is the deeply disconcerting history of oppression, discrimination, exploitation, and dehumanization of African Americans in the United States.

The BLM movement, then, both is and is not about confrontations between African Americans and the police and the fate of George Floyd and others because of such confrontations. Because there is not space within a brief chapter to provide an overview of the long history of oppression against Black people, the following section primarily focuses on the central issue: the treatment of African Americans within the criminal justice system. As P. Copeland (2016) noted, "Beyond policing, the [BLM] Movement is confronting the systemic violence of mass-criminalization, mass-incarceration, and mass-detention and deportation" of those who are Black and other minorities (p. 5). Various additional chapters, including chapters 14, 24, and 30, all provide additional context for the BLM movement.

Movement Overview

Confrontations between law enforcement officers and African Americans are long-standing and have often led to social activism, mass organizing, demonstrations, or investigations (Hattery & Smith, 2018); yet, they have taken on particular importance with the increased availability of recording capability. Cell phones allow the capturing of visual images of events, as with George Floyd's death, which serves to focus public attention on individual cases.

Policies such as stop and frisk and racial profiling have fed the anger many Black people feel (Hinton, 2016). Such laws or surveillance activities are perceived to be racist and directed primarily at African American males (Hattery & Smith, 2018). In her 2010 book, *The New Jim Crow*, Michelle Alexander discussed the widespread incarceration of Black men, often for low-level drug offenses. The imprisonment of Black males grew extensively, starting in the 1980s, largely because of the President Ronald Reagan administration's harsh drug and crime policies. Importantly, even after leaving prison, ex-felons are severely limited in their ability to attain higher education or get a job; therefore, they are likely to resort to criminal activities. Added to this are the numerous public policies over the past century that have purposefully benefited suburban areas to the detriment of inner-city areas and that have often supported de facto discrimination, leaving many Black Americans with few employment opportunities and a decaying and toxic infrastructure (Hinton, 2016)

Although other deaths or beatings previously had led to calls for action and protests, the case of Michael Brown, Jr., in Ferguson, Missouri, particularly energized the BLM movement (Wolfe & Nix, 2015). In 2014, as a result of Brown's killing by officer Darren Wilson (in self-defense, according to the police), a lengthy demonstration took place in Ferguson (Bradley, Pulphus, & Jones, 2015). Although mainly peaceful, this protest turned violent at times. Movement leaders contended that the highly militant response of law enforcement played a strong role in "ramping up" emotions and exacerbated the potential for violence. The national media focused its gaze on Ferguson for several days, and some cable channels, such as CNN, provided continuous coverage.

A grand jury was convened but refused to indict the officer (Wright, 2018). As a result of Brown's death and the subsequent demonstrations, the U.S. Department of Justice investigated conditions in Ferguson and, in 2015, issued a report that set out recommendations for changes in law enforcement and the judiciary system (Hattery & Smith, 2018; U.S. Department of Justice, 2015). Unfortunately, the continuing need for investigations and reports demonstrates the staying power of this problem. For example, the Kerner Commission was formed following protests in the late 1960s and, at the time, noted that the nation was "moving toward two societies, one black, one white, separate and unequal" (cited in Adedoyin et al., 2019, p. 112). A similar investigation followed the 1991 beating of Rodney King in Los Angeles and other such cases. There is good reason to assume that once the media spotlight is removed and volatility lessens, things will return to a disconcerting and unstable version of "normalcy."

Potential Effects

Many states have passed policies designed to reform those areas of the criminal justice and judicial system that have a disproportionally adverse effect on African Americans (P. Copeland, 2016). Most such proposals are opposed by law enforcement authorities. Among the most contentious is the creation of citizen review boards to oversee police response with minorities. BLM supporters have contended that law enforcement authorities protect one another and cannot be counted on to hold their fellow officers accountable. They also have contended that prosecutors, who rely on good relations with law enforcement, are also often unwilling to hold law enforcement officers accountable. The demand for citizen review boards, therefore, is an effort to engage a panel of people outside of law enforcement to review engagement and police procedures.

The BLM movement has much pertinence to the social work profession. With our grounding in social activism and social justice, members of the profession need to be key players in efforts to support egalitarian treatment of African Americans and other minorities. Social workers are especially aware of issues, such as intersectionality, historical maltreatment, and implicit bias, and should be at the forefront of educating others about these issues and their relevance to BLM (Haley, 2020).

Recently, the call to "defund the police" has become particularly contentious. The term itself is contentious even among those supporting reform. Change in what we envision as the role of police affects the social work profession; for example, one recommendation is for social workers or other mental health professionals to respond to certain emergency calls or to act in conjunction with law enforcement personnel in such situations. Too often in the past, social work engagement with minorities has frequently supported systemic racism, often without professionals even being consciously aware of it. As Haley (2020) wrote, "Social work education and training overemphasize biomedical and psychological approaches that have failed to bring significant progress toward eradicating health inequities" among those who are marginalized (p. 12).

Some of the Department of Justice's recommendations in its report on Ferguson not only pertained to the need for reforms within law enforcement but also considered historical problems that set the stage for a contentious relationship between police and minority citizens. As with many suburban communities, Ferguson was developed as a "Whites only" community, and numerous federal (and other) policies, along with de facto discrimination ensured that the community would remain segregated for decades (Rothstein, 2014, 2017). As the community became more integrated, "White flight" occurred in much of the city when many businesses and citizens moved. This left the city with much smaller tax revenues, which it attempted to make up for through arrests (U.S. Department of Justice, 2015). As one might presume, these arrests, fines, and bail costs fell heavily on Black Americans living in Ferguson and surrounding communities.

Therefore, short-term policy changes need to take place, such as body-worn cameras and review of police engagement activities (such as choke holds). In addition, however, are more long-term issues that macro-level social workers have focused on for decades, such as community development within high poverty areas, racial bias training with schools and elsewhere, and expungement policies related to those who have been convicted of felonies. Again, BLM is about interactions between law enforcement personnel and African Americans, but it is also about much more.

References

Aaron, H. J., Lambrew, J. M., & Healy, P. F. (2008). *Reforming Medicare: Options, tradeoffs, and opportunities*. Washington, DC: Brookings Institution Press.

Abbott, E. (1924). *Immigration: Selected documents and case records*. Chicago: University of Chicago Press.

Abbott, E., & Breckinridge, S. P. (1921). *The administration of the Aid-to-Mothers law in Illinois*. Washington, DC: U.S. Government Printing Office.

Abramovitz, M. (1988). *Regulating the lives of women: Social welfare policy from colonial times to the present*. Boston: South End Press.

Abramovitz, M. (2005). The largely untold story of welfare reform and the human services. *Social Work, 50*, 175–186.

Abrams, D. E. (2003). *A very special place in life: The history of juvenile justice in Missouri*. Jefferson City: Missouri Juvenile Justice Association.

Ackerman, A. R., & Furman, R. (2012). Community based management for sex offenders in the US: An evidence based evaluation. *International Journal of Criminal Justice Sciences, 7*, 591–604.

Adedoyin, A. C., Moore, S. E., Robinson, M. A., Clayton, D. M., Boamah, D. A., & Harmon, D. K. (2019). The dehumanization of Black males by police: Teaching social justice—Black life really does matter. *Journal of Teaching in Social Work, 39*, 111–131.

Adelman, M., & Morgan, P. (2006). Law enforcement versus battered women: The conflict over the Lautenberg Amendment. *Affilia: Journal of Women and Social Work, 21*, 28–45.

Adoption Assistance and Child Welfare Act of 1980, P.L. 96-272, 94 Stat. 500 (1980).

Adler-Greene, L. (2019). Every Student Succeeds Act: Are schools making sure every student succeeds? *Touro Law Review, 35*, 11–23.

Adoption and Safe Families Act of 1997, P.L. 105-89, 111 Stat. 2115 (1997).

Age Discrimination in Employment Act of 1967, P.L. 90-202, 81 Stat. 602 (1967).

Aguilar, C. E., & Richerme, L. K. (2014). What is everyone saying about teacher evaluation? Framing the intended and inadvertent causes and consequences of Race to the Top. *Arts Education Policy Review, 115*, 110–120.

Aikman, D. (1936, May). The WPA racket in Pennsylvania. *American Mercury, 28*(149), 28–35.

Air Pollution Control Act of 1955, P.L. 84-159, 69 Stat. 322 (1955).

Alaska Native Claims Settlement Act of 1971, P.L. 92-203, 85 Stat. 688 (1971).

Alexander, M. (2010). *The new Jim Crow: Mass incarceration in the age of color blindness*. New York: New Press.

Alexander, R., Jr. (2000). Civil commitment of sex offenders to mental institutions: Should the standard be based on serious mental illness or mental disorder? *Journal of Health and Social Policy, 11*, 67–68.

Alexander, R., Jr., & Alexander, C. L. (1995). The impact of *Suter v. Artist M.* on foster care policy. *Social Work, 40*, 543–548.

Alexander-Eitzman, B., Pollio, D. E., & North, C. S. (2013, January 14). The neighborhood context of homelessness. *American Journal of Public Health, 103*, 679–685.

Altmeyer, A. J. (1966). *The formative years of Social Security.* Madison: University of Wisconsin Press.

Altschuler, G. C., & Blumin, S. M. (2009). *The GI Bill: A new deal for veterans.* Oxford, England: Oxford University Press.

Altshuler, S. (2007). Everything you never wanted to know about special education … and were afraid to ask (I.D.E.A.). *Journal of Social Work in Disability and Rehabilitation, 6*, 23–33.

Altshuler, S. J., & Schmautz, T. (2006). No Hispanic student left behind: The consequences of "high stakes" testing. *Children & Schools, 28*, 5–14.

American Psychiatric Association. (2013). *Diagnostic and statistical manual of mental disorders* (5th ed.). Washington, DC: Author.

Americans with Disabilities Act of 1990, P.L. 101-336, 42 U.S.C. § 12101 et seq. (1990).

Anderson, E. A., & Koblinsky, S. A. (1995). Homeless policy: The need to speak to families. *Family Relations, 44*, 13–18.

Anderson, P. M. (1997). Continuing eligibility: Current labor market attachment. In C. J. O'Leary & S. A. Wander (Eds.), *Unemployment insurance in the United States: Analysis of policy issues* (pp. 125–157). Kalamazoo, MI: W. E. Upjohn Institute for Employment Research.

Andrews, C. M., Darnell, J. S., McBride, T. D., & Gehlert, S. (2013). Social work and implementation of the Affordable Care Act. *Health & Social Work, 38*, 67–71.

Andrias, K. (2019, Spring). A seat at the table: Sectoral bargaining for the common good. *Dissent, 66*(2), 30–36.

Androff, D. K., & Tavassoli, K. Y. (2012). Deaths in the desert: The human rights crisis on the U.S.–Mexico border. *Social Work, 57*, 165–173.

Anti-Drug Abuse Act of 1986, P.L. 99-570, 100 Stat. 3207 (1986).

Anti-Drug Abuse Act of 1988, P.L. 100-690, 102 Stat. 4181 (1988).

Anti-Negro Covenants II. (1947, August). *American City, 62*, 125–127.

Applebaum, R., & Payne, M. (2005, Spring). How Supplemental Security Income works. *Generations, 29*(1), 27–29.

Arena, J. (2012). *Driven from New Orleans: How nonprofits betray public housing and promote privatization.* Minneapolis: University of Minnesota Press.

Arsenault, R. (2011). *Freedom Riders: 1961 and the struggle for racial justice* (Rev. and abridged ed.). New York: Oxford University Press.

Azzi-Lessing, L. (2010). Growing together: Expanding roles for social work practice in early childhood settings. *Social Work, 55*, 255–263.

Bachman, S. S., & Gonyea, J. G. (2012). Improving health care delivery to aging adults with disabilities: Social work with dual eligible in a climate of health care reform. *Journal of Gerontological Social Work, 55*, 191–207.

Baird, V. (2020, September 3). Lessons from the pandemic. *New Internationalist.* Retrieved from https://newint.org/features/2020/08/11/big-story-covid-19-lessons-pandemic

Bakk, L. (2015). Medicare Part D coverage gap: Race, gender and cost-related medication nonadherence. *Social Work in Public Health, 30*, 473–485.

Baldwin, R. N. (1944). The Japanese-Americans in wartime. *American Mercury, 59*, 665–670.

Ball, R. M. (1998). Reflections on how Medicare came about. In R. D. Reischauer, S. Butler, & J. Lave (Eds.), *Medicare: Preparing for the challenges of the 21st century* (pp. 27–37). Washington, DC: National Academy of Social Insurance.

Barnes, A. R., Constantine Brown, J. L., & McCarty-Caplan, D. (2019). The unintended consequence of the Indian Child Welfare Act: American Indian trust in public child welfare. *Children and Youth Services Review, 98*, 221–227.

Bartik, T. J. (2001). *Jobs for the poor: Can labor demand policies help?* New York: Russell Sage Foundation.

Bates, V. E. (1966). Social work and Head Start: Toward an operational definition. *Child Welfare, 45*(2), 74–80.

Bauer, Y. (1994). *Jews for sale? Nazi–Jewish negotiations, 1933–1945.* New Haven, CT: Yale University Press.

Beck, R. (2015). *We believe the children: A moral panic in the 1980s.* New York: Public Affairs.

Beers, C. W. (1930). *A mind that found itself* (5th ed.). Garden City, NY: Doubleday, Doran.

Begos, K., Deaver, D., Railey, J., & Sexton, S. (2012). *Against their will: North Carolina's sterilization program and the campaign for reparations.* Apalachicola, FL: Gray Oak Books.

Béland, D. (2003). *Social Security: History and politics from the New Deal to the privatization debate.* Lawrence: University Press of Kansas.

Bendetsen, K. R. (1942). The Japanese evacuation: Democracy protects basic rights of evacuees. *Vital Speeches of the Day, 8*, 541–544.

Bennett, L. W. (1995). Substance abuse and the domestic assault of women. *Social Work, 40*, 760–771.

Berkowitz, C. D. (2010). Sex offender registration: Balancing the rights of the individual with the public good—A commentary on Comartin, Kernsmith & Miles (2010). *Journal of Child Sexual Abuse, 19*, 226–230.

Bertram, E., Blachman, M., Sharpe, K., & Andreas, P. (1996). *Drug war politics: The price of denial.* Berkeley: University of California Press.

Berzin, S. C., & O'Connor, S. (2010). Educating today's school social workers: Are school social work courses responding to the changing context? *Children & Schools, 32*, 237–249.

Beverly, S. G. (2002). What social workers need to know about the Earned Income Tax Credit. *Social Work*, 47, 259–266.

Bevington, D. (2009). *The rebirth of environmentalism: Grassroots activism from the spotted owl to the polar bear*. Washington, DC: Island Press.

Biggerstaff, M. A., Morris, P. M., & Nichols-Casebolt, A. (2002). Living on the edge: Examination of people attending food pantries and soup kitchens. *Social Work, 47*, 267–277.

Blahous, C. P., III. (2000). *Reforming Social Security for ourselves and our posterity*. Westport, CT: Praeger.

Bland, T. S. (1999). Managing employee absenteeism: Interplay of the ADA, FMLA, and workers' compensation. *Labor Law Journal, 50*, 156–167.

Blaustein, S. J., Cohen, W. J., & Haber, W. (1993). *Unemployment insurance in the United States: The first half century*. Kalamazoo, MI: W. E. Upjohn Institute for Employment Research.

Blaustein, S. J., O'Leary, C. J., & Wander, S. A. (1997). Policy issues: An overview. In C. J. O'Leary & S. A. Wander (Eds.), *Unemployment insurance in the United States: Analysis of policy issues* (pp. 1–43). Kalamazoo, MI: W. E. Upjohn Institute for Employment Research.

Bliss, D. L., & Meehan, J. (2008). Blueprint for creating a social work-centered disaster relief initiative. *Journal of Social Service Research, 34*, 73–85.

Board of Education of the Hendrick Hudson Central School District v. Rowley, 458 U.S. 176 (1982).

Bold, C. (1999). *The WPA Guides: Mapping America*. Jackson: University Press of Mississippi.

Boulton, M. (2014). *Failing our veterans: The G.I. Bill and the Vietnam generation*. New York: New York University Press.

Bowen, E. A., & Redmond, H. (2016). Teaching note—No peace without justice: Addressing the United States' war on drugs in social work education. *Journal of Social Work Education, 52*, 503–508.

Bowman, S. W. (2018). The kids are alright: Making a case for abolition of the juvenile justice system. *Critical Criminology, 26*, 393–405.

Boyd, D. J. (1998). Medicaid devolution: A fiscal perspective. In F. J. Thompson & J. J. DiIulio, Jr. (Eds.), *Medicaid and devolution: A view from the states* (pp. 56–105). Washington, DC: Brookings Institution Press.

Boyle, J. R., & Weishaar, M. (2001). *Special education law with cases*. Boston: Allyn & Bacon.

Bradley, S. M., Pulphus, J., & Jones, J. (2015). Ferguson, USA: A scholar's unforeseen connection and collision with history. *Western Journal of Black Studies, 39*, 273–280.

Brady Handgun Violence Prevention Act, P.L. 103-159, 107 Stat. 1536 (1994).

Brannon, Y. N., Levenson, J. S., Fortney, T., & Baker, J. N. (2007). Attitudes about community notification of sexual offenders and the non-offending public. *Sex Abuse, 19*, 369–379.

Bratt, R. G. (1994). *Rebuilding a low-income housing policy.* Philadelphia: Temple University Press.

Brodyn, A. (2019). Family feuds: The relationships between legal changes and media framing concerning the family. *Sociological Quarterly, 60*, 606–627.

Brooks, R. L. (2004). *Atonement and forgiveness: A new model for Black reparations.* Berkeley: University of California Press.

Brophy, A. L. (2006). *Reparations pro & con.* New York: Oxford University Press.

Brown, L. D. (1990). The medically uninsured: Problems, policies, and politics. *Journal of Health Policy, Politics and Law, 15*, 413–426.

Brown, T. J. (1996). Franklin Pierce's land grant veto and the Kansas–Nebraska session of Congress. *Civil War History, 42*, 95–115.

Brown, T. J. (1998). *Dorothea Dix: New England reformer.* Cambridge, MA: Harvard University Press.

Brown v. Board of Education, 347 U.S. 483 (1954).

Buck v. Bell, 274 US 200 (1927).

Buell, R. L. (1923). The development of anti-Japanese agitation in the United States II. *Political Science Quarterly, 38*, 57–81.

Bullard, R. D. (2002). Anatomy of environmental racism. In E. Hofrichter (Ed.), *Toxic struggles: The theory of practice of environmental justice* (pp. 25–35). Salt Lake City: University of Utah Press.

Burke, V. J. (1974). *Nixon's good deed: Welfare reform.* New York: Columbia University Press.

Burkhauser, R. V., & Daly, M. C. (2017). The Supplemental Security Income Disabled Children Program: Improving employment outcomes in adulthood. In R. Doar (Ed.), *A safety net that works: Improving federal programs for low-income Americans* (pp. 147–159). Washington, DC: American Enterprise Institute.

Burnes, D., Henderson, C. R., Sheppard, C., Zhao, R., Pillemer, L., & Lachs, M. S. (2017). Prevalence of financial fraud and scams among older adults in the United States: A systematic review and meta-analysis. *American Journal of Public Health, 107*, e13–e21.

Burt, E. V. (2004). *The Progressive Era: Primary documents from 1890–1914.* Westport, CT: Greenwood Press.

Bussey, M., & Lucero, N. M. (2013). Re-examining child welfare's response to ICWA: Collaborating with community-based agencies to reduce disparities for American/Alaskan Native children. *Children and Youth Services Review, 35*, 394–401.

Butler, E. (2004). The legislation takes away basic rights. In R. H. Mayer (Ed.), *The Civil Rights Act of 1964* (pp. 66–70). San Diego: Greenhaven Press.

Cacho, L., & Saviano, R. (2014). *Slavery, Inc.: The untold story of international sex trafficking*. New York: Counterpoint Press.

California's anti-Japanese campaign. (1920, July 31). *The Literary Digest, 66*, 14–15.

Carlson, A., & Senauer, B. (2003). The impact of the Special Supplemental Nutrition Program for Women, Infants, and Children on child health. *American Journal on Agricultural Economics, 85*, 479–491.

Carlson, B. E., Stromwall, L. K., & Lietz, C. A. (2013). Mental health issues in recently returning women veterans: Implications for practice. *Social Work*, 58, 105–114.

Carson, R. (1962). *Silent spring*. Boston: Houghton Mifflin.

Carter, E. W., Brock, M. E., & Trainor, A. A. (2014). Transition assessment and planning for youth with severe intellectual and developmental disabilities. *Journal of Special Education, 47*, 245–255.

Carter, G. L. (1997). *The gun control movement*. New York: Twayne Publishers.

Cassel, C. K. (2005). *Medicare matters: What geriatric medicine can teach American health care*. Berkeley: University of California Press.

Ceglowski, D. (1998). *Inside a Head Start center: Developing policies from practice*. New York: Teachers College Press.

Centers for Disease Control and Prevention. (n.d.). *United States COVID-19 cases, deaths, and laboratory testing (NAATs) by state, territory, and jurisdiction* [Maps, charts, and data provided by CDC, updated Mon-Sat by 8 pm ET]. https://covid.cdc.gov/covid-data-tracker/#cases_casesper100klast7days

Certo, N. J., Luecking, R. G., Murphy, S., Brown, L., Courey, S., & Belanger, D. (2008). Seamless transition and longer-term support for individuals with severe intellectual disabilities. *Research and Practice for Persons with Severe Disabilities, 22*, 85–95.

Cesnales, N. L., Thyer, B. A., & Albright, D. L. (2017). Differences in health-related quality of life among persons living with HIV/AIDS. *Journal of Human Behavior in the Social Environment, 27*, 198–205.

Chamberlain, P., & Moore, K. (2000). Models of community treatment for serious juvenile offenders. In J. Crane (Ed.), *Social programs that work* (pp. 258–276). New York: Russell Sage Foundation.

Chaney, C. (2020). Family stress and coping among African Americans in the age of COVID-19. *Journal of Comparative Family Studies, 51*, 254–273.

Chanmugam, A., Kemter, A. J., & Goodwin, K. H. (2015). Exceptional services for children in domestic violence shelters: Perspectives of shelter personnel. *Child and Adolescent Social Work Journal, 32*, 405–415.

Child Abuse Prevention Act, 1973: Hearings Before the Subcommittee on Children and Youth of the Committee on Labor and Public Welfare, United States Senate, 93rd Congress, 1st Session. (1973). Washington, DC: U.S. Government Printing Office. Retrieved from https://files.eric.ed.gov/fulltext/ED081507.pdf

Child Abuse Prevention and Treatment Act, P.L. 93-247, 88 Stat. 4 (1974).

Chinese Exclusion Act of 1882, P.L. 47-126, 22 Stat. 58 (1882).

Chipungu, S. S. (2003). Child welfare policies and African-American families. In T. Bent-Goodley (Ed.), *African-American social workers and social policy* (pp. 55–68). New York: Haworth Social Work Practice Press.

Chisholm, J. F. (2006). Cyberspace violence against girls and adolescent females. In F. L. Denmark, H. H. Krause, E. Halpern, & J. A. Sechzer (Eds.), *Violence and exploitation against women and girls* (pp. 74–88). Boston: Blackwell.

Civil Rights Act of 1964, P.L. 88-352, 78 Stat. 241, 42 U.S.C. §§ 1981–2000.

Civil Rights—Public Accommodations: Hearings Before the Committee on Commerce, United States Senate, 88th Congress, 1st Session. (1963, July 1). [Testimony of Attorney General Robert Kennedy.] Washington, DC: U.S Government Printing Office.

Cohen, A. (2009). *Nothing to fear: FDR's inner circle and the hundred days that created modern America.* New York: Penguin Books.

Cohen, J., Segal, D. R., & Temme, L. V. (1992). The impact of education on Vietnam-era veterans' occupational attainment. *Social Science Quarterly, 73*, 397–409.

Cole, N. L. (2021). The school-to-prison pipeline has caused great harm to communities of color. In L. Sorensen (Ed.), *The prison industrial complex* (pp. 95–104). New York: Greenhaven.

Colello, K. J. (2011). Older Americans Act: Title III Nutrition Services Program. In J. N. Palamino (Ed.), *The Older Americans Act: Provisions, funding and programs* (pp. 35–45). New York: Nova Science.

Coleman-Jensen, A. J. (2010). U.S. food insecurity status: Toward a refined definition. *Social Indicators Research, 95*, 215–230.

Colker, R. (2013). *Disabled education: A critical analysis of the Individuals with Disabilities Education Act.* New York: New York University Press.

Collier, C. W. (2013, Summer). Gun control in America: An autopsy report. *Dissent, 60*(3), 81–86.

Comartin, E. B., Kernsmith, P. D., & Kernsmith, R. M. (2009). Sanctions for sex offenders: Fear and public policy. *Journal of Offender Rehabilitation, 48*, 605–619.

Community Mental Health Centers Act, P.L. 88-164, 77 Stat. 290 (1963).

Comprehensive Drug Abuse Prevention and Control Act of 1970, P.L. 91-513, 84 Stat. 1236 (1970).

Comprehensive Education and Training Act of 1974, P.L. 93-203, 87 Stat. 839 (1974).

Comprehensive Environmental Response, Compensation, and Liability Act, P.L. 96-510, 94 Stat. 2767 (1980).

Copeland, C. W. (2012). Rulemaking requirements and authorities in the Patient Protections and Affordable Care Act (PPACA). In R. Kipp & V. Caputo (Eds.), Rules and rulemaking in the Patient Protection and Affordable Care Act (pp. 1–32). New York: Nova Science.

Copeland, P. (2016). Let's get free: Social work and the movement for Black lives. *Journal of Forensic Social Work, 5*, 3–19.

Coronavirus Aid, Relief, and Economic Security Act, P.L. 116-136, 134 Stat. 281 (2020).

Coyle, D. C. (1939, March). The WPA—Loafers or workers? *Forum and Century,* pp. 170–174. Available from WPA Records, Records of the Statistics Division, Entry 27, Box 40, National Archives II in College Park, MD.

Crook, C. (2015). Educating America's homeless youth through reinforcement of the McKinney-Vento Homeless Assistance Act. *Faulkner Law Review, 6,* 395–408.

Cross, E. L. (2020). COVID-19 journal entry: The perspective of a bachelor of science social work student in field placement. *Reflections, 26,* 41–44.

Cross, S. L. (2006). Indian family exception doctrine. Still losing children despite the Indian Child Welfare Act. *Child Welfare, 85,* 671–690.

Culpin, M. (1920). *Psychoneuroses of war and peace.* Cambridge, England: Cambridge University Press.

Curran, T. J. (1975). *Xenophobia and immigration, 1820–1930.* Boston: Twayne.

d'Amora, D. (2016, November/December). SNAP judgment. *Mother Jones,* 14–16.

D'Angelo, K, Libal, K, Seymour, N., & Hamel, R. (2017). After the "Great Recession": Excluding "able-bodied" adults from food entitlements in the United States. *Journal of Policy Practice, 16,* 452–471.

Daniels, R., & Kitano, H.H.L. (1970). *American racism: Exploration of the nature of prejudice.* Englewood Cliffs, NJ: Prentice Hall.

Darnell, J. S. (2013). Navigators and assisters: Two case management roles for social workers in the Affordable Care Act. *Health & Social Work, 38,* 123–126.

Davis, A. J. (1930). The evolution of the institution of Mothers' Pensions in the United States. *American Journal of Sociology, 35,* 573–587.

Davis, A. J. (Ed.). (2018). *Policing the Black man: Arrest, prosecution, and imprisonment.* New York: Vintage Books.

Day, P. D. (2006). *A new history of social welfare* (5th ed.). Boston: Allyn & Bacon.

DeConde, A. (2001). *Gun violence in America: The struggle for control.* Boston: Northeastern University Press.

Defense of Marriage Act of 1996, P.L. 104-199, 110 Stat. 2419 (1996).

Deford, M. A. (1935). The Japanese in Hawaii. *American Mercury, 35,* 332–340.

Delavega, E. (2016). The Earned Income Tax Credit: Estimating non-claims rates among eligible participants and why it matters to social workers. *Journal of Policy Practice, 15,* 145–161.

DeLiema, M., Navarro, A., Enguidanos, S., & Wilber, K. (2015). Voices from the frontline: Examining elder abuse from multiple professional perspectives. *Health & Social Work, 40,* e15–e24.

Dempsey, J. X., & Kerr, O. (2005). Sections 209, 212, and 220: Access to wire and electronic communications. In S. A. Baker J. Kavanagh (Eds.), *Patriot debates: Experts debate the USA Patriot Act* (pp. 31–44). Chicago: American Bar Association.

Deutsch, A. (1973). *The shame of the states* (reprint). New York: Arno Press. (Original work published 1948)

DiNitto, D. M. (2005). *Social welfare: Politics and public policy* (6th ed.). Boston: Pearson Education.

Dix, D. L. (1863). Memorial of Miss Dix. In *Reports of the Illinois State Hospital for the Insane, 1847–1862* (pp. 2–34). Chicago: F. Fulton.

Dix, D. L. (1976). Memorial to the legislature of Massachusetts, 1843. In M. Rosen, G. R. Clark, & M. S. Kivitz (Eds.), *The history of mental retardation: Collected papers* (Vol. 1, pp. 4–30). Baltimore: University Park Press. (Original work published 1843)

Dixon, L., & Goldman, H. (2004). Forty years of progress in community mental health: The role of evidence-based practices. *Administration and Policy in Mental Health, 31*, 381–392.

Does Housing First work? (2020, May). *Congressional Digest, 99*(5), 10–12.

Dolgoff, R., & Feldstein, D. (2007). *Understanding social welfare: A search for social justice* (3rd ed.). Boston: Pearson.

Domestic Violence Offender Gun Ban (Lautenberg Amendment), P.L. 104-208, 110 Stat. 3001 (1996).

Domhoff, G. W. (2009). The little-known origins of the Social Security Act: How and why corporate moderates created old-age insurance. In L. Rogne, C. L. Estes, B. R. Grossman, B. A. Hollister, & E. Solway (Eds.), *Social insurance and social justice: Social Security, Medicare, and the campaign against entitlements* (pp. 47–59). New York: Springer.

Donley, A. M., & Wright, J. D. (2018). The health of the homeless. *Sociology Compass, 12*(1), Article e12550.

Douglas, P. H. (1936). *Social Security in the United States: An analysis and appraisal of the federal Social Security Act*. New York: Whittlesey House.

Downey, K. (2009). *The woman behind the New Deal: The life and legacy of Frances Perkins—Social Security, unemployment insurance and the minimum wage*. New York: Anchor Books.

Dreier, P., Mollenkopf, J., & Swanstrom, T. (2004). *Place matters: Metropolitics for the twenty-first century* (2nd ed.). Lawrence: University Press of Kansas.

Drew, E. (1999). *The corruption of American politics: What went wrong and why*. Woodstock, NY: Overlook Press.

Dreyfuss, R. (1996, November/December). The end of Social Security as we know it? *Mother Jones,* 51–52, 54–58.

Drimmer, J. C. (1993). Cripples, overcomers, and civil rights: Tracing the evolution of federal legislation and social policy for people with disabilities. *UCLA Law Review, 40*, 1341–1410.

Drug-Free Workplace Act of 1988, P.L. 100-690, 102 Stat. 4304 (1988).

Dudziak, M. (1986). Oliver Wendell Holmes as a eugenic reformer: Rhetoric in the writing of constitutional law. *Iowa Law Review, 71*, 833–867.

Duke, J. (2010). Exploring homeowner opposition to public housing developments. *Journal of Sociology and Social Welfare, 37*, 49–74.

Earned Income Tax Credit, P.L. 94-12, 89 Stat. 32 (1975).

Economic Opportunity Act of 1964, P.L. 88-452, 78 Stat. 508 (1964).

Edsforth, R. (2000). *The New Deal: America's response to the Great Depression*. Malden, MA: Wiley-Blackwell.

Education for All Handicapped Children Act of 1975, P.L. 94-142, 89 Stat. 773.

Edwards, A. L., & Few-Demo, A. L. (2014). Implementing ASFA with vulnerable African American families: A community capacity approach. *Child Welfare, 93*, 27–43.

Eigenberg, H. M. (2001). *Woman battering in the United States: Till death do us part*. Prospect Heights, IL: Waveland Press.

88 Cong. Rec. Pt. 1, 1419–1420 (1942, February 18).

88 Cong. Rec. Pt. 2, 1565 (1942, February 24).

Elementary and Secondary Education Act of 1965, P.L. 89-313, 20 U.S.C. §§ 2701–3386.

El-Hai, J. (2005). *The lobotomist: A maverick medical genius and his tragic quest to rid the world of mental illness*. Hoboken, NJ: Wiley.

Ellwood, W. N. (1994). *Rhetoric in the war on drugs: The triumphs and tragedies of public relations*. Westport, CT: Praeger.

Emergency Immigration Act of 1921, P.L. 67-5, 42 Stat. 5.

Employment Non-Discrimination Act of 1995, H.R. 1863. Retrieved from https://www.congress.gov/bill/104th-congress/house-bill/1863

ENDA Overview: Sexual orientation and gender identity discrimination. (2013, December). *Congressional Digest, 92*(10). Retrieved from http://congressionaldigest.com/issue/lgbt-rights-in-the-workplace/enda-overview/

End of the "melting-pot" theory. (1924, June 7). *The Literary Digest, 81*, 15.

Erickson, P. E. (2000). Federal child abuse and child neglect policy in the United States since 1974: A review and critique. *Criminal Justice Review, 25*, 77–92.

Erwin, M. J., Gershon, R.R.M., Tiburzi, M., & Lin, S. (2005). Reports of intimate partner violence made against police officers. *Journal of Family Violence, 20*, 13–19.

Estes, C. L., Rogne, L., Grossman, B. R., Solway, E., & Hollister, B. A. (2009). Introduction: We're all in this together: Social insurance, social justice and social change. In L. Rogne, C. L. Estes, B. R. Grossman, B. A. Hollister, & E. Solway (Eds.), *Social insurance and social justice: Social Security, Medicare, and the campaign against entitlements* (pp. xxv–xxxi). New York: Springer.

Estey, J. A. (1937, March 1). Unemployment insurance and the mobility of labor. *Social Forces*, 417–422.

Every Student Succeeds Act, P.L. 114-95, 129 Stat. 1802 (2015).

Faber, D., & O'Connor, J. (2002). Capitalism and the crisis of environmentalism. In E. Hofrichter (Ed.), *Toxic struggles: The theory of practice of environmental justice* (pp. 12–23). Salt Lake City: University of Utah Press.

Fair Housing Act of 1968, P.L. 90-284, 82 Stat. 73 (1968).

Fair Labor Standards Act of 1938, P.L. 75-718, 52 Stat. 1060 (1938).

Family and Medical Leave Act, P.L. 103-3, 107 Stat. 6 (1993).

Family Support Act, P.L. 100-485, 102 Stat. 2343 (1988).

Federal Food and Drugs Act of 1906, 34 Stat. 768, Chapter 3915 (1906).

Federal Insurance Contributions Act, 26 U.S.C. 3128 (1954).

Federal Water Pollution Control Act of 1948, P.L. 80-845, 62 Stat. 1155 (1948).

FallCreek, S., & Gilbert, N. (1981, May). Aging network in transition: Problems and prospects. *Social Work, 26*, 210–216.

Federal Gun Control Act of 1968, P.L. 90-618, 82 Stat. 1213-2 (1968).

Feeble minded boys committed under new law. (1915, 19 November). *Chicago Tribune*, p. 5.

Fine, T. S. (2006). The Family Medical Leave law: Feminist social policy? *Journal of Policy Practice, 5*, 49–66.

Firearm Owners' Protection Act of 1986, P.L. 99-308, 100 Stat. 449 (1986).

Fleary, S. A., Joseph, P., Zhang, E., & Quirion, C. (2019). "They give you back that dignity": Understanding the intangible resources that make a transitional house a home for homeless families. *Journal of Social Distress and the Homeless, 28*, 72–84.

Fodor, M. D. (2001). *Megan's Law: Protection or privacy?* Berkeley Heights, NJ: Enslow.

Food and Nutrition Act, P.L. 110-246, 122 Stat. 1651 (2008).

Food Stamp Act of 1964, P.L. 88-525, 78 Stat. 703 (1964).

Food Stamp Act of 1964: Hearing before the Committee on Agriculture and Forestry, United States Senate, 88th Congress, 2nd Session. (1964, June 18 and 19).

Food Stamp timeline: Evolution of the current program. (2010). *Congressional Digest*, 89(10), 297.

Ford, M. E., & Schwamm, J. B. (1992). Expanding eligibility for Supplemental Security Income based on childhood disability: The *Zebley* decision. *Child Welfare, 71*, 307–318.

Fowler, R. (2013, June). The deep roots of Workers' Comp [Cover story]. *Tennessee Bar Journal, 49*(6), 10–16.

Frazer, E. (1923, June 16). Our foreign cities: New York. *The Saturday Evening Post*, pp. 6–7, 136–138, 141–142.

Freeman, W., & Watts, J. W. (1950). *Psychosurgery in the treatment of mental disorders and intractable pain* (2nd ed.). Springfield, IL: Charles C Thomas.

Friedland, R. B. (2005, Spring). How Medicare works. *Generations, 29*(1), 30–34.

Frydl, K. J. (2009). *The GI Bill.* Cambridge, NY: Cambridge University Press.

Galton, F. (1870). *Hereditary genius.* New York: D. Appleton.

Garfield, J. R. (1912, June 12–19). A program of action for a children's protective society. In *Proceedings of the National Conference of Charities and Correction* (pp. 33–40). Fort Wayne, IN: Fort Wayne Printing.

Gedicks, A. (2005). Resource wars against Native peoples. In R. D. Bullard (Ed.), *The quest for environmental justice: Human rights and the politics of pollution* (pp. 168–187). San Francisco: Sierra Club Books.

Gerstel, N., & McGonagle, K. (1999). Job leaves and the limits of the Family Medical Leave Act: The effects of gender, race, and family. *Work and Occupations, 26*, 510–534.

Gitnik, L. J. (1996). Will the interaction of the Family and Medical Leave Act and the Americans with Disabilities Act leave employees with an "undue hardship"? *Washington University Law Quarterly, 74*, 283–315.

Goetz. E. G. (2003). *Clearing the way: Deconcentrating the poor in urban America*. Washington, DC: Urban Institute Press.

Goffman, E. (1961). *Asylum: Essays on the social situation of mental patients and other inmates*. Garden City, NY: Anchor Books.

Goldberg, G. S., & Collins, S. D. (2001). *Washington's new poor law: Welfare reform and the roads not taken – 1935 to the present*. New York: Apex Press.

Gollaher, D. (1995). *Voice for the mad: The life of Dorothea Dix*. New York: Free Press.

Goodgame, D. (1994, December 19). Reining in the rich. *Time*, 35–38.

Gorin, S. H. (2011). The Affordable Care Act: Background and analysis [Editorial]. *Health & Social Work, 36*, 83–86.

Gorin, S. H. (2012). Why we should keep the Social Security retirement age [Editorial]. *Health & Social Work, 37*, 67–70.

Gorin, S. H., & Armstrong, R. (2012). The truth about Social Security and Medicare [Editorial]. *Health & Social Work, 37*, 3–7.

Gorn, E. J. (2001). *Mother Jones: The most dangerous woman in America*. New York: Hill and Wang.

Goshe, S. (2013). Malleable mandates: Liberal ideology and the politics of protection and punishment in the Juvenile Justice and Delinquency Prevention Act. *Western Criminology Review, 14*, 39–50.

Goss, K. A. (2006). *Disarmed: The missing movement for gun control in America*. Princeton, NJ: Princeton University Press.

Gowan, M. A., & Zimmermann, R. A. (1996). The Family and Medical Leave Act of 1993: Employee rights and responsibilities, employer rights and responsibilities. *Employee Responsibilities and Rights Journal, 9*, 57–71.

Graham, L. M. (2009). Reparations, self-determination, and the seventh generation. In M.L.M. Fletcher, W. T. Singel, & K. E. Fort (Eds.), *Facing the future: The Indian Child Welfare Act at 30* (pp. 50–89). East Lansing: Michigan State University Press.

Grant, J. (2009). A profile of substance abuse, gender, crime and drug policy in the United States and Canada. *Journal of Offender Rehabilitation, 48*, 654–668.

Grant, M. (1933). *The conquest of a continent*. New York: Charles Scribner's Sons.

Green, E. C. (2003). *This business of relief: Confronting poverty in a southern city, 1740–1940*. Athens: University of Georgia Press.

Greenbaum, S., Hathaway, W., Rodriguez, C., Spalding, A., & Ward, B. (2008). Deconcentration and social capital: Contradictions of a poverty alleviation policy. *Journal of Poverty, 12*, 201–228.

Greenfield, M. (1968). *Medicare and Medicaid: The 1965 and 1967 Social Security amendments.* Berkeley, CA: Institute of Governmental Studies.

Greenstein, R. (2001). Enhancing WIC's effectiveness. In D. J. Besharov & P. Germanis (Eds.), *Rethinking WIC: An evaluation of the Women, Infants, and Children Program* (pp. 109–125). Washington, DC: AEI Press.

Grob, G. N. (1991). *From asylum to community: Mental health policy in modern America.* Princeton, NJ: Princeton University Press.

Grob, G. N. (1994). *The mad among us: A history of the care of America's mentally ill.* New York: Free Press.

Grossman, J. R. (1989). *Land of hope: Chicago, Black southerners, and the Great Migration.* Chicago: University of Chicago Press.

Hakim, D. (2021, May 11). In rebuke to N.R.A., federal judge dismisses bankruptcy case. *New York Times.* Retrieved from https://www.nytimes.com/2021/05/11/us/nra-bankruptcy.html

Haley, J. M. (2020). Intersectional and relational frameworks: Confronting anti-Blackness, settler colonialism and neoliberalism in U.S. social work. *Journal of Progressive Human Services, 31*(3), 210–225.

Hamilton, L., Wingrove, T., & Woodford, K. (2019). Does generous welfare policy encourage dependence? TANF asset limits and duration of program participation. *Journal of Children and Poverty, 25*, 101–113.

Handler, J. F., & Hasenfeld, Y. (2007). *Blame welfare, ignore poverty and inequality.* New York: Cambridge University Press.

Harnack, L., Valluri, S., & French, S. A. (2019). Importance of the Supplemental Nutrition Assistance Program in rural America. *American Journal of Public Health, 109*, 1641–1645.

Harrington, M. (1962). *The other America: Poverty in the United States.* New York: Macmillan.

Harrison Narcotics Tax Act, P.L. 63-223, 38 Stat. 785 (1914).

Hartman, A. (1993). Family preservation under attack. *Social Work, 38*, 509–512.

Hasson, R. G., III, Crea, T. M., McRoy, R. G., & Lê, Â. H. (2019). Patchwork of promises: A critical analysis of immigration policies for unaccompanied undocumented children in the United States. *Child & Family Social Work, 24*, 275–282.

Hattery, A. J., & Smith, E. (2018). *Policing Black bodies: How Black lives are surveilled and how to work for change.* Lanham, MD: Rowman & Littlefield.

Hauser, E. O. (1941). America's 150,000 Japanese. *American Mercury, 53*, 689–697.

Hegar, R., & Scannapieco, M. (1995). From family duty to family policy: The evolution of kinship care. *Child Welfare, 74*, 200–216.

Helfer, R. E. (1985). Where to now, Henry? A commentary on the battered child syndrome. *Pediatrics, 76*, 993–997.

Henwood, B. F., Matejkowski, J., Stefancic, A., & Lukens, J. M. (2014). Quality of life after *housing first* for adults with serious mental illness who have experienced chronic homelessness. *Psychiatry Research, 220*, 549–555.

Herman, B. (2007). CAPTA and early childhood intervention: Policy and the role of parents. *Children & Schools, 29*, 17–24.

Hernandez, J. P., & Potocky, M. (2014). Ryan White CARE Action Part D: Matches and gaps in political commitment and local implementation. *Social Work in Public Health, 29*, 267–284.

Herzberg, L. (2013). Shared decision-making: A voice for the Lakota people. *Child and Family Social Work, 18*, 477–486.

Hill, H. D., & Romich, J. (2018). How will higher minimum wages affect family life and children's well-being? *Child Development Perspectives, 12*, 109–111.

Hindman, H. D. (2006). Unfinished business: The persistence of child labor in the US. *Employment Responsibilities and Rights Journal, 18*, 125–131.

Hinton, E. (2016). *From the war on poverty to the war on crime: The making of mass incarceration in America.* Cambridge, MA: Harvard University Press.

Hitler, A. (1971). *Mein Kampf* (R. Manheim, trans.). Boston: Houghton Mifflin. (Original work published 1925)

Hoch, C., & Slayton, R. A. (1989). *New homeless and old: Community and the skid row hotel.* Philadelphia: Temple University Press.

Hoefer, R., & Curry, C. (2012). Food security and social protection in the United States. *Journal of Policy Practice, 11*, 59–76.

Hogan, S. R., Speiglman, R., & Norris, J. C. (2010). The effects of eliminating Supplemental Security Income drug addiction and alcoholism eligibility on the mental health of low-income substance abusers. *Social Work in Public Health, 25*, 438–453.

Holahan, J. F., & Cohen, J. F. (1986). *Medicaid: The trade-off between cost containment and access to care.* Washington, DC: The Urban Institute.

Holahan, J., & Weil, A. (February, 2007). Toward real Medicaid reform. *Health Affairs, 26*(Suppl. 2), 254–270.

Homeland Security Act of 2002, P.L. 107-296, 116 Stat. 2135 (2002).

Hopkins, H. L. (1938, June). The WPA looks forward: A statement and a forecast. *Survey Midmonthly, 24*(6), 195–198.

Hopper, K. (2003). *Reckoning with homelessness.* Ithaca, NY: Cornell University Press.

Housing Act of 1949, P.L. 171-338, 63 Stat. 432 (1949).

Housing and Community Development Act of 1974, P.L. 93-383, 88 Stat. 633 (1974).

Howard, D. S. (1973). *The WPA and federal relief policy.* New York: Da Capo Press.

Howell, J. C. (2003). *Preventing and reducing juvenile delinquency: A comprehensive framework.* Thousand Oaks, CA: SAGE.

H.R. 5—117th Congress: Equality Act (2021, 25 February). Retrieved from https://www.govtrack.us/congress/bills/117/hr5

Hunt, H. A. (2003/2004). Benefit adequacy in state workers' compensation programs. *Social Security Bulletin, 65*(4), 24–30.

Hunter, M.J.B. (2009). A practitioner's view from thirty years on the cutting edge of the Indian Child Welfare Act. In M.L.M. Fletcher, W. T. Singel, & K. E. Fort (Eds.), *Facing the future: The Indian Child Welfare Act at 30* (pp. 111–126). East Lansing: Michigan State University Press.

Hurst, P. (Director). (1921). *Shadows of the West* [Film]. Motion Picture Producing Company of America.

Immigration Act of 1924, P.L. 68-139, 43 Stat. 153 (1924).

Inciardi, J. A. (2008). *The war on drugs IV: The continuing saga of the mysteries and miseries of intoxification, addiction, crime, and public policy* (4th ed.). Boston: Pearson.

Indian Child Welfare Act, P.L. 95-608, 92 Stat. 3069 (1978).

Indian Self-Determination and Education Assistance Act of 1975, P.L. 93-638, 88 Stat. 2203 (1975).

Individuals with Disabilities Education Act of 1990, P.L. 101-476, 20 U.S.C. §§ 1400–1482.

Individuals with Disabilities Education Improvement Act of 2004, P.L. 108-446, 20 U.S.C. §§ 1400–1482.

In re Gault, 387 U.S. 1, 87 S. Ct. 1428 (1967).

"The international Jew: The world's foremost problem." (1920). *The Dearborn Independent,* pp. 23, 28–29.

Jacob Wetterling Crimes Against Children and Sexually Violent Offender Registration Act, P.L. 103-322, 108 Stat. 2038 (1994).

Jacobs, B. G., Harney, K. R., Edson, C. L., & Lane, B. S. (1986). *Guide to federal housing programs* (2nd ed.). Washington, DC: Bureau of National Affairs.

Jacoway, E. (2007). *Turn away thy son: Little Rock, the crisis that shocked the nation.* New York: Free Press.

Janoski, J. M. (2013). Extraordinary and unusual circumstances: Compensability of psychological injuries under South Carolina's workers' compensation law. *South Carolina Law Review, 64,* 1063–1084.

Jasper, M. C. (2005). *Your rights under the Family and Medical Leave Act.* Dobbs Ferry, NY: Oceana.

Jeglic, E. L., Mercado, C. C., & Levenson, J. S. (2012). The prevalence and correlates of depression and hopelessness among sex offenders subject to community notification and residence restriction legislation. *American Journal of Criminal Justice,* 37, 46–59.

Jennings, P. K. (2006). The trouble with the Multiethnic Placement Act: An empirical look at transracial adoption. *Sociological Perspectives, 49,* 559–581.

Jensen, G. F., & Rojek, D. G. (1998). *Delinquency and youth crime* (3rd ed.). Prospect Heights, IL: Waveland Press.

Jenson, J. M. (2007). Aggression and violence in the United States: Reflections on the Virginia Tech shootings. *Social Work Research, 31,* 132–134.

Jones, B. J. (2009). Differing concepts of "permanency": The Adoption and Safe Families Act and the Indian Child Welfare Act. In M.L.M. Fletcher, W. T. Singel, & K. E. Fort (Eds.), *Facing the future: The Indian Child Welfare Act at 30* (pp. 127–145). East Lansing: Michigan State University Press.

Jones, B. J., Tilden, M., & Gaines-Stoner, K. (2008). *The Indian Child Welfare Act handbook: A legal guide to the custody and adoption of Native American children* (2nd ed.). Chicago: American Bar Association.

Jones, E., & Wessely, S. (2005). *Shell shock to PTSD: Military psychiatry from 1900 to the Gulf War*. Hove, England: Psychology Press.

Jones, P. (2010). Responding to the ecological crisis: Transformative pathways for social work education. *Journal of Social Work Education, 46*, 67–84.

Jozefowisz-Simbeni, D.M.H., & Israel, N. (2006). Services to homeless students and families: The McKinney-Vento Act and its implications for school social work practice. *Children & Schools, 28*, 37–44.

The Jukes in 1915. (1916). *Journal of Heredity, 7*, 469–474.

Juvenile Justice and Delinquency Prevention Act of 1974, P.L. 93-415, 88 Stat. 1109 (1974).

Kahan, K., & Wentworth, G. (2012, January 2). Out of work and out of luck. *The Nation*, pp. 17–19.

Kahan, M. (2006). "Put up" on platforms: A history of twentieth century adoption policy in the United States. *Journal of Sociology and Social Welfare, 33*, 51–72.

Kaplan, R. L. (2011). Older Americans, Medicare and the Affordable Care Act: What's really in it for elders? *Generations, 35*(1), 19–25.

Karger, H., & Rose, S. R. (2010). Revisiting the Americans with Disabilities Act after two decades. *Journal of Social Work in Disability and Rehabilitation, 9*, 73–86.

Katz, M. B. (1996). *In the shadow of the poorhouse: A social history of welfare in America* (2nd ed.). New York: Basic Books.

Katznelson, R. (2005). *When affirmative action was White: An untold history of racial inequality in twentieth-century America*. New York: W. W. Norton.

Kelly, D. R. (2016). Stopping the bully: An analysis of Texas House Bill 1942. *Children & Schools, 38*, 163–169.

Kelso, R. W. (1969). *The history of public poor relief in Massachusetts 1620–1920* (Reprinted ed.). Montclair, NJ: Patterson Smith.

Kempe, C. H., & Helfer, R. E. (Eds.). (1972). *Helping the battered child and his family.* Philadelphia: J. B. Lippincott.

Kennedy, S. (1973). *Jim Crow guide to the U.S.A.* (2nd ed.). Westport, CT: Greenwood Press.

Keogh, B. K., & Barkett, C. J. (1978). Children's rights in assessment and school placement. *Journal of Social Issues, 34*, 87–100.

Kero, K., & Ernst, J. S. (2019). Social services for older adults: Utilization and future directions. *Medsurg Nursing, 28*, 323–326.

Kerr-Mills Social Security Act, P.L. 86-778, 74 Stat. 924 (September 13, 1960).

Kevles, D. J. (1985). *In the name of eugenics*. New York: Alfred A. Knopf.

Khanani, I., Elam, J., Hearn, R., Jones, C., & Maseru, N. (2010). The impact of prenatal WIC participation on infant mortality and racial disparities. *American Journal of Public Health, 100*, S204–S209.

Kleck, G. (1997). *Targeting guns: Firearms and their control*. New York: Aldine de Gruyter.

Kline, W. (2001). *Building a better race: Gender, sexuality and eugenics from the turn of the century to the baby boom*. Berkeley: University of California Press.

Kohl, H., Sanders, B., & Blumenthal, R. (2012). Elder abuse: What is the federal role? *Generations, 36*(3), 106–110.

Kohn, A. (2004). NCLB and the effort to privatize public education. In D. Meier & G. Wood (Eds.), *Many children left behind* (pp. 79–97). Boston: Beacon Press.

Kolivoski, K. M., Goodkind, S., & Shook, J. J. (2017). Social justice for crossover youth: The intersection of the child welfare and juvenile justice systems. *Social Work, 62*, 313–321.

Kopels, S., & Rycraft, J. R. (1993). The U.S. Supreme Court rules on reasonable efforts: A blow to child advocacy. *Child Welfare, 72*, 397–405.

Kornfeld, S. K. (2018). A need not being met: providing paid family and medical leave for all Americans. *Family Court Review, 56*, 165–179.

Koyama, J. (2015). When things come undone: The promise of dissembling education policy. *Discourse: Studies in the Cultural Politics of Education, 36*, 548–559.

Kraut, A. M. (1994). *Silent travelers: Germs, genes and the "immigrant menace."* New York: Basic Books.

Krieg, J. P. (1992). *Epidemics in the modern world*. New York: Twayne.

Krishnan, L., Ogunwole, M., & Cooper, L. A. (2020). Historical insights on coronavirus disease 2019 (COVID-19), the 1918 influenza pandemic, and racial disparities: Illuminating a path forward. *Annals of Internal Medicine, 173*, 474–481.

Kuanliang, A., & Sorensen, J. (2007). Are we tough enough? Trends in juvenile sentencing. In M. D. McShane & F. P. Williams, III (Eds.), *Youth violence and delinquency: Monsters and myths: Vol. 2. Juvenile justice* (pp. 17–27). Westport, CT: Praeger.

Kwon, I. G., Scott, B. Safranski, S. R., & Bae, M. (1997). The effectiveness of gun control laws: Multivariate statistical analysis. *American Journal of Economics and Sociology, 56*, 41–50.

Lagana-Riordan, C., & Aguilar, J. P. (2009). What's missing from No Child Left Behind? A policy analysis from a social work perspective. *Children & Schools, 31*, 135–144.

Land-Grant Bill for Indigent Insane Persons, S. 44 33rd Cong. (1854).

Lang, K. (2019–2020). Apply, deny, appeal: The difficult process of claiming disability benefits. *Generations, 43*(4), 18–24.

Larson, A. (1989). Tensions of the next decade. In J. F. Burton, Jr. (Ed.), *New perspectives in workers' compensation* (pp. 21-43). Cornell, NY: ILR Press.

Lathrop, J. C. (1912, June 12–19). The Children's Bureau. In *Proceedings of the National Conference of Charities and Corrections* (pp. 30–33). Fort Wayne, IN: Fort Wayne Printing.

Laughlin, H. H. (1925). The eugenical sterilization of the feeble-minded. *Journal of Psycho-Asthenics, 31*, 210–218.

Lawlor, E. F. (2003). *Redesigning the Medicare contract: Politics, markets, and agency*. Chicago: The University of Chicago Press.

Lazariu-Bauer, V., Stratton, H., Pruzek, R., & Woelfel, M. L. (2004). A comparative analysis of effects of early versus late prenatal WIC participation on birth weight: NYS, 1995. *Maternal and Child Health Journal, 8*, 77–86.

Leake, R., Potter, C., Lucero, N., Gardner, J., & Deserly, K. (2012). Findings from a national needs assessment of American Indian/Alaska Native child welfare programs. *Child Welfare, 91*, 47–63.

Leatherwood, D., & Payne, C. (2016). Putting No Child Left Behind behind us: Rethinking education and inequality. *Social Service Review, 90*, 562–570.

Lee, J. Y, Rozier, R. G., Norton, E. C. Kotch, J. B., & Vann, W. F. (2004). Effects of WIC participation on children's use of oral health services. *American Journal of Public Health, 94*, 772–776.

Lens, V. (2002). TANF: What went wrong and what to do next. *Social Work, 47*, 279–290.

Lercara, B. (2016). The Adoption and Safe Families Act: Proposing a "best efforts" standard to eliminate the ultimate obstacle for family reunification. *Family Court Review, 54*, 657–670.

Leuchtenburg, W. E. (1963). *Franklin D. Roosevelt and the New Deal: 1932–1940*. New York: Harper & Row.

Levine, M., & Levine A. G. (2011). Who said the Government can't do anything right? The World War II GI Bill, the growth of science, and American prosperity. *American Journal of Orthopsychiatry, 81*, 149–156.

Levinson, J., & Tewksbury, R. (2009). Collateral damage: Family members of registered sex offenders. *American Journal of Criminal Justice, 34*, 54–68.

Libal, K., Tomczak, M., Spath, R., & Harding, S. (2014). Hunger in a "land of plenty": A renewed call for social work action. *Social Work, 59*, 366–369.

Lieberman, T. (2013, October 14). The real hunger games. *The Nation*, pp. 12–17.

Lightner, D. L. (1999). *Asylum, prison, and poorhouse: The writings and reform work of Dorothea Dix in Illinois*. Carbondale: Southern Illinois University Press.

Lim, Y., DeJohn, T. V., & Murray, D. (2012). Free tax assistance and the Earned Income Tax Credit: Vital resources for social workers and low-income families. *Social Work, 57*, 175–184.

Limb, G. E., & Brown, E. F. (2008). An examination of the Indian Child Welfare Act section of State Title IV-B Child and Family Services Plans. *Child and Adolescent Social Work Journal, 25*, 99–110.

Lindsey, D. (1994). Mandated reporting and child abuse facilities: Requirements for a system to protect children. *Social Work Research, 18*, 41–54.

Lindstrom, M. J., & Smith, Z. A. (2001). *The National Environmental Policy Act: Judicial misconstruction, legislative indifference, and executive neglect.* College Station: Texas A&M University Press.

Lloyd, J. L. (2019). From farms to food deserts: Food insecurity and older rural Americans. *Generations, 43*(2), 24–32.

Loevy, R. D. (1997). The impact and aftermath of the Civil Rights Act of 1964. In R. D. Loevy (Ed.), *The Civil Rights Act of 1964: The passage of the law that ended segregation* (pp. 333–354). New York: SUNY Press.

Loevy, R. D. (2004). Who were the heroes? What was the impact? In R. H. Mayer (Ed.), *The Civil Rights Act of 1964* (pp. 66–76). San Diego: Greenhaven Press.

Loewen, J. W. (2006). *Sundown towns: A hidden dimension of American racism.* New York: Touchstone.

Logan, T. K., Cole, J., Shannon, L., & Walker, R. (2006). *Partner stalking: How women respond, cope, and survive.* New York: Springer.

Lyons, E. (1970). *The red decade* (2nd ed.). New York: Arlington House.

Mabli, J., & Worthington, J. (2014). Supplemental Nutrition Assistance Program participation and child food security. *Pediatrics, 133*, 610–619.

Macek, S. (2006). *Urban nightmares: The media, the right, and the moral panic over the city.* Minneapolis: University of Minnesota Press.

Mackelprang, R. W., Mackelprang, R. D., & Thirkill, A. D. (2005). Bioterrorism and smallpox: Policies, practices, and implications for social work. *Social Work, 50*, 119–127.

Main, C. T. (2007). *Bulldozed: "Kelo," eminent domain and the American lust for land.* New York: Encounter Books.

Maioni, A. (1998). *Parting at the crossroads: The emergence of health insurance in the United States and Canada.* Princeton, NJ: Princeton University Press.

Malthus, T. R. (1967). *An essay on the principle of population* (reprinted ed.). New York: Dutton. (Original work published 1798)

Mannes, M. (1995). Factors and events leading to the passage of the Indian Child Welfare Act. *Child Welfare, 74*, 164–282.

Markward, M. J., & Biros, E. (2001). McKinney revisited: Implications for school social work. *Children & Schools, 23*, 182–187.

Marsh, J. C. (2005). Bush plan takes the security out of Social Security. *Social Work, 50*, 99–100.

Martin, E. G., Pollack, H. A., & Paltiel, A. D. (2006). Fact, fiction, and fairness: Resource allocation under the Ryan White CARE Act. *Health Affairs, 25*, 1103–1112.

Mayerson, A. (1993). The history of the ADA: A movement perspective. In L. O. Gostin & H. A. Beyer (Eds.), *Implementing the Americans with Disabilities Act: Rights and responsibilities of all Americans* (pp. 17–24). Baltimore: Paul H. Brookes.

Mazumder, B. (2011, April). How did Unemployment insurance extensions affect the unemployment rate in 2008–10. *Chicago Federal Letter, 285*. Retrieved from https://www.chicagofed.org/~/media/publications/chicago-fed-letter/2011/cflapril2011-285-pdf.pdf

McAdams, T., Moussavi, F., & Klassen, M. (1992). Employee appearance and the Americans with Disabilities Act: An emerging issue? *Employee Responsibility and Rights Journal, 5*, 323–337.

McCarter, S. A. (2011). Disproportionate minority contact in the American juvenile justice system. Where are we after 20 years, a philosophy shift, and three amendments? *Journal of Forensic Social Work, 1*, 96–107.

McCarter, S. A., & Bridges, J. B. (2011). Determining the age of jurisdiction for adolescents: The policy debate. *Journal of Policy Practice, 10*, 168–184.

McDonnell, L. M. (2005). No Child Left Behind and the federal role in education: Education or revolution? *Peabody Journal of Education, 80*, 19–38.

McEldowney, R., & Jenkins, C. L. (2005). Efforts to reform Medicaid in a time of fiscal stress: Are we shuffling chairs on the decks of the *Titanic*? *Journal of Health and Social Policy, 21*, 1–16.

McHugh, M. C., & Frieze, I. H. (2006). Intimate partner violence: New directions. In F. L. Denmark, H. H. Krause, E. Halpern, & J. A. Sechzer (Eds.), *Violence and exploitation against women and girls* (pp. 121–138). Boston: Blackwell.

McKay, M. M. (1994). The link between domestic violence and child abuse: Assessment and treatment considerations. *Child Welfare, 73*, 29–39.

McKinney-Vento Homeless Assistance Act, P.L. 100-77, 101 Stat. 482 (1987).

McKinney-Vento Homeless Education Assistance Improvements Act of 2001, P.L. 107-110, 115 State 1989 (2002).

McKinnon, J. (2008). Exploring the nexus between social work and the environment. *Australian Social Work, 61*, 256–268.

McNeal, C., & Amato, P. R. (1998). Parents' marital violence: Long-term consequences for children. *Journal of Family Issues, 19*, 123–139.

McRoy, R., & Griffin, A. (2012). Transracial adoption policies and practices: The US experience. *Adoption & Fostering, 36*, 38–49.

McWey, L. M., Henderson, T. L., & Tice, S. N. (2006). Mental health issues and the foster care system: An examination of the impact of the Adoption and Safe Families Act. *Journal of Marital and Family Therapy, 32*, 195–214.

McWilliams, C. (1935). Once again the "yellow peril." *The Nation, 140*, 735–736.

Mead, L. M. (2000). Are welfare employment programs effective? In J. Crane (Ed.), *Social programs that work* (pp. 277–309). New York: Russell Sage Foundation.

Mechanic, D. (1999). *Mental health and social policy: The emergence of managed care* (4th ed.). Boston: Allyn & Bacon.

Medicare, P.L. 89-97, 79 Stat. 286 (1965).

Medicare Prescription Drug, Improvement, and Modernization Act, P.L. 108-173, 94 Stat. 2647 (2003).

Mencher, S. (1967). *Poor law to poverty program: Economic security policy in Britain and the United States.* Pittsburgh, PA: University of Pittsburgh Press.

Mendenhall, A. N. (2006). A guide to the Earned Income Tax Credit: What everyone should know about EITC. *Journal of Poverty, 10*, 51–68.

Menzel, P. T. (1992). Oregon's denial: Disabilities and the quality of life. *Hastings Center Report, 22*(6), 21–25.

Messing, J. T., Ward-Lasher, A., Thaller, J., & Bagwell-Gray, M. E. (2015). The state of intimate partner violence intervention: Progress and continuing challenges. *Social Work, 60*, 305–313.

Meyer, B. D. (2017). The Earned Income Tax Credit. In R. Doar (Ed.), *A safety net that works: Improving federal programs for low-income Americans* (pp. 1–18). Washington, DC: American Enterprise Institute.

Meyer-Emerick, N. (2001). *The Violence Against Women Act of 1994: An analysis of intent and perception.* Westport, CT: Praeger.

Miller, K. (1996). Gimme shelter: the communication of America's homeless. In E. B. Ray (Ed.), *Communication and disenfranchisement: Social health issues and implications.* (pp. 79–93). Mahway, NJ: Lawrence Erlbaum.

Millett, J. D. (1938). *The Works Progress Administration in New York City.* Chicago: Public Administration Service.

Mills v. Board of Education, 348 F. Supp. 866 (D.D.C. 1972).

Minimum wage overview: Provisions of the Fair Labor Standards Act. (2013, May). *Congressional Digest, 92*(5), 3–10.

Mitchell, M. (2010). Gender and unemployment insurance: Why women receive unemployment benefits at lower rates than men and will unemployment insurance reform close the gap? *Texas Journal of Women and the Law, 20*, 55–74.

Mnookin, S. (2011). *The panic virus: The true story behind the vaccine-autism controversy.* New York: Simon & Schuster.

Moe, T. M. (2003). The future of school vouchers. In P. E. Peterson (Ed.), *The future of school choice* (pp. 135–155). Stanford, CA: Hoover Institution Press.

Molloy, P. (1951, September 8. The relief chiselers are stealing us blind. *The Saturday Evening Post,* pp. 32–33, 142–144.

Monheit, A. C., & Short, P. F. (1989). Mandating health coverage for working Americans. *Health Affairs, 8*(4), 23–38.

Moniz, C., & Gorin, S. (2007). *Health and mental health care policy: A biopsychosocial perspective* (2nd ed.). Boston: Pearson.

Monroe, A. (1996, November/December). Safe and secure? *Mother Jones,* 53.

Monroe, P. A., Garand, J. C., & Teeters, H. (1995). Family leave legislation in the U.S. House: Voting on the Family and Medical Leave Act of 1990. *Family Relations, 44*, 46–55.

Moon, M. (1993). *Medicare now and in the future*. Washington, DC: Urban Institute Press.

Mooradian, J. K. (2007). "You can't go home again": Disproportionate confinement of African American delinquents. In M. D. McShane & F. P. Williams, III (Eds.), *Youth violence and delinquency: Monsters and myths: Vol. 2. Juvenile justice* (pp. 99–117). Westport, CT: Praeger.

Morrissey, S. (2016). Motherhood, poverty, and the WIC program in urban America. Lanham, MD: Lexington Books.

Morse, A. D. (1967, November 28). Voyage to doom. *Look*, 64–70.

Mosher, C. J., & Akins, S. (2007). *Drugs and drug policy: The control of consciousness alteration*. Thousand Oaks, CA: SAGE.

Mucciaroni, G. (2008). *Same sex, different politics: Success and failure in the struggles over gay rights*. Chicago: University of Chicago Press.

Murray, C. (1984). *Losing ground: American social policy, 1950–1980*. New York: Basic Books.

Naleppa, M. J., & Reid, W. J. (2003). *Gerontological social work: A task-centered approach*. New York: Columbia University Press.

Nam, C. B. (1964, January 1). Impact of the "GI bills" on the educational level of the male population. *Social Forces, 43*(1), 26–32.

Nash, G. B. (2004). Poverty and politics in early American history. In B. G. Smith (Ed.), *Down and out in early America* (pp. 1–37). University Park: Penn State University Press.

National Coalition for the Homeless. (2008, June). *McKinney-Vento Act* (Fact Sheet No. 18). Washington, DC: Author.

National Commission on Excellence in Education. (1983, April). *A nation at risk* [Report]. Retrieved from https://www2.ed.gov/pubs/NatAtRisk/intro.html

National Environmental Policy Act of 1969, P.L. 91-190, 83 Stat. 852 (1969).

National Housing Act, P.L. 73-479, 48 Stat. 1246 (1934).

National Labor Relations Act, P.L. 74-198, 49 Stat. 449 (1935).

National Mental Health Act, P.L. 79-487, 60 Stat. 421 (1946).

Nerenberg, L. (2008). *Elder abuse presentation: Emerging trends and promising strategies*. New York: Springer.

Nestle, M. (2019). The Supplemental Nutrition Assistance Program (SNAP): History, politics, and public health implications. *American Journal of Public Health, 109*, 1631–1635.

Netting, F. E., Huber, R., Paton, R. N., & Kautz, J. R., III. (1995). Elder rights and the Long-Term Care Ombudsman Program. *Social Work, 40*, 351–357.

Nissen, L. B. (2020). An open letter to social work students in the time of COVID-19: The future is calling. *The New Social Worker*, 10–12. Retrieved from https://www.socialworker.com/feature-articles/practice/open-letter-social-work-students-covid-19/

No Child Left Behind Act of 2001, P.L. 197-110, 30 Stat. 750 (2001).

Noah, T. (1982, September). Bring back the WPA. *The Washington Monthly*, pp. 38–46.

Noe, K., Smith, P. C., & Younis, M. (2012). Calls to reform the U.S. hospice system. *Ageing International, 37*, 228–237.

Nofz, M. P. (1986). Social services for older rural Americans: Some policy concerns. *Social Work, 31*, 85–91.

Novak, M. (2006). *Issues in aging.* Boston: Pearson.

Obama, B. (2011, February). "We are not a nation that says, 'don't ask, don't tell.'" *Vital Speeches of the Day*, pp. 81–82.

Obergefell v. Hodges, 576 U.S. 644 (2015).

Oberlander, J. (2008). *The political life of Medicare.* Chicago: University of Chicago Press.

O'Brien, G. V. (2003). Indigestible food, conquering hordes, and waste materials: Metaphors of immigrants and the early immigration restriction debate in the U.S. *Metaphor and Symbol, 18*, 33–47.

O'Brien, G. V. (2004). Rosemary Kennedy: The importance of a historical footnote. *Journal of Family History, 29*, 225–236.

O'Brien, G. (2009). Metaphors and the pejorative framing of marginalized groups: Implications for social work education. *Journal of Social Work Education, 45*, 29–46.

O'Brien, G. V. (2011). Eugenics, genetics and the minority group model of disabilities: Implications for social work advocacy. *Social Work,* 56, 347–354.

O'Brien, G. V. (2013). *Framing the moron: The social construction of feeble-mindedness during the American eugenics era.* Manchester, England: Manchester University Press.

O'Brien, G. V. (2018). *Contagion and the national body: The organism metaphor in American thought.* London: Routledge.

O'Brien, G. V. (2019). *Metaphor analysis in public policy and private practice: A social work perspective.* Washington, DC: NASW Press.

O'Brien, G. V., & Ellegood, C. (2005). The Americans with Disabilities Act: A decision tree for social service administrators. *Social Work, 50*, 271–279.

O'Brien, G. V., & Koerkenmeier, M. (2001). Persons with HIV/AIDS in the workplace: Implications for employee assistance professionals. *Employee Assistance Quarterly, 16*, 9–23.

O'Brien, G. V., & Maue, M. E. (2002). Direct threat issues in the employment of persons with disabilities: Implications for the social work profession. *Journal of Social Work in Disability and Rehabilitation, 1*(1), 39–51.

Occupational Health and Safety Act of 1970, P.L. 91-596, 84 Stat. 1590 (1970).

O'Connor, S. (2001). *Orphan trains: The story of Charles Loring Brace and the children he saved and failed.* Boston: Houghton Mifflin.

O'Connor v. Donaldson, 422 U.S. 563 (1975).

Ogawa, D. M. (1971). *From Japs to Japanese: An evolution of Japanese-American stereotypes.* Berkeley, CA: McCutchan.

Oh, S., DiNitto, D. M., & Kim, Y. (2018). Substance use and use disorders and treatment receipt among adults and families receiving Temporary Assistance for Needy Families (TANF), 2003–2014. *Addictive Behaviors, 85*, 173–179.

Older Americans Act: A Staff Summary by the Select Committee on Aging. (1979, July). U.S. House of Representatives, 96th Congress, 1st Session. Washington, DC: U.S. Government Printing Office.

Older Americans Act Amendments of 2000, P.L. 106-501, 114 Stat. 2226 (2000).

Older Americans Act of 1965, P.L. 89-73, 79 Stat. 218.

O'Leary, C. J., & Rubin, M. A. (1997). Adequacy of the weekly benefit amount. In C. J. O'Leary & S. A. Wandner (Eds.), *Unemployment insurance in the United States: Analysis of policy issues* (pp. 163–205). Kalamazoo, MI: W. E. Upjohn Institute for Employment Research.

Olsen, E. O. (2017). Reducing poverty by reforming housing policy. In R. Doar (Ed.), *A safety net that works: Improving federal programs for low-income Americans* (pp. 87–106). Washington, DC: American Enterprise Institute.

Olsen, L., & DeBoise, T. (2007). Enhancing school readiness: The early Head Start model. *Children & Schools, 29*, 47–50.

Olson, L. K. (2003). *The not-so-golden years: Caregiving, the frail elderly, and the long-term care establishment*. Lanham, MD: Rowman & Littlefield.

Olson-Raymer, G. (1983). The role of the federal government in juvenile delinquency prevention: Historical and contemporary perspectives. *Journal of Criminal Law and Criminology, 74*, 578–600.

135 Cong. Rec., Pt. 14, S.10722 (1989, September 7).

142 Cong. Rec., 6126–6128 (1990, May 14).

Owens, A. (2015). Housing policy and urban inequality: Did the transformation of assisted housing reduce poverty concentration. *Social Forces, 94*, 325–348.

Ozawa, M. N. (1995). The Earned Income Tax Credit: Its effect and its significance. *Social Service Review, 69*, 563–582.

Ozawa, M. N. (2002). SSI and adults with disabilities: Background, trends and a study of participation. *Journal of Disability Policy Studies, 13*, 153–162.

Ozawa v. United States, 260 US 178 (1922).

Padilla, Y. C., Shapiro, E. R., Fernández-Castro, M. D., & Faulkner, M (2008). Our nation's immigrants in peril: An urgent call to social workers. *Social Work, 53*, 5–8.

Palley, E. (2008). Federal school law and social work practice. *School Social Work Journal, 33*, 16–34.

Paradise, V. I. (1922). Three per cent. *Harper's Monthly Magazine, 144*, 505–514.

P.A.R.C. v. Commonwealth of Pennsylvania, 334 F. Supp. 279 (E.D. PA 1972).

Parish, S. L. (2013). Why dismantling the safety net for children with disabilities and their families is a poor idea [Guest Editorial]. *Health & Social Work, 38*, 195–198.

Park, Y. (2008). Facilitating injustice: Tracing the role of social workers in the World War II internment of Japanese Americans. *Social Service Review, 82*, 447–483.

Paschall, K. W., Gershoff, E. T., & Kuhfeld, M. (2018). A two decade examination of historical race/ethnicity disparities in academic achievement by poverty status. *Journal of Youth and Adolescence, 47*, 1164–1177.

Patel, K., & Rushefsky, M. (2006). *Health care politics and policy in America* (3rd ed.). Armonk, NY: M. E. Sharp.

Patient Protection and Affordable Care Act, P.L. 111-148, 124 Stat. 119 (2010).

Patterson, G. T. (2009). An examination of evidence-based practice interventions for public emergencies. *Journal of Evidence-Based Social Work, 6*, 274– 287.

Paulson, M. J., & Blake, P. R. (1969). The physically abused child: A focus on prevention. *Child Welfare, 48*, 86–95.

Payne, J. S., Payne, R. A., Mercer, C. D., & Davison, R. A. (1973). *Head Start: A tragicomedy with epilogue*. New York: Behavioral Publications.

Peláez, A. L., Marcuello-Servós, C., de Mesa, J. C., & Kalixto, P. A. (2020). The more you know, the less you fear: Reflexive social work practices in times of COVID-19. *International Social Work, 63*, 746–752.

Pelts, M. D. (2014). A look back at the Defense of Marriage Act: Why same-sex marriage is still relevant for social work. *Affilia: Journal of Women and Social Work, 29*, 237–247.

Peña, D. G. (2002). Endangered landscapes and disappearing peoples? In J. Adamson, M. M. Evans, & R. Stein (Eds.), *The environmental justice reader: Politics, poetics and pedagogy* (pp. 58–78). Tucson: University of Arizona Press.

Perrin, J. M., & Stein, R.E.K. (1991). Reinterpreting disability: Changes in Supplemental Security Income for children. *Pediatrics, 88*, 1047–1051.

Personal Responsibility and Work Opportunity Reconciliation Act of 1996, P.L. 104-193, 110 Stat. 2105 (1996).

Peter, W. W. (1934). Germany's sterilization program. *American Journal of Public Health and the Nation's Health, 24*, 187–191.

Petersen, D. T., & Massengill, D. (1991, March). Employer response to the Drug-Free Workplace Act of 1988: A preliminary look. *Labor Law Journal, 42*(3), 144–151.

Petruy, E., & Dalin, H. (2020). The future of elder justice: A perspective from the administration for community living. *Generations, 44*(1), 98–100.

Pfaelzer, J. (2007). *Driven out: The forgotten war against Chinese Americans*. New York: Random House.

Phelan, J. D. (1919). The Japanese evil in California. *North American Review, 210*, 323–328.

Phillips, C. M., & Mann, A. (2013). Historical analysis of the Adoption and Safe Families Act of 1997. *Journal of Human Behavior in the Social Environment, 23*, 862–868.

Pilcher, F. H. (1894). Superintendent's report. In *Seventh biennial report of the superintendent, Kansas Asylum for Idiotic and Imbecile Youth at Winfield* (pp. 7–8). Topeka, KS: Press of the Hamilton Printing Company.

Pink, R. (2012). Child rights, right to water and sanitation, and human security. *Health and Human Rights, 14*(1), 1–10.

Pinto, S., & Gutelius, B. (2021). Platform power to the people. *Stanford Social Innovation Review, 19*(1), 26–33.

Pitt, C. (2011). U.S. Patriot Act and racial profiling: Are there consequences of discrimination? *Michigan Sociological Review, 25,* 53–69.

Piven, F. F., & Cloward, R. A. (1971). *Regulating the poor: The functions of public welfare.* New York: Vintage Books.

Placek, P. J., & Hendershot, G. E. (1974). Public welfare and family planning: An empirical study of the "brood sow" myth. *Social Problems, 21,* 658–671.

Poindexter, C. C. (1999). Promises in the plague: Passage of the Ryan White Comprehensive AIDS Resources Emergency Act as a case study for legislative action. *Health & Social Work, 24,* 35–41.

Polivka, L. J. (2012). A future out of reach? The growing risk in the U.S. retirement security system. *Generations, 36,* 12–17.

Pollack, D., & Kleinman, T. (2016). *Social work and the courts: A casebook* (3rd ed.). New York: Routledge.

The Poor Relief Act 1601, 43 Eliz. c 2.

Popenoe, P. (1934). The progress of eugenic sterilization. *Journal of Heredity, 25,* 19–26.

Popenoe, P. (1996). Family caps. *Society, 33*(5), 25–27.

Popenoe, P., & Johnson, R. H. (1933). *Applied eugenics.* New York: Macmillan.

Proctor, R. (1988). *Racial hygiene.* Cambridge, MA: Harvard University Press.

The pros and cons of reauthorizing the Violence Against Women Act. (2019, June). *Congressional Digest, 98*(6), 13–30.

Pulido, M. L. (2012). The ripple effect: Lessons learned about secondary traumatic stress among clinicians responding to the September 11th terrorist attacks. *Clinical Social Work Journal, 40,* 307–315.

Quinn, A., & Otteson, M. (2019) Strengthening the voice of those with mental health issues: A community approach to developing a mental health identification system. *Social Work, 64,* 216–223.

Raines, J. C. (2006). The new IDEA: Reflections on the reauthorization for social workers. *School Social Work Journal, 31,* 1–17.

Rank, M. R., & Hirschl, T. A. (2005). Likelihood of using Food Stamps during the adulthood years. *Journal of Nutritional Education and Behavior, 37,* 137–146.

Reese, W. J. (2005). *America's public schools from the common school to "No Child Left Behind."* Baltimore: Johns Hopkins University Press.

Rehabilitation Act of 1973, P.L. 93-112, 87 Stat. 355 (1973).

Reid, T. R. (2010). *The healing of America: A global quest for better, cheaper, and fairer health care* (2nd ed.). New York: Penguin Books.

Reilly, P. R. (1991). *The surgical solution: A history of involuntary sterilization in the United States.* Baltimore: Johns Hopkins University Press.

Reiss, A. J., & Roth, J. A. (2001). Understanding and preventing violence. In L. Nisbet (Ed.), *The gun control debate: You decide* (2nd ed., pp. 182–214). Amherst, NY: Prometheus Books.

Reno, V., Williams, C. T., & Sengupta, I. (2003/2004). Workers' compensation, Social Security Disability Insurance, and the offset: A fact sheet. *Social Security Bulletin, 65*(4), 3–6.

Ritenhouse, D. (2011). What's orientation got to do with it? The best interest of the child standard and legal bias against gay and lesbian parents. *Journal of Poverty, 15*, 309–329.

Rivers, D. L., & Rivers, K. T. (2012). The President Obama healthcare scorecard: The Affordable Care Act in real life. *National Social Science Journal, 38*, 73–79.

Robert T. Stafford Disaster Relief and Emergency Assistance Act, P.L. 93-288, 102 Stat. 4689 (1988).

Roberts, D. (1997). *Killing the Black body: Race, reproduction and the meaning of liberty.* New York: Pantheon Books.

Roberts, D. (2002). *Shattered bonds: The color of child welfare*. New York: Basic Books.

Roberts-DeGennaro, M. (2001). Welfare reform: Impact on children under age 18 receiving SSI. *Journal of Health and Social Policy, 14*, 1–23.

Robie, T. R. (1934). Selective sterilization for race culture. In H. F. Perkins et al. (Eds.), *A decade of progress in eugenics* (pp. 201–209). Baltimore: Williams and Wilkins.

Robinson, M. B., & Scherlen, R. G. (2007). *Lies, damned lies and drug war statistics: A critical analysis of national drug control policy.* Albany: State University of New York Press.

Rogozen, S. (2017). Prioritizing diversity and autonomy in the polygamy legalization debate. *UCLA Women's Law Journal, 24*, 107–149.

Romich, J. L. (2017). Is raising the minimum wage a good idea? Evidence and implications for social work [Commentary]. *Social Work, 62*, 367–369.

Roog, S. A., Knight, T. A., Koob, J. J., & Kraus, M. J. (2004). The utilization and effectiveness of the Family Medical Leave Act of 1993. *Journal of Health and Social Policy, 18*, 39–52.

Rose, E. (2010). *The promise of preschool: From Head Start to universal pre-kindergarten.* Oxford, England: Oxford University Press.

Rosenbaum, S. (2009). Insurance discrimination on the basis of health status: An overview of discrimination practices, federal law, and federal reform options. *Journal of Law, Medicine and Ethics, 37*(s2), 101–120.

Rosenberg, J., & Karabell, Z. (2003). *Kennedy, Johnson and the quest for justice.* New York: W. W. Norton.

Ross, E. A. (1913). American and immigrant blood. *Century Magazine, 87*, 225–232.

Rossi, P. H. (1998). *Feeding the poor: Assessing federal food aid.* Washington, DC: AEI Press.

Rothman, D. J. (1971). *The discovery of the asylum: Social order and disorder in the new republic.* Glenview, IL: Scott, Foresman.

Rothstein, R. (2014, October 15). The making of Ferguson, Public policies at the root of its troubles. *Economic Policy Institute.* Retrieved from https://www.epi.org/publication/making-ferguson/

Rothstein, R. (2017). *The color of law: The forgotten history of how our government segregated America.* New York: Liveright.

Rowell, C. H. (1913). The Japanese in California. *The World's Work, 26,* 196–197.

Roy, S., & Kaur, N. (2020). Issues and challenges with COVID-19: Interventions through social work practice and perspectives. *Journal of Social Work Values & Ethics, 17,* 85–91.

Rubin, L. B. (2008). The untold health care story: How they crippled Medicare. *Dissent, 55*(3), 51–54.

Rudalevige, A. (2003). No Child Left Behind: Forging a congressional compromise. In P. E. Peterson & M. R. West (Eds.), *No Child Left Behind? The politics and practice of school accountability* (pp. 23–49). Washington, DC: Brookings Institution Press.

Ryan White Comprehensive AIDS Resources Emergency Act of 1990, P.L. 101-381, 104 Stat. 576.

Ryu, J. H., & Bartfield, J. S. (2012). Household food insecurity during childhood and subsequent health status: The Early Childhood Longitudinal Study—Kindergarten cohort. *Research and Practice, 102,* e50–e55.

Sacco, L. N. (2013). The Violence Against Women Act: Overview, legislation, and federal funding. In S. P. Zimmerman (Ed.), *Federal responses to domestic violence: The Family Violence Prevention and Services Act and the Violence Against Women Act* (pp. 53–69). New York: Novinka.

Sales, E. (1995). Surviving unemployment: Economic resources and job loss duration in blue-collar households. *Social Work, 40,* 483–494.

Samantrai, K. (1992). To prevent unnecessary separation of children and families: Public Law 96-272—Policy and practice. *Social Work, 37,* 295–302.

Sanchez, T. R. (2006). The Triangle fire: A simulation-based lesson. *The Social Studies, 97*(2), 62–68.

Sauer, M., & Okerblom, J. (1993, September 6). Trial by therapy. *National Review,* pp. 30–39.

Schlaifer, C., & Freeman, L. (1991). *Heart's work: Civil War heroine and champion of the mentally ill, Dorothea Lynde Dix.* New York: Paragon House.

Schmitz, C. L., Matyók, T., Sloan, L. M., & James, C. (2012). The relationship between social work and environmental sustainability: Implications for interdisciplinary practice. *International Journal of Social Welfare, 21,* 278–286.

Scotch, R. K. (2001). *From good will to civil rights: Transforming federal disability policy* (2nd ed.). Philadelphia: Temple University Press.

Seaberg, J. R. (1986). "Reasonable efforts": Toward implementation in permanency planning. *Child Welfare, 65,* 469–302.

Sealander, J. (2003). *The failed century of the child: Governing America's young in the twentieth century.* Cambridge, England: Cambridge University Press.

Sedo, K. J. (2007). Workers' compensation, Social Security Disability, SSI, and genetic testing. *Journal of Law, Medicine and Ethics, 35,* 74–79.

Seipel, M.M.O. (1999). Social consequences of malnutrition. *Social Work, 44*, 416–425.

Servicemen's Readjustment Act of 1944, P.L. 346-268, S.1767 (1944).

Sex Offender Registration and Notification Act, P.L. 109-248, 120 Stat. 587 (2006).

Shaefer, H. L., & Wu, L. (2011, June). Unemployment Insurance and low-educated, single, working mothers before and after welfare reform. *Social Service Review, 85*(2), 205–228.

Shaffer, E.T.H. (1923, September). A new South - The Negro migration. *The Atlantic Monthly*, pp. 403–409.

Shakespeare, T. (1994). Cultural representation of disabled people: Dustbins for disavowal. *Disability and Society, 9*(3), 283–299.

Shannon, B. D. (1997). The impact of the courts on mental health policy and services. In T. R. Watkins & J. W. Callicutt (Eds.), *Mental health policy and practice today* (pp. 49–68). Thousand Oaks, CA: SAGE.

Shapiro, J. P. (1989, September 18). Liberation day for the disabled. *U.S. News and World Report*, pp. 20–24.

Shapiro, J. P. (1993). *No pity: People with disabilities—Forging a new civil rights movement.* New York: Three Rivers Press.

Shapiro, J. P. (1998, July 6). The Americans With Minor Disabilities Act. *U.S. News and World Report*, pp. 41–42.

Sheridan, T. F. (1998). Changing the system: Don't mourn—Organize! In D. Aronstein & B. Thompson (Eds.), *HIV and social work* (pp. 541–560). New York: Haworth Press.

Shilts, R. (1988). *And the band played on: Politics, people, and the AIDS epidemic.* New York: Quality Paperback Book Club.

Shin, S. H., & Choi, S. (2007). State response to substance-abusing TANF recipients: The challenge for welfare policy. *Journal of Policy Practice, 6*, 65–83.

Should Congress limit the present scope of the federal Food Stamp program? (1975, May). *Congressional Digest, 54*(5), 140–159.

Shubik, C., & Kendall, J. (2007). Rethinking juvenile status offense laws: Considerations for congressional review of the Juvenile Justice and Delinquency Prevention Act. *Family Court Review, 45*, 384–398.

Shugarman, L. R., & Whitenhill, K. (2011). The Affordable Care Act proposes new provisions to build a stronger continuum of care. *Generations, 35*(1), 11–18.

Sinclair, U. (1981). *The jungle* (rev. ed.). Toronto: Bantam Books. (Original work published 1906)

Skipp, C., & Campo-Flores, A. (2009, August 3). A bridge too far. *Newsweek*, pp. 46–51.

Slovak, K. (2002). Gun violence and children: Factors related to exposure and trauma. *Health & Social Work, 27*, 104–112.

Smith, G. E., & Pear, T. H. (1917). *Shell shock and its lessons.* Manchester, England: Longmans, Green.

Smith, J. D., & Nelson, K. R. (1989). *The sterilization of Carrie Buck.* Far Hills, NJ: New Horizon Press.

Smith, R. M. (2003). *From blackjacks to briefcases: A history of commercialized strikebreaking and unionbusting in the United States.* Athens: Ohio University Press.

Smith, Z. A. (2000). *The environmental policy paradox.* Upper Saddle River, NJ: Prentice Hall.

Smith-Osborne, A. (2009). Mental health risk and social ecological variables associated with educational attainment for Gulf War veterans: Implications for veterans returning to civilian life. *American Journal of Community Psychology, 44*, 327–337.

Social Security Act of 1935, P.L. 74-271, 49 Stat. 620 (1935).

Soergel, A. (2020, January 2). 24 U.S. states will see a minimum wage increase in 2020. *U.S. News and World Report.* Retrieved from https://wtop.com/news/2020/12/24-u-s-states-will-see-a-minimum-wage-increase-in-2021/

Specht, H., & Courtney, M. E. (1994). *Unfaithful angels: How social work has abandoned its mission.* New York: Free Press.

Spencer, H. (1904). *The study of sociology.* New York: D. Appleton.

Stadum, B. (1995). The dilemma in saving children from child labor: Reform and casework at odds with families' needs (1900–1938). *Child Welfare, 74*, 33–55.

Stein, T. J. (2007). *Child welfare and the law.* New York: Longman.

Steiner, J. F. (1917). *The Japanese invasion: A study in the psychology of inter-racial contacts.* Chicago: A. C. McClurg.

Stoddard, L. (1922). *The rising tide of color against White world-supremacy.* New York: Charles Scribner's Sons.

Storrs, L.R.Y. (2000). *Civilizing capitalism: The National Consumers' League, women's activism, and labor standards in the New Deal era.* Chapel Hill: University of North Carolina Press.

Strange vagaries of shell-shock—Real and camouflaged. (1918, June 8). *The Literary Digest, 57*, 65–66.

Strasser, M. (2010). Life after DOMA. *Duke Journal of Gender Law and Poverty, 17*, 399–424.

Strickland, J. (2014). Teaching the history of slavery in the United States with interviews: "Born in slavery: Slave narratives from the Federal Writers' Project, 1936-1938." *Journal of American Ethnic History, 33*, 41–48.

Sullivan, A. (1997). *Same-sex marriage: Pro and con.* New York: Vintage Books.

Sullivan v. Zebley, 493 U.S. 521 (1990).

Supplemental Nutrition Assistance Program: Food Stamp eligibility and benefits. (2010, December). *Congressional Digest, 89*(10), 295–296.

Suter v. Artist M., 503 U.S. 347 (1992).

Svihula, J., & Estes, C. L. (2009). Social Security privatization: The institutionalization of an ideological movement. In L. Rogne, C. L. Estes, B. R. Grossman, B. A. Hollister, & E. Solway (Eds.), *Social insurance and social justice: Social Security, Medicare, and the campaign against entitlements* (pp. 217–228). New York: Springer.

Sweeping law for rights of disabled. (1990). *Congressional Quarterly Almanac, 46*, 447–461.

Sylves, R. (2008). *Disaster policy and politics: Emergency management and Homeland Security*. Washington, DC: CQ Press.

Szasz, T. S. (1970). *The manufacture of madness*. New York: Harper Colophon Books.

Takaki, R. (1989). *Strangers from a different shore: A history of Asian Americans*. New York: Penguin Books.

Takamura, J. C. (1999). Getting ready for the 21st century: The aging of America and the Older Americans Act. *Health & Social Work, 24*, 232–238.

Takamura, J. C. (2000). The aging of America and the Older Americans Act. In S. M. Keigher, A. E. Fortune, & S. L. Witkin (Eds.), *Aging and social work: The changing landscapes* (pp. 127–136). Washington, DC: NASW Press.

Taylor, D. E. (2014). *Toxic communities: Environmental racism, industrial pollution, and residential mobility*. New York: New York University Press.

Teaf, H. M., Jr. (1938, June). Work relief and the workers. *Survey Midmonthly*, 199–201.

A technical assistance manual on the employment provisions (Title I) of the Americans with Disabilities Act. (1992). [Printed for the United States Equal Employment Opportunity Commission.] Washington, DC: U.S. Government Printing Office.

Terwilliger, G. J., III. (2005). Controlling the border: A matter of safety, sovereignty, and fairness. In S. A. Baker & J. Kavanagh (Eds.), *Patriot debates: Experts debate the USA Patriot Act* (pp. 113–118). Chicago: American Bar Association.

Thomas, D. S., & Nishimoto, R. S. (1946). *The spoilage: Japanese American evacuation and resettlement*. Berkeley: University of California Press.

Thomas, T. (2011). *The registration and monitoring of sex offenders: A comparative study*. London: Routledge Press.

The threatened inundation from Europe. (1920, December 18). *The Literary Digest, 67*(12), 7–9.

Tiefenthaler, J., Farmer, A., & Sambira, A. (2005). Services and intimate partner violence in the United States: A county-level analysis. *Journal of Marriage and Family, 67*, 565–578.

Tiffany, F. (1891). *Life of Dorothea Lynde Dix*. Boston: Houghton, Mifflin.

Torrey, E. F. (1988). *Nowhere to go: The tragic odyssey of the homeless mentally ill.* New York: Harper & Row.

Trattner, W. I. (1999). *From poor law to welfare state: A history of social welfare in America* (6th ed.). New York: Free Press.

Treffert, D. A. (1973). Dying with their rights on [Letter to the editor]. *American Journal of Psychiatry, 130*, 1041.

Trenkamp, B., & Wiseman, M. (2007). The Food Stamp program and Supplemental Security Income. *Social Security Bulletin, 67*(4), 71–87.

Trent, J. W., Jr. (1994). *Inventing the feeble mind: A history of mental retardation in the United States*. Berkeley: University of California Press.

Tsai, J., Lee, C.Y.S., Byrne, T., Pietrzak, R. H., & Southwick, S. M. (2017). Changes in public attitudes and perceptions about homelessness between 1990 and 2016. *American Journal of Community Psychology, 60*, 599–606.

Tucker, A. (2010). A matter of fairness: How denying mental-mental claims frustrates the central purposes of workers' compensation law. *Journal of Legal Medicine, 31*, 467–484.

Turnbull, H. R., III. (1993). *Free appropriate public education: The law and children with disabilities*. Denver: Love.

Underwood, J. K., & Mead, J. F. (1995). *Legal aspects of special education and pupil services*. Boston: Allyn & Bacon.

United States v. Windsor, 570 U.S. 744 (2013).

U.S. Const. amend. II.

U.S. Const. amend. V.

U.S. Const. amend. XIII.

U.S. Const. amend. XIV.

U.S. Const. art. IV, § 1.

U.S. Department of Justice, Civil Rights Division. (2015, March 4). *Investigation of Ferguson police department*. Retrieved from https://www.justice.gov/sites/default/files/opa/press-releases/attachments/2015/03/04/ferguson_police_department_report.pdf

U.S. sales of dog and cat food holding up under pressure. (2009, May). *Pets International*. Retrieved from http://www.packagedfacts.com/docs/pf_petsinternational_sept2009.pdf

USA Patriot Act, P.L. 107-56, 115 Stat. 272 (2001).

van Wormer, K. (2006). The case for restorative justice: A crucial adjunct to the social work curriculum. *Journal of Teaching in Social Work, 26*, 57–69.

Ventry, D. J., Jr. (2001). The collision of tax and welfare politics: The political history of the Earned Income Tax Credit. In B. D. Meyer & D. Holtz-Eakin (Eds.) *Making work pay: The Earned Income Tax Credit and its impact on America's families* (pp. 15–47). New York: Russell Sage Foundation.

Vieira, E. R., Vaccaro, J. A., Zarini, G. G., & Huffman, F. G. (2017). Health indicators of US older adults who received or did not receive meals funded by the Older Americans Act. *Journal of Aging Research*, Article 2160819. doi:10.1155/2017/2160819

Vinovskis, M. A. (2005). *The birth of Head Start: Preschool policies in the Kennedy and Johnson administrations*. Chicago: The University of Chicago Press.

Violence Against Women Act, P.L. 103-322, 108 Stat. 1796 (1994).

Violent Crime Control and Law Enforcement Act, P.L. 103-322, 108 Stat. 1796 (1994).

Virginia McMartin et al. v. Children's Institute International, Court of Appeals of California, Second Appellate District, Division Five (August 10, 1989).

Vose, C. E. (1959). *Caucasians only: The Supreme Court, the NAACP, and the restrictive covenant cases*. Berkeley: University of California Press.

Voting Rights Act of 1965, P.L. 89-110, 79 Stat. 437 (1965).

Waldinger, G. (1982). Subsidized adoption: How paid parents view it. *Social Work, 27*, 516–521.

The war on drugs is lost. (1996, February 12). *National Review*, pp. 34–48.

Washington, H. A. (2006). *Medical Apartheid: The dark history of medical experimentation on Black Americans from colonial times to the present*. New York: Harlem Moon.

Washko, M. M., Schack, R. W., Goff, B. A., & Pudlin, B. (2011). Title V of the Older Americans Act, the Senior Community Service Employment Program: Participation demographics and service to racially/ethnically diverse populations. *Journal of Aging and Social Policy, 23*, 182–197.

Weil, A., & Hill, I. (2003). The State Children's Health Insurance Program: A new approach to federalism. In J. Holahan, A. Weil, & J. M. Wiener (Eds.), *Federalism & health policy* (pp. 293–323). Washington, DC: Urban Institute Press.

Welfare reform: Can the states fly solo? (1996, November–December). *Policy Review*, pp. 44–49.

Wellman, N. S., & Kamp, B. (2004). Federal food and nutrition assistance programs for older people. *Generations, 28*(3), 78–85.

West, M. R., & Peterson, P. E. (2003). The politics and practice of accountability. In P. E. Peterson & M. R. West (Eds.), *No Child Left Behind? The politics and practice of school accountability* (pp. 1–19). Washington, DC: Brookings Institution Press.

Westman, J. C. (1996). The rationale and feasibility of licensing parents. *Society, 34*, 46–52.

Whalen, C., & Whalen, B. (1985). *The longest debate: A legislative history of the 1964 Civil Rights Act*. Washington, DC: Seven Locks Press.

Whaley, S. E., Koleilat, M., Whaley, M., Gomez, J., Meehan, K., & Saluja, K. (2012). Impact of policy changes on infant feeding decisions among low-income women participating in the Special Nutrition Program for Women, Infants, and Children. *American Journal of Public Health, 102*, 2269–2273.

Whelan, E. (2012, December 31). Federalism and marriage: The Supreme Court should stay out of the way. *National Review*, pp. 34–36.

Whitaker, R. (2002). *Mad in America: Bad science, bad medicine, and the enduring mistreatment of the mentally ill*. New York: Basic Books.

White, J. R. (2002). *Terrorism: An introduction* (3rd ed.). Belmont, CA: Wadsworth Thomson Learning.

Wilkins, B. T., Mullins, M. H., Mahan, A., & Canfield, J. P. (2016). Homeless liaisons' awareness about the implementation of the McKinney–Vento Act. *Children & Schools, 16*, 57–64.

Williams, J. (2006). *Enough: The phony leaders, dead-end movements, and culture of failure that are undermining Black America—And what we can do about it*. New York: Crown.

Williams, J. H. (2015). Marshalling social responses to environmental changes. *Social Work Research, 39*, 195–198.

Wilson, J. Q., & Sylvester, K. (1996, March–April). No more home alone. *Policy Review, 76*, 34–39.

Wise, W. E. (1935). *Jane Addams of Hull House*. New York: Harcourt, Brace.

Wisensale, S. K. (2006). Commentary: What role for the Family and Medical Leave Act in long-term care policy? *Family and Aging Policy, 18*, 79–92.

Wolfe, S. E., & Nix, J. (2015). The alleged "Ferguson effect" and police willingness to engage in community partnership. *Law and Human Behavior, 40*, 1–10.

Wong, K. C. (2007). *The impact of the USA Patriot Act on American society: An evidence based assessment*. New York: Nova Science.

Wood, C. (1991). Health care rationing: The Oregon experiment. *Nursing Economics, 9*, 239–244.

Woodward, C. V. (1957). *The strange career of Jim Crow*. New York: Oxford University Press.

Woolhandler, S., & Himmelstein, D. (2011). Healthcare reform 2.0. *Social Research, 78*, 719–730.

Wright, R. F. (2018). Elected prosecutors and police accountability. In A. J. Davis (Ed.), *Policing the Black man: Arrest, prosecution, and imprisonment* (pp. 234–254). New York: Vintage Books.

Yell, M. L., Katsiyannis, A., & Hazelkorn, M. (2007). Reflections on the 25th anniversary of the U.S. Supreme Court's decision in *Board of Education v. Rowley*. *Focus on Exceptional Children, 39*(9), 1–12.

Yoder, R. M. (1956, March 17). They get paid for not working. *The Saturday Evening Post, 31*, 116–118.

Youngberg v. Romeo, 457 U.S. 307 (1982).

Zigler, E., & Muenchow, S. (1992). *Head Start: The inside story of America's most successful educational experiment*. New York: Basic Books.

Zigler, E., & Styfco, S. J. (2004). Moving Head Start to the states: One experiment too many. *Applied Developmental Science, 8*, 51–55.

Zucchino, D. (1999). *Myth of the welfare queen*. New York: Simon & Schuster.

Index

About the Author

Gerald (Jerry) V. O'Brien, PhD, is a professor in the Social Work Department at Southern Illinois University Edwardsville, where he has taught for the past two decades. He received his BSW from the University of Missouri–St. Louis, his MSW from the University of Missouri–Columbia, and his PhD from the University of Illinois at Urbana–Champaign.

O'Brien teaches classes in community organizing, policy analysis, and research and disability studies at both the undergraduate and the graduate levels. His research focuses on disability history and policy with particular emphasis on eugenics as well as metaphor analysis in relation to social injustice and stigmatization. His articles have been published in *Social Work*, the *Journal of Social Work Education*, the *Journal of Sociology and Social Welfare*, *Metaphor and Symbol*, and other journals. This is his fourth book, following *Metaphor Analysis in Public Policy and Private Practice: A Social Work Perspective* (NASW Press, 2019), *Framing the Moron: The Social Construction of Feeble-Mindedness in the American Eugenic Era* (Manchester University Press, 2013), and *Contagion and the National Body: The Organism Metaphor in American Thought* (Routledge, 2018).